On Judaism

On Judaism

MARTIN BUBER

Edited by
NAHUM N. GLATZER

Foreword by
RODGER KAMENETZ

SCHOCKEN BOOKS   NEW YORK

COPYRIGHT © 1967 BY SCHOCKEN BOOKS INC.
Foreword copyright © 1995 by Rodger Kamenetz

"The Early Addresses" translated by Eva Jospe

Library of Congress Cataloging-in-Publication Data

Buber, Martin, 1878-1965.
  On Judaism / Martin Buber; edited by Nahum N. Glatzer;
foreword by Rodger Kamenetz.
    p. cm.
  Includes bibliographical references.
  ISBN 0-8052-1050-4 (pbk.)
  1. Judaism. 2. Judaism—20th century.
I. Glatzer, Nahum Norbert, 1903- . II. Title.
BM45.B814 1996
296—dc20 95-31333
CIP

Manufactured in the United States of America

First Schocken paperback edition published in 1972

2   3   4   5   6   7   8   9

Contents

Foreword

IN EARLY twentieth-century Europe, the received opinion among Western-educated Jewish intellectuals was that Kabbalah and Hasidism were stuff and nonsense. Part of their prejudice had to do with social discrimination—the assimilated Jews of Berlin and Prague were embarrassed by their brethren to the East, the so-called *ostjuden*, with their long beards, fur *shtreimls*, and fanatical devotion to prayer, God, and snuff. They were also influenced by the movement in Germany for a scientific Judaism, with its emphasis on rationality and horror at anything that smacked of superstition, such as magic, amulets, exorcisms, demons and dybbuks, and other lore of Jewish folk. To such a sensibility, the notion that an extremely powerful tradition of Judaism ever flourished in the shtetls of the Pale would have seemed utterly unlikely.

One great thinker changed that perception. In his midtwenties Martin Buber discovered the power of Hasidism, and thanks to his translations of its tales and legends, so did the rest of the German-speaking Jewish world. Although in some respects an heir to the scientific study of Judaism that preceded him, Buber had a strong taste for the mystical and he opened up for his audience of Jewish intellectuals the enduring significance to Judaism of its esoteric traditions.

As a consequence, when the first of his addresses on Judaism was delivered in 1909, Martin Buber at thirty-one was already an influential figure in the German-speaking Jewish world. He'd first risen to prominence from his stu-

dent days as an activist in Theodore Herzl's Zionist movement. Now, after several years of isolation during which he
produced his first versions of Hasidic tales, he turned once
again to the public arena to offer his audience the great
hope of a Judaism they could believe in.

The early speeches collected here represent, then, a
third major phase of Buber's career—his mission to young
Jewish intellectuals and artists before and during World
War I. The first three speeches were given at the invitation
of the Bar Kochbans, a society founded at Prague Univer-
sity in 1898, which proved to be the most influential Zionist organization in Central Europe. Others were given to a
similar group in Berlin.

Franz Kafka, who attended at least two of these lectures, captured in his stories the anxious social and psychological state of Buber's listeners. Highly secularized and
skeptical, deeply assimilated into German culture, they
were also guilty and uncertain about their relation to Jewishness. They understood Judaism as bondage to paternal
authority and as a system of archaic laws. Like Josef K. in
The Trial, they could neither live within the inherited system nor be wholly free of its emotional claims. Many
looked to Zionism for answers, among them Kafka's close
friends, the philosopher Hugo Bergmann and the writer
Max Brod. But in the years since Buber had first been active, the movement was losing its appeal, bogging down in
purely pragmatic considerations. At just this point Buber
was asked to give the first of his lectures. He offered up a
truly liberating vision of a Jewish renewal, combining
Zionism with the highest spiritual aspirations.

Gershom Scholem, the great scholar of Jewish mysticism, reflects back on those times—his teenage years—in
an essay written shortly after Buber's death in 1965. "When
I came to know him," Scholem writes, "he stood at the

zenith of his influence on Jewish youth in German-speaking
circles, during the years of World War I and shortly there-
after, when his words reached and moved a large audience."
Though sharply repudiating many of Buber's ideas, Scholem
felt that the "Addresses on Judaism" "exuded a considerable
magic in their time. I would be unable to mention any other
book about Judaism of these years, which even came close to
having such an effect . . . among a youth that here heard the
summons to a new departure that many of them took seriously enough to act on it." ("Martin Buber's Conception of
Judaism" in *On Jews and Judaism in Crisis*, p. 138.)

The early addresses could be read as Zionist history,
then. Or as a preamble to Buber's philosophy of encounter,
especially "The Holy Way" (1918) and "Herut: On Youth
and Religion." (1919) By 1916, Buber had already started
work on his philosophical masterwork, *I and Thou*.

But it would be untrue to their spirit to read them only
in the past tense. They must also be read in the present in-
dicative, as a response to the urgent needs of Jews today.

While very much in the spirit of Buber, such an assertion is also excruciatingly ironic. Momentous history separates us from his original audience: two world wars and the
rise of Nazism. When one adds the destruction of one-third
of the Jewish people in the Holocaust, then the irony grows
deeper, and more powerfully somber. These addresses cannot be read without a sense of foreboding, reflected by
Buber as well in the dedication of "The Holy Way" to his
close friend Gustav Landauer, a Jewish socialist pacifist
brutally kicked to death by soldiers of the German Reich in
the postwar chaos of 1919.

But one more event separates us from the original audience for the early addresses. That is the unimaginable success of the Zionist project to which Buber contributed so
much energy. From the start, Buber foresaw Jewish renewal

emerging from the life of a genuine community of Jews on Jewish soil. So it is also ironic that his words might now have a special significance for North American Jews today, who remain stubbornly in Diaspora unmoved by the promise of the promised land.

Nevertheless, I would like to claim Buber as a prophet of our contemporary Jewish renewal, and not only because he uses the phrase explicitly in his third lecture. In addressing the spiritual situation of highly assimilated, secular, well-educated young Jews of his time and place, he spoke—in essential terms—to the situation of most North American Jews today.

Essence is Buber's manner and mode—both the beauty and trouble of his work. His language mixes idealistic philosophy and romantic poetry into passages of great rhetorical skill, as well as infuriating imprecision. One can see why such a fiercely adamant literary sensibility as Kafka's was resistant to Buber's prose, but Kafka may have been more deeply influenced in literary terms than he would admit. The intensely symbolic realms of Kafka's tales trace their deed of origin to the even more elaborately symbolic tales of Rabbi Nachman, which Kafka read in Buber's translation. But when we consider that at the end of his brief life, the greatest practitioner of modern German prose was studying Hebrew so as to emigrate to Palestine—then we know Kafka's own life was a parable of the Jewish predicament Buber so deeply understood.

As Buber's own preface to the 1923 edition of the first eight lectures indicates, his message evolved—or as he says, became clarified in time. But basically throughout his lectures, Buber offers a vision of Judaism as a creative dynamic process. His working model is the early Hasidic movement—as Buber himself portrayed it.

In his early days of Zionist activism, he had affiliated himself with the cultural wing of the party led by Ahad Ha'am. But after his discovery of Hasidism, spirituality replaced culture. His program could be defined as Zionist neo-Hasidism—for this Jewish renewal community would find its life and norms nowhere else but in the land of Israel. Thus Buber offered the prospectus of a third religious path to a group alienated from both traditional Judaism, and its late rival, Reform.

The evolution of Buber's vision of the Jewish spirit is instructive. In a process that would sound familiar to many American Jews who came of age in the 60s, he seems to have discovered spirituality in other religions before looking for it in Judaism. His immersion in Christian mysticism at the turn of the century, and his studies of Hinduism and Buddhism, made it possible for him to appreciate Hasidic teachings when he fully encountered them around 1902. In 1905, he retreated from his Zionist party activities, removed himself to Florence, and immersed himself in Hasidic texts. As his childhood background included study of Hebrew—his grandfather was a well-known scholar of midrash and editor of its most distinguished published editions—Buber was unusually well-equipped to encounter Hasidic texts directly. He read Hasidism with unabashed subjectivity, for his goal was not scholarship but inspiration. He understood that interpretation, not translation, was required, and beyond that, a creative act of assimilation. Thus emerged Buber's *Tales of Rabbi Nachman* (1906) and *The Legend of the Baal Shem* (1908). Whatever Buber got wrong in the way of scholarly exactitude, he got the essential thing right. As the more historically oriented scholar Scholem admits, "Buber was the first Jewish thinker who saw in mysticism a basic feature and continuously operat-

ing tendency of Judaism." Thus in his work on Hasidism, as
in these lectures, Buber was a trailblazer. In both, he presented a strong image and ideal of a Jewish religion that
could be taken seriously by Jews who had rejected, as
Buber strongly rejected, the other two Jewish spiritual
paths then available, namely, Reform and Orthodoxy.

When Buber speaks in the first lecture, "Judaism and
the Jews," of "the miserable slavery" of "habitual inheritors" of traditional Judaism, or when he compares such
"avowed adherence" to the inertia of a stone "falling
through space," the rhetoric is vividly unfair. Buber's rejection of *halakha*, the path of Jewish law, was radical and
thoroughgoing.

Most historians of the religion consider Buber's non-
halakhic depiction of Judaism to be ahistorical. Observant
Jews find it anathema. But there is a third group—the large
majority—who live a contradiction. In their hearts, they believe that only halakhic Jews practice authentic Judaism,
but they themselves do not practice it. Such a stance can be
personally convenient, a sort of complacent incuriosity.
The core of Buber's message will unsettle such Jews as
much as it inspires them. His claim for an outlaw Judaism
also demands a whole commitment to a spiritual life.

Is Buber's Judaism purely a product of his own imagination, divorced from historical Jewish reality, as many
critics assert? Or has Buber touched the essence, the core of
Jewish spirituality, and found the standard against which
our contemporary practice should be measured?

Certainly Buber was no mere modernizer. As dismis-
sive as he was of traditional practices, he criticized even
more harshly the movement of liberal and "scientific" Judaism that preceded him, and that later proved dominant in
the United States as Reform Judaism. In the third lecture

Buber finds this reforming trend, "not a true renewal of Judaism, but its perpetuation in an easier, more elegant, Westernized, more socially acceptable form." He asks, "How could this feeble program dare to call itself a revival of prophetic Judaism?" (p.38)

Instead Buber views Judaism (in the first three lectures particularly) as a struggle between two opposing forces. They can be listed under various headings according to different stages of Jewish history: prophets versus priests, the Essenes versus rabbis, the *hasidim* versus the *mitnagdim*. In short, the forces of creative renewal and criticism versus the forces of institutional norms and continuity. The call of the present or the law of the past.

In the drama of his message, Buber often strays into blatantly dichotomous thinking, the fallacy of either-or. And his simplistic use of racial designations, as when he speaks of Jews (in "Renewal of Judaism") as "endowed with greater motor than sensory faculties" can be dismissed today as pseudoscientific pap. Writing within the dominant discourse of his time with its emphasis on racial stereotypes, he treads dangerously close to racial theories that in the hands of Nazis like Alfred Rosenberg proved disastrous to the Jewish people. But one has to see his purpose. Buber was seeking a basis in *blood*—in genetics—for an abiding mystery that he sensed but could not yet explain: the continuing spiritual quest of the Jewish people that has survived centuries of defeat and persecution. By calling attention to both the beauty and difficulty of the Jewish struggle for unity, Buber stirred an audience highly ambivalent about its Jewishness. Their greatest spiritual danger was not heresy, but indifference. Buber's lectures were not academic exercises; he was sounding a shofar.

Buber's chief biographer, Maurice Friedman, makes

the case for a continuing development of Buber's views of Judaism, from the formulations of his early Zionist years, which he later confessed to Chaim Weizmann were "too easy," through the early lectures on Judaism and beyond. From the very start Buber felt that his study of Judaism was not "entering a harbor, but setting out on the open sea." (Friedman, *Martin Buber's Life and Work: The Early Years 1878-1923*. New York: Dutton, 1981. p.76.)

If Buber figured his own development as adventuresome and dynamic, that reflected his view of Judaism as well. He saw in the Torah not a dogma, but a document of difficult spiritual struggles. Only at certain moments in its past had the Jewish people lived up to its own demanding ideals, its call for the unity of faith and deed. At other times and periods, Jews had clung stubbornly to the outward manifestations of Jewish practice, with no sense of inner content.

A brief history of the struggle is outlined in the fifth lecture, "Jewish Religiosity," given in November 1913 to the Free Jewish Club of Berlin, a group founded on the model of the Prague Bar Kochban Society. Here Buber makes a key distinction between religion and religiosity. Religiosity is the creative active spiritual longing, "the will to realize the unconditioned through action." Religion is simply the accumulation of laws and customs that arise from the religiosity of any given time. Thus, "religiosity is the creative, religion the organizing principle . . . religion means preservation, religiosity, renewal." For Buber, "renewal of Judaism means renewal of Jewish religiosity."

He did not consider Jewish law to be the essence of Judaism, only the byproduct of its religiosity. The laws of Moses, the customs of Temple service, the later rabbinic law—these are religion—and merely forms. Each reflected the spirit and needs of its own time but cannot claim a present authority solely on the weight of tradition. Rather, true religiosity is always current and searching. It demands unconditionality—as heard primarily in the voices of prophets, mystics, and heretics—of which, as Scholem asserts, Buber was certainly one.

Some readers might find his most heretical position to be his incorporation of early Christianity into the history of Jewish religiosity, as when he cites New Testament quotations as Jewish sources. In "Renewal of Judaism" he argues that what is "erroneously and misleadingly called early Christianity. . . could with greater justification be called original Judaism." The reason: what Jesus and John the Baptist proclaimed was "nothing else than, the renewal, in Judaism, of the religiosity of the deed."

Buber is not arguing for any "rapprochement" or merger between Judaism and Christianity—far from it. He utterly rejects Christianity's "syncretist" elements, including those that transformed it from a Jewish religion of deed to a cult of faith. He goes so far as to say, "whatever in Christianity is creative is not Christianity but Judaism." Nonetheless, he argues that Jews must give up their "superstitious horror of the Nazarene movement" in order to "place it where it belongs: in the spiritual history of Judaism."

Buber's disposition toward Christianity acknowledges his own spiritual and intellectual development. As mentioned, Buber might never have heard what he heard in Judaism had he not first encountered Christian mysticism. Certainly Buber's open attitude toward Christianity and his willingness to identify the Jewish elements within it won him a friendly audience among Christian theologians, far more so than among many Jews, a circumstance that

Scholem and other Jewish critics have noted with sly derision.

But here Buber was ahead of his time, for in the past thirty years our contemporary communications—our inter-connectivity—have made pluralism and multiculturalism impossible to ignore. The shtetls are no more, and their North American replacement, the Jewish neighborhood, is on the endangered species list. Only the mental shtetls are left, the prejudices and distances Jews feel from others, and they are breaking down rapidly, cell by cell. In North America Jews are spreading out geographically from their initial centers of settlement, intermarrying at a high rate. They have lost most obvious distinctive ethnic markers such as language or clothing. They have become Americans indistinguishable from other Americans. In such a highly assimilated environment, Buber's pioneer efforts to break the surface tension between Jews and Christians seems increasingly relevant.

Despite his primary emphasis on Zionism, Buber did foresee that renewal might well take place in Diaspora. While in the third lecture, "Renewal of Judaism" (1910), he looks ahead to "the establishment of a Jewish spiritual center" in the land of Israel, he doubts that such a center could "guarantee a renewal of Judaism . . . unless it were created not for the sake of renewal but out of and through renewal." Failing that, Buber looked for "absolute" renewal in the Diaspora. "It seems to me that the great ambivalence, the boundless despair, the infinite longing and pathetic inner chaos of many of today's Jews provide more propitious ground for the radical shakeup that must precede such a total renewal. . . ." The generation he addressed is long gone, but the ambivalence, longing, and chaos "of today's Jews" remain. Whether such anxieties will indeed prove "propitious" for Jewish renewal is unclear though in recent years a number of voices have called for such renewal in

North America in different accents: feminist, political, environmental, and mystical.

Most of the Jewish audience for Buber's first six lectures did not have his skills in Hebrew or his knowledge of Jewish texts. By seeking the essence of Judaism, by stripping away or rejecting large parts of the rabbinic tradition, Buber described a Judaism that was provisional and ungrounded in many respects. There is always a strong tension in Jewish thought between essentialism and particularism. Everyone recalls the story of Rabbi Hillel who when asked by a pagan to teach the Torah while standing on one foot replied, "Love thy neighbor as thyself, the rest is commentary." Not everyone remembers what Hillel said next, namely, "Now go and study." Caught up in the intoxication of renewal, it's easy to forget to study. This was Hugo Bergmann's criticism of the first three speeches at the time and Scholem's criticism more than a half century later. In form, they echo similar critiques of the havurah and Jewish renewal movements today. Enthusiasm without solid grounding in Jewish textual study is emptyheaded. Yet at certain points in religious history, the need for enthusiasm is overriding. Judaism has plenty of teachers and plenty of books—but how does it find motivated students, especially today when our pluralistic society offers seekers a spiritual supermarket, from astrology and Buddhism, to Hinduism, Sufism, yoga, and zen? Moreover, large numbers of Jews, in fact the majority, do not take Judaism seriously as a religion. In a recent survey, one out of five Jews when asked their religion answered, none. So today, as in Buber's time, Jews need to hear an authoritative assertion of a unique spiritual power to Judaism. Buber's early addresses inspired a generation of German and German–speaking Jews to identify themselves with the Jewish people. They retain the power to inspire today.

Buber revised his ideas and refined them in his second series of three lectures. After the first war, he began his collaboration with Franz Rosenzweig: a translation of the Torah into German and equally important, his support of Rosenzweig's Frankfurt Lehrhaus for Jewish learning. The Lehrhaus was a center for adult Jewish education where serious learning was combined with a certain religious fervor. It later become the model for similar efforts in the United States. In part through his collaboration with Rosenzweig, Buber worked to ground his vision of Judaism more thoroughly on Biblical sources. This is reflected, for instance, in the eighth lecture ("Herut: On Youth and Religion"), where Buber underscores the importance of studying the Hebrew text of the Bible.

Buber's enduring insight is that Judaism is a process, not a conclusion; a religion of presence, and not simply an historical religion. The relevance of this approach came home to me when I interviewed a number of Jews who turned to Buddhism in the 70s and 80s, Jews who in my view articulate the spiritual hunger of many in their generation. For far too many, Judaism had been presented in the post-Holocaust era as a religion with a great past, but no real presence. Many of them sought direct religious experiences, which they found through practices of meditation.

As a young man, Buber also experimented with meditation and what Friedman calls "ecstatic" experiences. Later he came to feel strongly that the pursuit of such special mental states took a person away from the human world of encounter, and that it is only through our encounters with the human that we can encounter God. Thus for Buber, Jewish spirituality centers on the authenticity of human encounters and not on the cultivation of special feelings of holiness or ecstasy. As Buber states several times in these

lectures, Judaism is a call to unity, not dualism, one that demands a Judaism of deeds, not of mental states.

For traditional Jews, the deeds required are adumbrated
in Torah and Talmud—they are the mitzvot, the commandments. But Buber remained adamantly outside the law because, as he explained in his correspondence with
Rosenzweig in the early twenties, he felt an inevitable contradiction between obedience to the law and the experience
of revelation. Buber could "not believe that revelation is
ever a formulation of law. It is only through man, in his
self-contradiction, that revelation becomes legislation."
"For me," Buber wrote, "though man is a law-receiver, God
is not a law-giver, and therefore the Law has no universal
validity for me, but only a personal one. I accept therefore,
only what I think is being spoken to me. . . ." As he formulated the question in another letter, "I must ask myself
again and again: Is this particular law addressed to me and
rightly so?"

Certainly this searching question has found its home
within the theology of Reform, Conservative, and Recon-
structionist Judaism, though one wonders if it is asked with
the same seriousness and intensity by many of the rank and
file. In any case, recent years have seen an aesthetic drift
toward formality in the synagogues of liberal branches of
Judaism, with increased emphasis on Hebrew prayer, and
the addition of more traditional customs and practices. Perhaps Buber would have been surprised by this trend, or by
the strength and resiliency of Orthodoxy, and especially the
evolution of the modern Orthodox movement. If by forms
we include rituals and religious practices, then such forms
have proven to have more inherent vitality in recent years
than Buber allowed for. His early view of the relation of
form and content—with form always stultifying, and content always renewing—seems too simplistic. As the Ameri-

can poet Robert Creeley once put it, "form is never more than an extension of content." Form is not always content's enemy, then, but often its wrestling partner, even at times, its wrestling angel.

If Buber seems in the present lectures too thoroughgoing in his condemnation of traditional Judaism, he nevertheless underlined a very strong tendency within tradition, and his warning of the potential stultification of the law and dogma is our clearest echo of the prophet's voices of old. Perhaps Buber's lack of universal acceptance in the Jewish world can itself be counted a sign of his authenticity as a Jewish voice. We Jews have always been more willing to accept our prophets once they are safely in books.

As an early Zionist, Buber placed his hopes for a new Judaism in the land of Israel, a community based on the soil and living a life informed by that relationship which he believed would evolve and shape a new spiritual form of Judaism. So far this has not yet happened for two reasons: the Holocaust that killed one-third of the Jewish people in Europe also killed almost two-thirds of the most learned teachers of Judaism. Since then the life and death struggle for survival has left Israel with little energy to turn inward and contemplate its spiritual task. But if the current process toward peace succeeds, then perhaps Buber's prophecy for Zionism will yet come to pass.

Meanwhile what Buber as a European did not fully address was the possibility of a newly enlivened Diaspora Judaism in North America. How do his ideas, addressed long ago to a young Kafka or Scholem, speak to us here and now?

Certainly his concept of "Jewish renewal," which is essential to his third lecture, is alive and well today. Arthur Waskow, a leading Jewish author and social activist, popularized the phrase in the early 70s and along with Rabbi

Zalman Schachter-Shalomi has continuously promoted over the past three decades a renewed Judaism based on community, ecology, feminism, and adaptations of Jewish mysticism. Waskow's exploration of creative midrash in a havurah setting—what he calls "God-wrestling"—is clearly in the spirit of Buber's thought as is Rabbi Schachter-Shalomi's adaptation of Hasidic thought to contemporary psychology. More broadly speaking, the entire havurah and "Jewish Catalog" movement of the late 60s and 70s seems to have adopted many elements of Buber's vision, including a reformulation of Hasidism, a disaffection with received forms and hierarchies, and most of all, a quest for a meaningful contemporary Judaism—an existential Judaism. Many of these same ideas have been given a political dimension in the pages of *Tikkun* magazine. What Buber did not at all anticipate, but which seems to be the most vital and creative area of Jewish renewal today, is the emergence of a feminist Judaism as reflected in the practices and innovations of Jewish women today as well as in the writings of thinkers such as Rachel Adler and Judith Plaskow.

Buber would not have left today's Jewish renewal movements unscathed. His formulation of genuine religiosity is severe; he would not let anyone confuse a momentary spiritual high with a true encounter. There's no magic formula: it's not simply a matter of enlivening prayer practices with slices of yoga or silent Buddhist meditation, nor are there any easy ways to assimilate past modes of Jewish spirituality. Buber well understood the dangers of make-believe—and no doubt its temptations. We hear the severity of his internal standards in the following comment, "It would have been an impermissible masquerading had I taken on the Hasidic manner of life . . . I who had a wholly other relation to Jewish tradition, since I must distinguish in my innermost being between what is commanded me and what is not commanded me." The self-examination required to determine what is commanded us is difficult. To Buber there is the relative life and the unconditional—there's no such thing as in-between. He warned that precisely because it has no ready rules, the true Jewish spiritual path is not easy. (Friedman, p.309) In regard to the future synthesis of Jewish renewal, he tells us in the third lecture, "We know that it will come; we do not know how it will come." And adds, "We can only be prepared."

In a sense Buber provided guidelines for Jewish renewal today. In his second lecture, "Judaism and Mankind," he distinguishes Jews as unique among the nations of mankind in their striving for unity out of a psychological and social dualism. The theme of the ideal of unity continues in the third lecture, where he defines it as the desire to unite reality into a single concept, to "see the forest more truly than the trees, the sea more truly than the wave." The "peak of this spiritual process" is the "God-idea of the prophets," namely "a transcendent unity . . . the world-creating, world-ruling, world-loving God." But this idea could not be sustained. Rather as "the relative life"—which we know as Jewish history—continues, "the idea becomes diluted, fades" into "lifeless schema" characteristic of "later priestly rule and the beginnings of rabbinism." Buber sees most of Jewish history as "the battle between schema and longing" with only a few moments in which the "active unitary tendency arises." Buber finds this battle raging among the Talmudic masters, the early Christian movement, in "the discourse of the Midrashin" and "in the soul of the kabbalah." And for a moment "it rose once again" in Hasidism.

Buber analyzes what he describes as the failure of Hasidism in the fourth lecture, "The Spirit of the Orient and

Judaism," and develops this idea in the fifth lecture as well. He blames the movement's decay on the Hasidic adherence to halakha, to preserving the Talmudic fence around Torah. Hasidism "did not dare touch the fence" and "consequently it was incapable of taking over the functions of a genuine fight for the spirit." Instead, "the fence was broken and trampled down not by an elemental force pressing forward toward new creation, but by a pale, feeble attempt at reform." In short, Reform Judaism. Buber concludes—and his words seem equally meaningful today—that "we live in the uncertain state that follows" with "no foundation laid" for a new structure for Judaism.

"Nevertheless," Buber affirms, "this foundation exists and continues to exist, unshaken. It is the Jew's own soul."

Between the time Buber wrote those words and the appearance of the four later essays collected here, which date from 1942 to 1951, every Jew's soul had been severely shaken. The trauma of the Holocaust and the religious implications of the establishment of the state of Israel continue to raise serious questions. In the later essays, Buber himself movingly calls into question his own lifelong philosophy of dialogue. One senses Buber's tremendous anguish as he wonders out loud whether, in the postwar era, the Jewish people can yet fulfill their mission. In "Judaism and Civilization" he asks, "Are we still truly Jews? Jews in our lives? Is Judaism still alive?"

These questions still resound with immediacy. And while no one can be certain of the answers I can't help thinking that so long as Jews ask such powerful questions of themselves, the struggle for Jewish renewal lives on.

Rodger Kamenetz
April 1995
Baton Rouge, Louisiana

Publisher's Note

THE FIRST three of the "Early Addresses" were delivered between 1909 and 1911 and published under the title *Drei Reden über das Judentum* ("Three Addresses on Judaism"), Frankfurt am Main, 1911. The second three addresses were delivered between 1912 and 1914 and published in the book *Vom Geist des Judentums* ("The Spirit of Judaism"), Leipzig, 1916. The seventh lecture, *Der heilige Weg* ("The Holy Way") was delivered in May, 1918, and published in Frankfurt am Main, 1919. The eighth address, Herut: On Youth and Religion, was published under the title *Cheruth*, Vienna, 1919. The collection of the eight addresses with a new preface appeared under the title *Reden über das Judentum*, Frankfurt am Main, 1923; a second edition was published by Schocken Verlag, Berlin, 1932. The present English version is based on a text of this second edition as revised by Buber for the definitive edition of his Jewish writings in *Der Jude und sein Judentum*, Cologne, 1963.

Of the "Later Addresses," the first appeared in Buber's *Ha-Ruah veha-Metziut*, Tel Aviv, 1942. The English translation by I. M. Lask (in Buber's *Israel and the World*, New York, 1948) was used in the present volume after adjustments had been made to follow Buber's final revision of his German text. The last three addresses were published under the title *At The Turning*, London and New York, 1952. The English rendition of the latter volume was used for the present volume by permission of the publishers, Routledge and Kegan Paul.

THE EARLY ADDRESSES
1909-1918

Preface to the 1923 Edition

THE ADDRESSES collected here have something essential in common, though I myself have only gradually become aware of this fact. Basically, all of them deal with Judaism as a phenomenon of religious reality.

To emphasize this point, they are presented here together; also, many an inexact, or indeed inaccurate, expression in the early addresses is clarified in the later ones, in correspondence with my own progress toward clarity. However, having gained any decisive clarity only after (and but shortly after) the last of these addresses had been delivered, I thought to preface them with an explanation that should clear up, insofar as it is possible, misunderstandings based upon my previous inexactness. This preface is intended as an explanation rather than a correction, for I can describe what has happened to me only as a process of clarification, but not a conversion. An explanation, I said—not an interpretation; for inherent in the process of clarification was the fact that my words became clear to myself, that I now understood what it was that I had then felt compelled to say, and that my inadequate words were adequate, after all.

The addresses deal with Judaism as a phenomenon of religious reality. By this I mean that there exists a re-

ligious reality, and that it has become manifest in and
through Judaism; in fact, Judaism exists for the sake of
this reality. Consequently, the question here is not
whether we understand Judaism to be a culture or a teaching, a historical or psychic phenomenon; it may include
these as well as other components. But it can be fully defined only by that religious reality which becomes manifest in it, and any definition not including this reality
would miss what is meant here. One conclusion, however, follows: that we must not understand Judaism to
be an abstraction.

A phenomenon of religious reality—should it not
suffice to say a religious phenomenon? This would, once
again, be inexact. For today we describe as "religious"
essentially something that takes place in man's inner life,
as well as the expressions of this something insofar as
they reflect this inner life. I, however, am referring to
something that takes place between man and God, that
is, in the reality of their relationship, the mutual reality
of God and man.

With this, I have already stated that by the term
"God" I mean not a metaphysical idea, nor a moral ideal,
nor a projection of a psychic or social image, nor anything at all created by, or developed within, man. I do
mean God, whom man, however, possesses only in ideas
and images; but these ideas and images are not the work
of free creation; they are products of divine-human encounters, of man's attempts to grasp the inexplicable as
and when it happens to him. They are the traces of the
mystery. "It is not God who changes, only theophany," it
is stated in the last of these addresses. Theophany, however, is no Over There; it happens to man, who has as
great a share in it as God. Images and ideas do emanate
from it; what is revealed in it, however, is neither image
nor idea, but God. Religious reality is called precisely

that because it constitutes an undiminished relationship to God Himself. Man does not possess God Himself, but he encounters God Himself.

Our generation is inclined to see in religion a peculiar form of human creativity, a form that in one way or another belongs to a regular cultural enterprise, without which man's spiritual life would somehow be incomplete, and which, otherwise, is morphologically determined by its own time. God as the "object" of religion is, accordingly, regarded as the product of a semiartistic interpretation of the world, as a fiction one may approve as worth preserving for the sake of its aesthetic value as much as for its manifold salutary effects—its strengthening of the courage to live, its safeguarding of morals, and its attestation to the existence of the spiritual element. But that from which all religion draws life, religious reality, precedes, and has a decisive effect upon, the morphology of every age. Religious reality lastingly endures at the core of a religion that is morphologically determined by a culture and its phases. Religion, therefore, subsists under a twofold influence: one external, which draws culture-imposed limits; the other internal, which removes, in accord with its origin, those limits. Though it no longer affects all realms of life directly, religious reality affects them through a definite religion from the moment it becomes embodied in that religion; theophany engenders history.

But if there were no religious reality, if God were only a fiction, it would be mankind's duty to demolish it; for I can hardly imagine anything more insipid and indecent than the sanctioned feigning that God exists, and whoever (in contrast to the honest atheist) programmatically proceeds as if God existed well deserves that God proceed as if he, the feigner, did not exist.

Inexact, then, is the statement in the fifth address

where I say that it does not depend on God but on man
whether God is "immanent" or "transcendent." Viewed
within the reality of history, it depends on that theophany
in which both God and man have a share. Viewed within
the reality of personal life, it depends on the relationship
between God and man, a relationship which, if it is real,
is mutual. An example, valid for both historical and personal reality: the sufferer does not want to be comforted
by God; he wants to savor Him in the very substance of
suffering. He "wants," I say; but he will learn that he
wants it only at the time of fulfillment, when God does
not speak to him from Over There but imparts Himself
to him from here, as the "spark" in the "shell," [1] as spirit
above chaos, as eternal life in temporal transitoriness.

The theophany which arms the liberated people,
Israel, for taking possession of their land appears as a
force descending from heaven, and the earthly event,
lightning and mountain-fire,[2] is evidenced in a movement
from "above" to "below." But there is also a theophany
of Exile, a never-being-abandoned despite shame and
degradation. In that theophany, revelation does not flash
from the cloud, but from the lowly things themselves; it
whispers to us in the course of every ordinary day, and it
is alive quite near us, quite close; the *shekhinah*[3] dwells
about us, sharing our exile and our wait, and our suffering heals and is hallowed through the immanence of the
Word. This is the history of Israel, as it is the history of
the human person; and it may well be the history of the
world, or that chapter of it which we have been given to
read and to write so far.

Inexact, then, is also the statement in the second address that "this God" had emerged from the striving for
unity. God cannot emerge—only a God-image, a God-
idea, can, and this, too, never from the human realm

alone but only from where the divine and the human elements touch, from their encounter. True, there can never
be a real "conception," that is, a conceiving of God, a
theophany, without the utmost co-creating participation
of an individual's or a people's whole personality, without
their special readiness that breaks out into ultimate, passionate action. But what is at work here is not something
that merely evolves around itself, not a myth-spewing
imagination, not a manufacturing of finished products
which the soul's workshop puts into spatial-temporal in-
finity. It is, rather, an honest movement in the direction
of God, a swinging toward Him without any reservations;
it is man's coming to meet Him.

Myth, where it really is myth and therefore different
from and greater than fable, is an account not imagined by
man but impressed upon him, impressed, that is, upon
that human being who is alive with a burning sense of
color and shape. It is not in the brain that divine images
originate, but in the eye, in the undivided human being's
faculty of vision which is touched by a ray of the Divine.
That is, divine images originate not in the depths of a
lonely soul, but rather on that plane of man's being which
is open to that which is other than man, though it can reflect it only in human terms. The mystery will leave us
unaffected only if, lacking the total involvement of our
whole being, we presume to deal with it in terms of an
"irreducible residue of the phenomenon," an "innermost
subjectivity of the thinking subject," or in similar ways.
But if we move toward it, if we confront it and address it,
it will come toward us; and this coming-toward-us mystery signifies our salvation.

I do not at all mean therefore that God is "later" than
individual man's or a people's religious experience [. . .].
An "experience" (*Erlebnis*) is of concern to me only inso-

far as it is an event or, in other words, insofar as it pertains
to the real God. The psychologizing of God and the psychic
effusiveness of the egotist who has cut himself off from
the totality of the actual world I find noteworthy only
as spectacles, as a dance on a tightrope between two cliffs.
What happens at the periphery, in the realm whose at-
traction and lure consist in assuming control over the
giddy nothingness, is always noteworthy but never important. And lastly, I sense in this peculiar, eventless,
experiencing a perversion that is more than a psychic one;
it is a cosmic perversion.

Intrinsically, what really matters is not the "experiencing" of life (*Erleben*)—the detached subjectivity—
but life itself; not the religious experience, which is part
of the psychic realm, but religious life itself, that is, the
total life of an individual or of a people in their actual
relationship to God and the world. To make the human
element absolute means to tear it out of life's totality, out
of reality; and if I have at any time contributed to this
"absolutizing"—so far as I know, unintentionally—I
now feel duty-bound to point out all the more emphatically the dimensions of reality.

Thirdly, to do so I must clarify a concept which,
though ultimately neither inexact nor imprecise, has in
some passages of these addresses turned out to be one or
the other: the concept of "the realization of God." This
term, which I can justify in a fundamental sense still to
be explained, becomes inexact when, as in our first address, we say that God must be transmuted from an abstract truth into a reality; for this term lures us into the
glittering notion that God is an idea which can become
reality only through man, and, furthermore, induces the
hopelessly wrong conception that God is not, but that He
becomes—either within man or within mankind. I call

such a theory, manifest today in a variety of guises, hope-lessly wrong, not because I am not certain of a divine *becoming* in immanence, but because only a primal cer-tainty of divine *being* enables us to sense the awesome meaning of divine becoming, that is, the self-imparting of God to His creation and His participation in the destiny of its freedom, whereas without this primal certainty there can be only a blatant misuse of God's name. [. . .]

We ought to understand that to "realize God" means to prepare the world for God, as a place for His reality —to help the world become God-real (*gottwirklich*); it means, in other and sacred words, to make reality one. This is our service in the Kingdom's becoming.

Are we capable of that much? We are capable of do-ing our share in effecting this one thing for whose sake we are on earth, the one thing that God will not achieve without us.

All men are, in some way, no matter how dimly, aware of this our human task. But once it was heard by a peo-ple, as a people; having, through this summons, become a people, it inviolably preserved its knowledge, despite all its own defects, weaknesses, and failures.

All men are, at some time, no matter how fleetingly, aware of an encounter with God. But one particular seg-ment of humanity is enduringly aware of it; with the in-nermost certainty of their living conscience, they are aware of it, not alone in their blessings, but even more in their every downfall and at each moment of dissolution.

All men, somewhere, in some loneliness of their pain or of their thought, come close to God; there is no in-vulnerable heathen. But the Jew, bound up with the world, immured in the world, dares to relate himself to God in the immediacy of the I and Thou—as a Jew.

This is Judaism's primal reality.

This people had once been the first to respond to the One who spoke, where previously only the single individual had responded. It will not, after all its failures and even in the midst of its failures, cease to prepare itself anew for His word that is yet to come.

I

Judaism and the Jews

THE QUESTION I put before you, as well as before myself, is the question of the meaning of Judaism for the Jews.

Why do we call ourselves Jews? Because we are Jews? What does that mean: we are Jews? I want to speak to you not of an abstraction but of your own life, of our own life; and not of our life's outer hustle and bustle, but of its authenticity and essence.

Why do we call ourselves Jews? Only out of inherited custom—because our fathers did so? Or out of our own reality?

Out of inherited custom? Tradition constitutes the noblest freedom for a generation that lives it meaningfully, but it is the most miserable slavery for the habitual inheritors who merely accept it, tenaciously and complacently. What meaning does this tradition have for us— this name, watchword, marching order: Judaism? What sort of community is this we bear witness to when we call ourselves Jews? What is the significance of this journey of ours through the abyss—do we fall, through the millennia's nebulous space, into oblivion, or will some power carry us to fulfillment? What does it mean for us to want perpetuity, not merely as human beings—human spirit

and human seed—but, in defiance of both Time and this
particular time, as Jews?

In the great storehouse of theory all sorts of impres-
sive and accommodating answers lie ready for those clever
people who do not want to make the business of living
more difficult for themselves by facing these questions in
too great depth or for too long. Two such answers are:
religion and nationhood. But, as we view them, these
answers are nothing but disguised questions.

Is there a Jewish religion?

As I have already said, my question is not concerned
with life's outer forms but with its inner reality. Judaism's
significance for the Jew is only as great as its inner reality.

Is there an inherently Jewish religiosity? Is there, not
dogma or norm, not cult or rule, but, alive in men of
today and manifest in a community of Jews, a unique
relationship to the unconditioned (*zum Unbedingten*)
which can be called essentially Jewish?

We know that a Jewish religiosity did once exist. It
existed in the age that let Jacob wrestle with God for His
blessing,[1] and in the one that had Moses die in the kiss of
God; in the age, too, of primitive Christianity, an age
bold enough to elevate a man who attained perfection
unto the status of God's own son; and in the age in which
late Hasidism dared, in the shared existence and shared
effort of men, to forge God's destiny on earth.

But our own time? Where is there among Jews a divine fervor that would drive them from the purposive busyness of our society into an authentic life, a life that bears
witness to God, that, because it is lived in His name, trans-
mutes Him from an abstract truth into a reality? To be
sure, today, too, there is something like avowed adherence—no, all sorts of adherences: adherence out of
loyalty; adherence out of pride; adherence out of inertia,
as the stone, falling through space, adheres to its direction.

But where is there fulfillment? Where a community dominated not by Jewish inertia (called "tradition"), nor by
Jewish adaptability (that "purified," that is, soulless,
"Judaism" of a "humanitarianism" embellished with
"monotheism"), but by Jewish religiosity in its immediacy, by an elemental God-consciousness?

As for inner reality, Jewish religiosity is a memory,
perhaps also a hope, but it is not a presence.

The other answer maintains that Jews are a nation.
Certainly, they are a nation; just as there is, formally, a
Jewish religion, so there is, in effect, a Jewish nationality:
it is manifest in the life of the Jews among the nations.
We are not, however, inquiring into Judaism's effect upon
the self of the Jews but into its inner reality. How does
national existence manifest itself here? The stance the
Jew, suffering and reacting, assumes toward the non-
Jewish world, the effect this world has upon him as a Jew,
and the way in which he, in turn, works this out for himself—all this may have contributed to the molding of his
character through seventy generations, but it does not
constitute a basic element of his inner Judaism. Otherwise he would be a Jew merely by defiance, a Jew not by
his very essence but by proclamation of the nations; and
at a nod from these nations his Judaism would no longer
be a living substance, but merely remembered suffering
and a remembered image, like traces years and fate have
left in our face. It must be something else: autonomous
reality. But what is it that causes a man's nation to become
an autonomous reality in his soul and in his life? What
causes him to feel his nation not only around but within
himself?

The individual adult repeats, on a higher level, a
process already run through by the child. The child first
experiences the world around him and only gradually
discovers his I, only gradually learns to differentiate be-

tween the mass of objects and his body as a separate existence. This process of perceptual orientation repeats, as it
were, its rhythm in the later process of intellectual orientation. There, individual man first experiences the changing world of impressions and influences, the world around
him, and last of all discovers his own self, the enduring
substance amidst all the changes.

At first, the individual finds himself in a cosmos constituted by his impressions, with the I contributing merely
the feeling-tone. Out of this cosmos two great areas assume particular actuality for him because of their distinct
outline and clarity: his native surroundings, earth and
sky in their familiar specialness; and a circle of people
who draw him into that circle and let him participate,
while communicating to him the basic form of social inter-
course, their language, as well as their basic form of doing things, their mores. On these three constant elements
within his experience—native surroundings, language,
and mores—the individual's sense of belonging to a community is built. This community reaches farther than the
primal community of family, or the community of friends,
born of choice. The individual feels that he belongs to
those whose constant elements of experience are the same
as his, and on this level he perceives them, in their totality,
as his people.

Many remain on this level. But we are interested in
taking a look at the one who proceeds from there. What
leads him on is an innate desire, blunted in some people
but growing and maturing in others, for perpetuity, for
lasting substance, for immortal being. He discovers that
there is constancy not only in the forms of experience,
but also a constancy of existence which steadily sustains
all experience. As the child discovers the I of his physical
being last, so the adult discovers the I of his spiritual being last, as an enduring substance.

The child, discovering his I, comes to know that he is
limited in space; the adult, that he is unlimited in time.
As man discovers his I, his desire for perpetuity guides
his range of vision beyond the span of his own life. This
is the time of those uniquely far-reaching, mute emotions
which will never recur with the same force, not even
when they become clarified and rounded out into an idea:
immortality of the soul, immortality of faculty, immortality of action and deed. Stirred by the awesomeness of
eternity, this young person experiences within himself the
existence of something enduring. He experiences it still
more keenly, in its manifestness and its mystery, with all
the artlessness and all the wonder that surrounds the mat-
ter-of-fact, when he discerns it: at the hour when he discovers the succession of generations, when he envisions
the line of fathers and of mothers that had led up to him.
He perceives then what commingling of individuals, what
confluence of blood, has produced him, what round of
begettings and births has called him forth. He senses
in this immortality of the generations a community of
blood, which he feels to be the antecedents of his I, its
perseverance in the infinite past. To that is added the discovery, promoted by this awareness, that blood is a deep-
rooted nurturing force within individual man; that the
deepest layers of our being are determined by blood; that
our innermost thinking and our will are colored by it.
Now he finds that the world around him is the world of
imprints and of influences, whereas blood is the realm of a
substance capable of being imprinted and influenced, a
substance absorbing and assimilating all into its own form.
And he therefore senses that he belongs no longer to the
community of those whose constant elements of experience he shares, but to the deeper-reaching community of
those whose substance he shares. Once, he arrived at a
sense of belonging out of an external experience; now,

out of an internal one. On the first level, his people represented the world to him; now they represent his soul. The
people are now for him a community of men who were,
are, and will be—a community of the dead, the living, and
the yet unborn—who, together, constitute a unity. It is
this unity that, to him, is the ground of his I, this I which
is fitted as a link into the great chain [. . .]. Whatever
all the men in this great chain have created and will create he conceives to be the work of his own unique being;
whatever they have experienced and will experience he
conceives to be his own destiny. The past of his people
is his personal memory, the future of his people his personal task. The way of his people teaches him to understand himself, and to will himself.

This insertion in the great chain is individual man's
natural position in relation to his people, subjectively
seen. But the natural subjective situation does not always correspond to a natural objective one. Such a natural
objective situation is present when the people to whom
individual man feels he belongs on the first level and those
to whom he feels he belongs on the second level are one
and the same; when the community of those who share
with him the same constant elements and the community
of those who share the same substance are one and the
same; when the homeland where he grew up is also the
homeland of his blood; when the language and the ways
in which he grew up are, at the same time, the language
and the ways of his blood; when the people that gave him
the form of his experience is the same as that which gives
him the content of his experience.

This natural objective situation is not present in the
Jew's, especially the Western Jew's, relationship to his
people. All the elements that might constitute a nation
for him, that might make this nation a reality for him, are
missing; all of them: land, language, way of life. Neither

the land he lives in, whose nature encompasses him and molds his senses, nor the language he speaks, which colors his thinking, nor the way of life in which he participates and which, in turn, shapes his actions, belongs to the community of his blood; they belong instead to another community. The world of constant elements and the world of substance are, for him, rent apart. He does not see his substance unfold before him in his environment; it has been banished into deep loneliness, and is embodied for him in only one aspect: his origin.

That his substance can, nevertheless, become a reality for the Jew is due to the fact that his origin means more than a mere connection with things past; it has planted something within us that does not leave us at any hour of our life, that determines every tone and every hue in our life, all that we do and all that befalls us: blood, the deepest, most potent stratum of our being.

The forces that carve man's life are his inwardness and his environment: his disposition to assimilate impressions, and the matter creating these impressions. But the innermost stratum of man's disposition, which yields his type, the basic structure of his personality, is that which I have called blood: that something which is implanted within us by the chain of fathers and mothers, by their nature and by their fate, by their deeds and by their sufferings; it is time's great heritage that we bring with us into the world. We Jews need to know that our being and our character have been formed not solely by the nature of our fathers but also by their fate, and by their pain, their misery and their humiliation. We must feel this as well as know it, just as we must feel and know that within us dwells the element of the prophets, the psalmists, and the kings of Judah.

Every person among us capable of looking back upon his life, and inside it, will discern the vestiges of this force.

Whoever realizes the pathos of his inner struggles will discover that there still lives within him an element whose
great national prototype is the struggle of the prophets
against the people's straying inclinations. In our longing
for a pure and unified life we hear the sound of that call
which once awakened the great Essene and early Christian
movements. But we also sense our fathers' fate, debasing us, in the irony of the modern Jew, an irony stemming
from the fact that, for centuries, we did not hit back when
our face was slapped. Instead, inferior in number and in
strength, we turned aside, feeling tautly superior as "intellectuals." And this very intellectuality—out of touch
with life, out of balance, inorganic, as it were—fed on the
fact that, for millennia, we did not know a healthy, rooted
life, determined by the rhythm of nature.

And what good does it do us to realize all this?

In those stillest of hours when we sense the ineffable,
we become aware of a deep schism in our existence. This
schism will seem insuperable to us so long as the insight
that our blood is the creative force in our life has not yet
become a living, integral part of us. To attain unity out of
division we must become aware of the significance of this
blood within us, for in the hustle of our days we are conscious only of the world around us, and of its effects. Let
the vision of those stillest hours penetrate even more
deeply: let us behold, let us comprehend, ourselves. Let
us get hold of ourselves: let us draw our life into our
hands, as a pail out of a well; let us gather it into our hands,
as one gathers scattered corn. We must come to a decision, must establish a balance of powers within us.

Where individual man, in his relationship to the people,
finds himself in a natural objective situation, his life runs
its course in harmony and secure growth. Where no such
situation exists, individual man becomes divided; and
the more aware he is, the more honest, and the more deci-

siveness and clarity he demands of himself, the deeper
the conflict. He finds himself inescapably confronted by
a choice between the world about him and the world
within him; between the world of impressions and the
world of substance; between environment and blood; between the memory of his lifespan and the memory of millennia; between the objectives of society and the task of
releasing his own potential. Choice does not mean that
one must expel, relinquish, or overcome the one or the
other; it would be senseless, for instance, to try to shed the
culture of the world about us, a culture that, in the final
analysis, has been assimilated by the innermost forces of
our blood, and has become an integral part of ourselves.
We need to be conscious of the fact that we are a cultural admixture, in a more poignant sense than any other
people. We do not, however, want to be the slaves of this
admixture, but its masters. Choice means deciding what
should have supremacy, what should be the dominant in
us and what the dominated.

That is what I should like to call the personal Jewish
question, the root of all Jewish questions, the question we
must discover within ourselves, clarify within ourselves,
and decide within ourselves.

It has been said (by Moritz Heimann[2]), "Whatever a
Jew, stranded on the most lonely, most inaccessible is-
land, still considers to be 'the Jewish question', that, and
that alone, is it." Yes, that, and that alone, is it.

Whoever, faced with the choice between environment
and substance, decides for substance will henceforth have
to be a Jew truly from within, to live as a Jew with all the
contradiction, all the tragedy, and all the future promise
of his blood.

When out of our deepest self-knowledge we have thus
affirmed ourselves, when we have said "yes" to ourselves
and to our whole Jewish existence, then our feelings will

no longer be the feelings of individuals; every individual among us will feel that he is the people, for he will feel the people within himself. We shall therefore not view Judaism's past as the past of a community to which we belong, but shall behold in it the early history of our lives, and by so doing will discern, in a different way than before, our growth and our direction. By the same token, we shall become aware of the present. Those people out there—the miserable, stooped people dragging their feet, peddling their wares from village to village, not knowing where tomorrow's livelihood will come from nor why they should go on living, and those dull, nearly stupefied masses, being loaded aboard ship, not knowing whereto or why[3]—we shall perceive them, all of them, not merely as our brothers and sisters; rather, made secure within himself, every one of us will feel: these people are part of myself. It is not together with them that I am suffering; *I* am suffering these tribulations. My soul is not by the side of my people; my people *is* my soul. And by the same process, every one of us will then become aware of the future of Judaism and feel: I want to go on living; I want my future—a new, total life, a life for my own self, for my people within me, for myself within my people. For Judaism has not only a past; despite all it has already created, it has, above all, not a past but a future. Judaism has, in truth, not yet done its work, and the great forces active in this most tragic and incomprehensible of people have not yet written their very own word into the history of the world.

The self-affirmation of the Jew has its tragic aspects as well as its grandeur. For, as I have already said, along with our self-affirmation we become aware of all the degradation from which we must liberate our future generations. But we also perceive that there still dwell within us things that have not as yet been brought out, that there

are still present within us forces awaiting their day. And
to live as a Jew means to absorb this tragic aspect as well
as the grandeur of self-affirmation. What matters for the
Jew is not his credo, nor his declared adherence to an
idea or a movement, but that he absorb his own truth, that
he live it, that he purify himself from the dross of foreign rule, and that he find his way from division to unity.

When I was a child I read an old Jewish tale I could
not understand. It said no more than this: "Outside the
gates of Rome there sits a leprous beggar, waiting. He is
the Messiah." Then I came upon an old man whom I
asked: "What is he waiting for?" And the old man gave
me an answer I did not understand at the time, an answer I learned to understand only much later. He said:
"He waits for you."

II

Judaism and Mankind

WHEN HE is a member of a people that leads a secure, free, and full life on its own soil, individual man need never speculate about his relationship to that people. For, whether or not he is conscious of it, he belongs to his people, as a matter of course and inviolably, by his natural participation in its activities and its thinking, its language and its customs. But where a people is devoid of so free and full a life, the situation is different: the individual is not situated within a community from the very outset; he must instead find his own niche. His sense of belonging will only gradually lead him to a genuine belonging, to participation, in the life and labor of the community. This process will become intensified as he penetrates more deeply into his personal individuality, into the secret of his uniqueness; simultaneously, he will discover what he and no one else is called upon to contribute to his people.

Something similar can be said about the relationship of a people to mankind. A people whose place within mankind's structure is well defined, fixed, and secure, a people clearly and distinctly defined by its country, language, and way of life, need never speculate about its significance for mankind. Pursuing its own affairs, it serves mankind in its own way and needs no further proof of its right to exist.

This is not the condition of the Jewish people. Because it lost its natural home millennia ago, and because it no longer possesses a common language or a natural community, its right to exist and the need for its survival are questioned over and over again—with the questions coming even from within its own midst. Here we must recall what is unique and eternal about this people, recall that primal element of man's soul, that basic form of man's life, which has been realized in Judaism with greater purity and greater force, as well as more effectively, than in any other people. We must remember what this primal element, this basic form, has meant and continues to mean for mankind, and that mankind has needed, still needs, and forever will need Judaism as the most distinct embodiment, the exemplary representation, of one of the mind's most supreme elemental drives. There is more at stake here than the fate of a people or the worth of its peoplehood; at stake are archhuman and universally human matters.

To remember all this, we must grasp the problem of Judaism in all its depth, delving to its very bottom, down to where the eternal is born out of contradiction. For this is the nature and the fate of Judaism; that its most exalted element is tied to its most debased, and its most illustrious to its most shameful. Judaism is not simple and unequivocal, but permeated by contrasts. It is a polar phenomenon.

"This much is certain: play-actor or genuine human being; capable of beauty, yet ugly; lascivious as well as ascetic; charlatan or player-at-dice, fanatic or cowardly slave—the Jew is all of that." Jakob Wassermann[1] once summed up in these words what I consider to be the basic problem of Judaism, the enigmatic, awesome, and crea-

tive contradiction of its existence: its dualism. Whether
we observe this people itself, especially where it lives in
a closed community, or reconstruct its experience as it
found expression in its history, or search in its literature,
which is its essence-become-opus, we are repeatedly confronted, starkly and directly, by contrasts more extreme
than any that ever stood side by side in some other social structure—a most courageous truthfulness alongside
a deep-seated mendacity, ultimate readiness for sacrifice
next to greediest egotism. No other people has begotten
such base adventurers and betrayers, no other people
such exalted prophets and redeemers. And this did not
take place only at various historical periods. The sublime
is by no mean to be equated with original Judaism, nor
the debased with its degeneration (though one must not
overlook the historical element); rather, they have at all
times stood side by side. Indeed, often the yea wrestles
with the nay within the same individuals who, though singular upheavals, crises, and decisions, may attain either
of the two poles.

I said: these are often the same individuals. I should
have said: in one way or another, both, the yea as well as
the nay, dwell within the Jew. No other man has so great
an abundance of ability or so great an abundance of
inhibitions as does the Jew. The life-story of a people is,
after all, basically nothing more than the life-story of any
member of that people, in large projection; and whatever
the history of Judaism teaches us can be complemented
and affirmed, through self-observation, by every individual Jew, if only he is sufficiently unafraid, clearsighted,
and honest. And this, indeed, we must be: unafraid, clearsighted, and honest. For it does not befit us to elude the
reality of our existence; nor will there be any salvation
for us until we have confronted it, and withstood it.

But the fact that this issue enters the sphere of the

individual's life without leaving the sphere of the people's
life makes it obvious that it is basically greater than an
ethnic question, that it is a human (*menschheitliche*)
question.

It is a fundamental psychological fact that the multiplicity of man's soul appears to him, recurrently, as a
dualism; in fact, inasmuch as appearance and being mean
the same thing in the world of consciousness, it may be
said that this multiplicity repeatedly assumes the form
of dualism. Man experiences the fullness of his reality
and his potentiality as a living substance that gravitates
toward two poles; he experiences his inner progress as a
journey from crossroads to crossroads. No matter what
changing meaning-contents (*Inhalte*) or names the two
opposites of man's inner striving may have, no matter
whether the choice at the crossroads is perceived as a personal decision, an external necessity, or even a matter
of chance, the basic form itself remains unchanged. One
of the essential, determining facts of human life (perhaps
even the most essential), it conveys the awesomeness of
the primal dualism, and with it the source and significance of all things of the spirit. In no man, however, has
this basic form been, nor is it, as strong, as dominant, or
as central as it has been, and is, in the Jew. Nowhere has
it been realized in such purity and so fully; nowhere has
it had so determining an effect upon character and destiny; nowhere has it created anything as momentous, as
paradoxical, as heroic, as wondrous as this marvel: the
Jew's striving for unity (*Einheit*). It is this striving for unity that makes Judaism a phenomenon of mankind, that
transforms the Jewish question into a human question.

This is neither the place nor the time to delineate the
causes and development of the inordinate awareness of
dualism within Judaism; but whoever knows how to read
history will encounter this development again and

again, from the time of the first documents to the present. Its strongest expression, in the earliest period, is the myth of the Fall included in the Book of Genesis. This myth (whose originality is not questioned even by Assyriologists) posits the elements of good and evil, the most distinct and most effective of all the components of inner dualism, and it does so with incomparable power and clarity. It presents man's task as a choice, a decision, with his future dependent upon this decision. It expresses the insight of man, who is grounded in dualism. It must not, however, be assumed that the same held true for old Persian dualism. The latter is concerned only with objective, not with subjective, being. It is an interpretation of the world, not a self-discovery. The dualism of the Persians is part of reality, not guilt. In their view, man is divided, as is the world. For the Jew of antiquity, the world is not divided. Nor is man divided; he is, rather, separated; he has fallen, he has become inadequate and unlike God (*gott-ungleich*).[2] Objective being is unified for the Jew of antiquity, and Satan is God's servant. Subjective being is split, but the external world is split only insofar as it is subjective being's symbol. One might attempt to present the sin-consciousness in the Babylonian psalms of repentance as recognition of inner dualism, but the concern, here, is merely with unfulfilled rites and other external insubordination; nowhere is there as yet any intimation of a knowledge of good and evil.

I have chosen the classic example of the myth of sin and cannot give further examples here. But wherever one opens the great document of Jewish antiquity—whether one reads the tales of apostasy in the history books, or the calls to overcome injustice in the books of the prophets, or the constantly recurring outcry for purification through God in the psalms, or, in the Book of Job, the words of insight into the inevitable inner duality which cannot be

overcome by sheer will power, which the individual
wrestling with himself cannot escape, and from which
only redemption can liberate man, there will one find a
sense and knowledge of disunion and duality—and a striving for unity.

A striving for unity: for unity within individual man;
for unity between divisions of the nation, and between
nations; for unity between mankind and every living
thing; and for unity between God and the world.

And this God Himself had emerged from the striving
for unity, from the dark, impassioned striving for unity.
He had been disclosed not in nature but in the subject.
The believing Jew "did not ask for heaven or earth if only
he had Him,"* because he had drawn Him not out of
reality but out of his own yearning, because he had not
espied Him in heaven or earth but had established Him
as a unity above his own duality, as salvation above his
own suffering. The believing Jew (and the believing Jew
was the whole Jew) found his unity in his God; in God he
safely took himself back to that mythical time, to that
childhood-like time of an original, as yet undivided, existence when, as Job says, "God's converse was upon my
tent" (29:4). In God he safely took himself across that
time-to-come, that Messianic time of reunion; in Him he
redeemed himself from all duality.

For just as the idea of an inner duality is Jewish, so is
the idea of redemption from it. True, juxtaposed against
it is the Indian idea of redemption, purer and more unconditional; but this idea signifies not a liberation from the
soul's duality, but a liberation from its entanglement in
the world. Indian redemption means an awakening; Jewish redemption, a transformation. Indian redemption

* Thus Luther translated, freely, yet with magnificent faithfulness, Psalm 73:25.

means a divesting of all appearance; Jewish redemption,
a grasping of truth. Indian redempion means negation;
Jewish redemption, affirmation. Indian redemption progresses into timelessness; Jewish redemption means the
way of mankind. Like all historical views, it has less substance but more mobility. It alone can speak as Job does,
"I know that my redeemer liveth" (19:25), and, with
the psalmist, "Renew a steadfast spirit within me" (51:
12). The redemption idea of the Jew Jesus is rooted in it.
The Messianic ideal of Judaism took its human aspect
from it. And when, in Jewish mysticism, the original character of the God-idea changed, when the dualistic view
was carried over into the very concept of God, the Jewish
idea of redemption attained the high plane of the Indian:
it grew into the idea of the redemption of God, the idea of
the reunion of God's being (which is separated from
things) with God's indwelling, which—wandering, erring
about, dispersed—abides with things. It became the idea
of God's redemption through the creature: through every
soul's progress from duality to unity, through every soul's
becoming one within itself, God becomes One within
Himself.

It is this striving for unity that has made the Jew creative. Striving to evolve unity out of the division of his I, he
conceived the idea of the unitary God. Striving to evolve
unity out of the division of the human community, he conceived the idea of universal justice. Striving to evolve unity
out of the division of all living matter, he conceived the
idea of universal love. Striving to evolve unity out of the
division of the world, he created the Messianic ideal,
which later, again under the guiding participation of Jews,
was reduced in scope, made finite, and called socialism.

The Jew was denied immediate unity, an immediate,
artless, original experience of unity within the I and
within nature. He did not start out from, he arrived at,

unity. When Spinoza created the most unified world structure man's mind had ever conceived, he, too, experienced
unity not in nature but in the demand (*Forderung*), in the
creative will, in the unified I. His I had become one; thus,
he could posit unity for the world.

This, then, is the primal process within the Jew, the
process manifested in their personal lives with all the
forcefulness of their Asiatic genius by those great Jews in
whom the most profound Judaism came alive: unification of the soul. In those Jews the great idea of Asia became exemplary for the Occident—the Asia of boundlessness and of holy unity, the Asia of Lao-tse and of Buddha,
which is the Asia of Moses and of the Isaiahs, of Jesus
and of Paul.

The Jew's creative forces are set aflame by his striving for unity; his creative action is rooted in the unification of his soul. "Only by being undivided will you have a
share in the Lord your God," says the Midrash.[3] The creative Jews are the conquerors of duality, its positive overcoming: the yea rather than the nay, productivity rather
than despair, the triumph of yearning. They are the "Let
there be light!" of Judaism. In their life, in their work,
the people redeemed itself.

Once we have grasped this fully, we can perceive the
significance of what we call *galut,* exile. The great creative epoch was followed by that long span of years which
one can truly call the Age of Exile, for it expelled us from
the very core of our existence. It was the era of barren
intellectuality, an intellectuality that, far removed from
life and from a living striving for unity, fed on bookish
words, on interpretations of interpretations; poverty-
stricken, distorted, and sickly, it subsisted in a climate of
idea-less abstraction. Once the natural unity of land and
well-rooted community, the sustaining unity of the soil,
had prevented the inner duality from degenerating into

ambivalence and instability. Over and over it created the forces which strove for unity, and created unity. Now these forces were lost. The fruitful struggle within the community—the struggle, rousing and rallying, waged by those who had found unity against those who had let themselves drift along the tide of their dissipating inclinations, the creative struggle of the prophets and redeemers against the godless and the self-satisfied—had burned out. Now began the struggle, essentially necessary but actually sterile, against the influence of the world, the struggle for the preservation of a way of life. It was uncreative; indeed, it was increasingly directed against creativity itself, against all that was free, new, change-promoting. For it seemed that anything free, new, and change-promoting was bent on undermining the last vestiges of uprooted Judaism.

This conflict had originated in a basic drive for healthy self-assertion; but it degenerated into blind self-destruction. In this harsh, senseless fight of official Judaism against underground Judaism, with its accusations of heresy and lack of insight, the great ideas of unity were leveled down to a tradition increasingly devoid of spirit; and where the striving for unity worked toward new ideas, toward new forms, it was forcibly suppressed. In addition, there was the unspeakable torment of everyday living, the longest and most painful martyrdom ever suffered by any people on earth. In this everlasting torture, in this internal and external struggle, the striving for unity became paralyzed. The people remained unredeemed. The great hours of stillness and of strength, the hours in which Jewish men had once experienced the eternal schism and had taken flight from it, became rarer and rarer. Except for the world of ideas of one great thinker, this stillness and strength lived on only in the luminous inwardness of the Jewish heretics and mystics. There they created a

work of exalted mystery, and there they contributed to
an underground continuity. Relaying the torch from
hand to hand, heretics and mystics kept the soul of Judaism in readiness for the moment of liberation.

Has this moment come? Is there such a moment?

Judaism lives not only in its history, not only in the
present life of its people; it lives also, and above all, in
us. So long as we perceive the Judaism of antiquity within
ourselves, so long as we still find within ourselves the primal dualism and the striving for unity, we cannot believe
that the original process is finished, and that Judaism has
realized its intent. So long as the basic elements are present, so too is the momentous task. And it becomes the
personal task of every one of us, every man's ethos, to be
consummated in stillness and in purity. Every man whose
soul attains unity, who decides, within his own self, for
the pure and against the impure, for the free and against
the unfree, for the creative and against the uncreative,
every man who drives the moneylenders out of his temple, participates in the great process of Judaism. And just
as we must decide within ourselves, so must we also decide within our people, rejecting a common bond with
the nay-minded, the play-actors, the lustful, the dice play-
ers, the abject slaves. Expulsion of the negative is the road
to unification, for individual man as well as for the people. This does not mean a confrontation between nation-
alists and non-nationalists, or the like; these concerns are
superficial, nonessential. It means a confrontation between men who make choices and men of complacent laissez-faire; between men with goals and men with objectives; between the creative and the corroding—between
elemental Jews (*Urjuden*) and *galut* Jews. And by elemental Jew I mean the Jew who becomes conscious of the
great powers of elemental Judaism within himself, and
who decides for them, for their activation.

If, then, we relate ourselves to elemental Judaism's spirit, if we strive for unity within our soul and purify the people, we shall have helped to effect its liberation and to set Judaism free, once again, for its deed within mankind.

This, as we have seen, has always been and will continue to be Judaism's significance for mankind: that it confronts mankind with the demand for unity, a unity born out of one's own duality and the redemption from it. Judaism cannot give new materials, new meaning-contents to mankind, as other nations do, for the Jew's relationship to material existence, to things, is not strong enough. It can only offer, ever anew, a unification of mankind's diverse contents, and ever new possibilities for synthesis. At the time of the prophets and of early Christianity, it offered a religious synthesis; at the time of Spinoza, an intellectual synthesis; at the time of socialism, a social synthesis.

And for what synthesis is the spirit of Judaism getting ready today? Perhaps for a synthesis of all those syntheses. But whatever form it will take, this much we know about it: it will, once again, demand unity, in the face of man's thousandfold, conflict-ridden, bustling concerns. It will, once again, say to mankind: "All you are looking for and all you do, all you strive for and hurry after, all your accomplishments and all your works, all your sacrifices and all your pleasures—all this is devoid of meaning and substance without unity."

A Jew once said: "One thing above all is needed." [4] With this saying he expressed Judaism's soul which knows that all meaning-contents are null and void unless they grow into a unified one, and that in all of life this alone matters: to have such unity. The soul of Judaism has not always dwelled on the heights of such a view; but the times when it did profess it, in purity and strength, were the great, the eternal, moments of Jewish history. At those moments Judaism was the Orient's apostle to mankind, for it drew from its experience of inner duality, and its redemption from it, the power and the fervor to teach the world of man the one thing above all it needs. Judaism set up the great symbol of inner duality, the separation of good and evil: sin. But it also taught, over and over, the overcoming of this separation—in God, in whom, as the psalm says, "There is loving kindness and plenteous redemption" (130:7); in the life of the holy man, who no longer knows sin, the separation of good and evil, but is "pure of sin"; and in the Messianic world, in which, as it is said in the Book of Enoch, sin will forever be destroyed.[5] This, then, is, and continues to be, Judaism's fundamental significance for mankind: that, conscious as is no other community of the primal dualism, knowing and typifying division more than any other community, it proclaims a world in which dualism will be abolished, a world of God which needs to be realized in both the life of individual man and the life of the community: the world of unity.

III

Renewal of Judaism

WHEN I SPEAK of renewal I am well aware that this is a bold, indeed almost daring, term, which, being at variance with the current outlook upon life and the world, is unacceptable to it. All activities of the typical man of today are governed by the concept of evolution, that is, the concept of gradual change—or, as it is also called, progress—emerging from the collective effect of many small causes. This concept, which, as one begins to realize, can claim only a relative validity even in the realm of natural processes, has, to be sure, greatly stimulated and advanced the natural sciences, but its effect upon the realm of the mind and the will has been highly deleterious. Man's spirit has been as greatly depressed by a sense of inescapable evolution as it had once been depressed by the sense of inescapable predestination, induced by Calvinism. The extinction of heroic, unconditional living in our time must to a great extent be ascribed to this sense. Once the great doer expected to alter the face of the world with his deed, and to inform all becoming with his own will. He did not feel that he was subject to the conditions of the world, for he was grounded in the unconditionality (*Unbedingtheit*) of God, whose word he sensed in the decisions he made as clearly as he felt the blood in his veins. This confidence in the suprahuman has been undermined; man's consciousness of God and deed had already been stifled in his cradle; all one could hope for was to become the exponent of some small "progress." And whoever can no longer desire the impossible will be able to achieve nothing more than the all-too-possible. Thus, the power of the spirit was replaced by busyness, and the might of sacrifice by bargaining skill. And even the longing for a new heroic life was corrupted by this tendency of the time. The most tragic example of this corruption is probably the man who, though he longed for such a life more intensely than any other man, could not free himself from the dogma of evolution: Friedrich Nietzsche.

I am aware that, when I speak of renewal (*Erneuerung*), I am leaving the domain of our time and entering that of a new time, a time to come. For by renewal I do not in any way mean something gradual, a sum total of minor changes. I mean something sudden and immense —by no means a continuation or an improvement, but a return and a transformation. Indeed, just as I believe that in the life of individual man there may occur a moment of elemental reversal, a crisis and a shock, a becoming new that starts down at the roots and branches out into all of existence, so do I believe that it is possible for such an upheaval to take place in the life of Judaism too.

The last part of Isaiah has God say: "I create new heavens and a new earth" (65:17); and the author of the Apocalypse claims: "I saw a new heaven and a new earth" (21:1). This is no metaphor, but direct experience. It is the experience of a man whose essence has been renewed, and with it the essence of the world. His body is the same mind-endowed body it has always been, and no faculty that was not already there has entered it. But in his shattering experience all his capacities have been welded into one, and no other power equals the primal power of unity.

Precisely this is what I believe will take place in Judaism: not merely a rejuvenation or revival but a genuine and total renewal.

Even though the concept of renewal in this absolute sense has, in our time, remained largely alien to the minds of those who are concerned with the survival of Judaism, they nevertheless recognize that ours is a moment of the highest tension and of final decision, a moment that has two faces, one looking toward death, the other toward life. They also recognize that Judaism can no longer be preserved by mere continuation, but that there is need for intervention and transformation, for healing and liberation. But, true to the spirit of our time, they hold that what is needed, and is possible, is a relative—in other words, a gradual and partial—renewal. I can best describe the meaning the term renewal has for me by discussing how it is understood by these men, and by the intellectual movements they represent.

Essentially, there are two basic concepts of renewal. They differ in their view of the nature of renewal because they differ in their view of the nature of Judaism. One regards Judaism as a religious community, the other as a national one. I shall discuss both concepts not as they are viewed by their average followers but as they are seen by their most prominent representatives. In the case of the first, this is not easy, for I have not found a truly independent and superior mind among its adherents. I shall choose one of the best: Moritz Lazarus.[1] The second concept, on the other hand, proffers a representative personality: the modern Hebrew thinker Ahad Ha'am.[2]

Lazarus, a clever and amiable popular philosopher, is of special interest to us because of the recent, posthumous publication of his small volume, *Renewal of Judaism.*[3] With singular expectation I read on the title page the words that had for many years reposed in my mind as a dark and still unopened sanctuary. And at first it seemed that expectation would not be disappointed. A sentence on one of the first pages went straight to my heart: it stated that our goal should be "the revival, the true re-establishment of prophetic Judaism."

The magnitude of this goal made me tremble. "The true re-establishment of prophetic Judaism"! What had prophetic Judaism been if not a command to live unconditionally? An injunction not to pay lip service to God by a declaration of faith while serving the utilitarian ends of a petty life by one's deeds; not to go all the way in one's thinking, yet stop at the halfway mark in one's actions; but to be whole at all hours and in all things, and to realize the consciousness of God at all times, so that, as Amos says, we let "righteousness well up as a mighty stream" (5:24).

Never in the history of mankind had the watchword "All or nothing" been proclaimed with so powerful a voice. And this was now to be fulfilled. At last there would be Jews of the kind enjoined by the prophets, namely, unconditional men. We would free ourselves from the designing hustle and bustle of modern society and begin to transform our existence into true life. Though the half-hearted, the indolent, the greedy might continue to call themselves Jews, only those men who labored earnestly for the re-establishment of prophetic Judaism would really be Jews. Yes, no doubt of it, this had to lead to a renewal of Judaism—and to a renewal of mankind.

But I read on, and my dreams dissolved. For, alas, what was predicated further on was an altogether different matter. This "revival of prophetic Judaism" was basically nothing more than a Jewish variant of what Luther had meant when he spoke of a revival of evangelical Christianity. Rationalization of faith, simplification of dogma, modification of the ritual law—that was all. Negation, nothing but negation! No, it was wrong to drag in Luther's name by way of comparison; Luther's concept of evangelical life had been infinitely more creative. What was preached here was not reformation, only reform; not transformation, only facilitation; not a renewal of Judaism, but its perpetuation in an easier, more elegant, Westernized, more socially acceptable form. Truly, I prefer a thousandfold the gauche dullards who, in their simplemindedness, observe day after day and without any shortcuts every detail of what they believe to be the command of their God, of their fathers' God. How could this feeble program dare to call itself a revival of prophetic Judaism? The prophets, it is true, spoke of the futility of rituals; not, however, in order to facilitate religious life, but in order to proclaim the holiness of the deed. Only when we demand something other than this so-called "purified religion," only when we demand the wholly unconditioned deed, only then may we invoke the prophets of Israel.

A totally different, incomparably more profound and more authentic world is made known to us in the thinking of Ahad Ha'am. Something of the spirit of prophetic Judaism does truly reside in this world. It lacks this spirit's original fire and ecstatic power, and is steeped, instead, in talmudic problematics and Maimonidean abstractions. But, in the trueness of its inner vision and in the relentlessness of its demand, it is reminiscent of our prophetic heritage. Still, the idea of an absolute renewal is not to be found here either.

Ahad Ha'am anticipates a renewal with the establishment of a spiritual center of Judaism in Palestine. Whether such a center could truly come to life unless grounded upon a socioeconomic settlement has been debated back and forth. And, indeed, a colony can be built only upon natural social and economic living conditions; otherwise it remains an artificial structure which, in the

long run, cannot resist the continual onslaught of the sur-
rounding utilitarian world. This, however, is not the essential point here. Whatever its emergent form, a central Jewish settlement in Palestine would undoubtedly have great
significance, a significance unparalleled in history: the
possible development of a nucleus of a healthy Jewish
people which, in the course of generations, would undoubtedly beget cultural values as well. In all probability
such a settlement would also have an invigorating and cohesive influence on Jewish life in the Diaspora. But it
could not guarantee a renewal of Judaism in the absolute
meaning of the term; moreover, the center of the Jewish people would become the center of Judaism as well
only if it were created not for the sake of renewal but out
of and through renewal. An intellectual center can promote scholarly work; it can even disseminate and propa-
gate ideas, though it cannot create them. Indeed, it
could perhaps even become a social model. But it cannot
beget the only things from which I expect the absolute to
emerge—return and transformation, and a change in
all elements of life. In fact, it seems to me that the great
ambivalence, the boundless despair, the infinite longing and pathetic inner chaos of many of today's Jews provide more propitious ground for the radical shake-up that
must precede such a total renewal than does the normal
and confident existence of a settler in his own land.

But to comprehend the one thing that could bring about
the change of which I am speaking, we must recall what
this Judaism is whose renewal we desire. When we view it
as a religion, we touch only the most obvious fact of its
organizational form; we arrive at a deeper truth when we
call it a nationality; but we must look still deeper to perceive its essence. Judaism is a spiritual process, documented
in the internal history of the Jewish people as well as in the
works of the great Jews. We have too limited a notion of

this process if we identify it either with the Jewish precept of unity or with prophetic Judaism, as do Lazarus and Ahad Ha'am, each in his own language. The Jewish precept of unity is only one element, and prophetic Judaism only one phase, of the great spiritual process called Judaism. Only by grasping this process in its total magnitude, in the wealth of its elements and the manifold transmutations of its historical revelation, can we understand the meaning of what I here call renewal.

The spiritual process of Judaism manifests itself in history as the striving for an ever more perfect realization of three interconnected ideas: the idea of unity, the idea of the deed, and the idea of the future. When I speak of ideas I do not, of course, mean abstract concepts; I mean innate predispositions of a people's ethos that manifest themselves with such great force and so enduringly that they produce a complex of spiritual deeds and values which can be called that people's absolute life. Every greatly and singularly gifted people possesses such unique predispositions and, created by them, a world of unique deeds and values. It therefore lives, as it were, two lives: one transitory and relative, lived in the sequence of earthly days, of generations that come and go; the other (lived simultaneously) permanent and absolute, a life lived in the world of the wandering and searching human spirit. Whereas in the first, the relative life, all seems chance, and often terrifyingly meaningless, in the other, the absolute life, great, luminous outlines of meaning and exigency are revealed, step by step. The relative life remains the possession of the unconsciousness of the people; the absolute life becomes, directly or indirectly, part of the consciousness of mankind.

But there is no other people in whom this constant productivity of an absolute life, this spiritual process of peoplehood, has become as visible and distinct as in the

Jewish people. In the relative life of the Jewish people, in what is commonly called its history, as well as in the everyday aspect of its present, there is a superabundance of cross-purposes, of haste, obsession, torment; but out of all this emerge, radiant and taller than life, the goals, writing their indestructible signs on the firmament of eternity. And to the vision that penetrates the relative life and perceives the absolute, it is revealed that the profusion of the first exists solely in order for the second to arise from it, and that, fundamentally, the second is reality and the first merely variegated, manifold appearance. This becomes manifest in Judaism more clearly and unequivocally than anywhere else, and this precisely is why I am justified in calling Judaism a spiritual process.

This process, as I have already said, is evidenced in the striving for the realization of three ideas or tendencies. These ideas are interconnected; they are, in fact, a unified entity within the people's ethos, an entity to be sundered only for demonstration purposes, in order to show that, in history, at times one, at times another of these ideas is dominant. The striving for their realization is by no means a steady and constant stream. It is repeatedly weakened by effluences, afflicted with droughts, now becoming shallow in the broad, unobstructed plain, now winding through the narrows of a rocky wilderness, dashing against a thousand obstacles. The spiritual process of Judaism assumes the form of an ideological struggle (*Geisteskampf*), an eternally renewed inner struggle for the pure realization of these national tendencies. The struggle stems from the fact that the determining virtues in the life of individual man are nothing more than his reformed, redirected passions, elevated to ideality; by the same token, the determining ideas in the life of a people are nothing more than its inherent tendencies, elevated to the spiritual and the creative. And just as in the

life of individual man his passions, breaking into the realm
of virtue and disturbing its pure realization, resist a reforming and redirecting, so do a people's tendencies resist
spiritualization, tarnishing the purity of their realization—
that is, their elevation to the absolute life of the people.
Thus, the ideas actually struggle for their own selves, for
their liberation from the narrowness of the people's tendencies, for their independence, and for their realization.
I shall try to demonstrate this by outlining, though only
sketchily, the three ideas of Judaism—unity, deed, and
future—but I can single out only a few especially memorable phases of this ideological battle.

The idea of unity and the tendency toward it inherent in the nature of the people originate in the fact that
the Jew has at all times perceived more keenly the context
in which phenomena appear than the individual phenomena as such. He sees the forest more truly than the
trees, the sea more truly than the wave, the community
more truly than the individual. He is therefore more inclined to pensiveness than to imagery, and for the same
reason is also impelled to conceptualize the fullness of
things even before he has wholly experienced it. But he
does not stop with a concept; he is driven to press on to
higher units—to a highest unit that sustains as well as
crowns all concepts and binds them into one, just as the
phenomena had been bound into a single concept.

But there is a second, deeper source for the Jew's
unitary tendency, the one I have already mentioned: the
longing to rescue himself from his inner duality and raise
himself to absolute unity. Both sources converge in the
God-idea of the prophets. The idea of a transcendant
unity springs into being: the world-creating, world-ruling,
world-loving God. The whole pathos of the prophets, the
most powerful pathos in the history of mankind, serves
this idea. But this is a peak of the spiritual process. Gradu-

ally, the outer source grows stronger than the inner, the
penchant for conceptualization stronger than the faithfulness to one's yearning. The idea becomes diluted, fades,
until the living God is transmuted into the lifeless schema
characteristic of the later period of priestly rule and of
the beginning of rabbinism.

The unitary tendency, however, would not be dragged
down. The battle between schema and longing raged un-
ceasingly. Temporarily, there was a reconciliation in the
views of Philo[4]; it was followed by a new flare-up among
the talmudic masters; the struggle permeated the early
Christian movement, filled the discourse of the Midra-
shim, and was the soul of the Kabbalah. But during that
struggle the nature of the idea of unity underwent
changes. God, inclining toward the world, was met by the
hosts of His emanations, the *sephirot*,[5] coming to unite
Him with the world. His "indwelling," the *shekhinah*, de-
scended to the world in order to abide with it. Sparks of
the Divine fell into the soul of man. Transcendent unity
became immanent—the unity of the world-permeating,
world-animating, world-being God: *deus sive natura*.[6]

This was the God of Baruch Spinoza. Again a peak
was reached in the spiritual process; a synthesis between
the faculty of conceptualization and that of yearning was
found. But it was followed by still another decline; again
the battle raged. For a moment, the active unitary tendency rose once again, in Hasidism. Then the movement
weakened, the battle grew limp. The sterile period—our
period—begins. What happened to the battle-sustaining
forces? Desert sands are about our feet; as a desert generation we wander about, not knowing whereto. But our
longing is not dead. It raises its head, calling its desire into
the desert. It cries out in the desert as John the Baptist
once did, at a time like ours: for renewal.

Judaism's second idea is that of the deed. This tendency, inherent in the ethos of the people, stems from the fact that the Jew is endowed with greater motor than sensory faculties; his motor system works more intensely than his sensory system. He displays more substance and greater personality in action than in apperception, and he considers what he accomplishes in life more important than what happens to him. It is for this reason, to give an example, that the Jew's art is so rich in gesture, and that its expression is more specifically his own than its meaning-content. For this reason, too, he considers doing more essential than experiencing. Hence, even in antiquity, not faith but the deed was central to Jewish religiosity. This conception may in fact be viewed as the fundamental difference between Orient and Occident: for the Oriental, the decisive bond between man and God is the deed; for the Occidental, faith. The difference is especially pronounced and emphasized in the Jew. All the books of the Bible speak very little of faith, but so much the more of deeds. It should not, however, be assumed that this means a soulless glorification of works, or rituals devoid of inner significance; on the contrary, every deed, even the smallest and seemingly most negligible, is in some way oriented toward the Divine, and the words of a later period, "Let all your acts be done for the sake of God," [7] are already applicable here, and in an especially poignant sense. At the time of the most naive relationship to God, the prescribed acts stood for a mysterious, magic union with Him. Thus, animal sacrifice was a symbolic substitute for the offering of one's own life; the flame of the altar was perceived as the soul's emissary to heaven.

But the acts lost their meaning; and yet the injunction still demanded continued observance of what had become meaningless, because, as Yohanan ben Zakkai[8] explains, God has "set up a statute, and has issued a decree." [9] Thus, out of the religiosity of the deed arose the ritual law. The deed-tendency rebelled against this inflexibility. In self-segregation, it founded life-communities which, instead of observing a law that had lost its meaning, wanted to practice, once again, the living deed that binds man to God. The earliest known community of this kind must have been that of the Rehabites, mentioned in the Book of Jeremiah.[10] Their ideas and organization were, apparently, misinterpreted, probably not unintentionally, by the law-observing redactors of the canon. In all likelihood an unbroken chain of tradition links the Rehabites to the Essenes, the antiquity of whose traditions are attested by historians. Along the way, the deed-tendency grew; the idea of the deed became ever purer, the concept of a bond with God ever greater and holier.

At the same time, however, the ritual law became more rigid and alienated from life, whereupon the movement spread from the self-segregated communities to the very core of the people and set ablaze the revolution of ideas that today, erroneously and misleadingly, is called early, original, Christianity. It could with greater justification be called original Judaism—though in a different sense than that of the historical term—for it is much more closely related to Judaism than to what is today called Christianity. It is a peculiar phenomenon of *galut* psychology that we not only tolerate the fact that this significant chapter was torn out of our history of ideas, but that we ourselves aided and abetted the tearing. We did all this only because syncretist elements attached themselves, though purely superficially, to this movement, so that not much was left of the original substance. Whatever was not eclectic, whatever was creative in the beginnings of Christianity, was nothing but Judaism. This revolution of ideas had burst into flame in a Jewish land; it had first stirred in the womb of ancient Jewish communal societies;

it had been spread by Jewish men; the people they addressed were, as is repeatedly proclaimed, the Jewish people and no other; and what they proclaimed was nothing else than the renewal, in Judaism, of the religiosity of the deed.

It was only in the syncretistic Christianity of the West that faith, as it is known ιo the Occidental, assumed primary importance; to earliest Christianity, the deed was central. As for the meaning-content of this striving toward the deed, it is clearly attested in one of the most original parts of the Gospels, which points most indubitably to a creative personality. In the first chapter of the Sermon on the Mount, it is stated: "Do not think that I have come to abolish the law or the prophets; I have not come to abolish but to fulfill" (Matthew 5:17). The meaning of this statement emerges from the subsequent comparison between the old and new teaching: it is not at all the intention of the new teaching to be new; it wants to remain the old teaching, but a teaching grasped in its absolute sense. It wants to restore to the deed the freedom and sanctity with which it had originally been endowed, a freedom and sanctity diminished and dimmed by the stern rule of the ritual law, and to release it from the straits of prescriptions that had become meaningless, in order to free it for the holiness of an active relationship with God, for a religiosity of the deed. And to rule out any misunderstanding, Matthew adds: "For I say to you truly: until heaven and earth vanish, neither the smallest letter nor a tittle of the law shall vanish, until all of this be done." This means: until the teachings of unconditionality (*Unbedingtheit*) are fulfilled in all their purity, and with all the power of one's soul; until the world is sanctified, is God-informed, through the absolute deed.

Early Christianity teaches what the prophets taught: the unconditionality of the deed. For all great religiosity

is concerned not so much with what is being done as
with whether it is being done in human conditionality or
divine unconditionality. And this chapter, the original
Sermon on the Mount, closes with the words which, significantly, paraphrase a verse of Leviticus: "Therefore you
shall be perfect, even as your Father in heaven is perfect" (11:14). Are not these words, and particularly the
words "even as," a Jewish creed in the innermost meaning of the term? And may we not answer those who are
currently recommending to us a "rapprochement" with
Christianity: "Whatever in Christianity is creative is not
Christianity but Judaism; and this we need not reapproach;
we need only to recognize it within ourselves and to take
possession of it, for we carry it within us, never to be lost.
But whatever in Christianity is not Judaism is uncreative,
a mixture of a thousand rites and dogmas; with this—
and we say it both as Jews and as human beings—we do
not want to establish a rapprochement." We may, however, give this answer only when we have overcome our
superstitious horror of the Nazarene movement, and
when we have placed it where it belongs: in the spiritual
history of Judaism.

However, this movement, which has had so great a
significance for the absolute life of the Jewish people,
has, in its relative life, remained an episode, unable to
put a stop to the increasing ossification of the law. But the
battle for the deed-idea did not let up. In ever new forms
it filled the millennia. It was dialectical as well as inward, public as well as hidden. In the places of learning
it spoke the language of keen intellects; in the homes, the
language of women. It assumed large proportions in the rejected heretics, and small ones in the small audacities of
the ghetto. And thus it flickered and burned around the
becrowned corpse of the law, until another great movement arrived, a movement that cut to the very core of

truth and stirred the very core of the people: Hasidism.

Original Hasidism—which has almost as little in common with the Hasidism of today as early Christianity has with the Church—can be understood only if one is aware that it is a renewal of the deed-idea. To Hasidism, the true meaning of life is revealed in the deed. Here, even more distinctly and profoundly than in early Christianity, what matters is not what is being done, but the fact that every act carried out in sanctity—that is, with God-oriented intent—is a road to the heart of the world. There is nothing that is evil in itself; every passion can become a virtue, every inclination "a vehicle of God." It is not the matter of the act that is decisive but its sanctification. Every act is hallowed, if it is directed toward salvation (*Heil*). The soul of the doer alone determines the character of his deed. With this, the deed does in truth become the life-center of religiosity. Simultaneously, the fate of the world is placed in the hands of the doer. The fallen divine sparks,[11] the erring souls dispersed in things and beings, are liberated through the deed that is sanctified by its intention. By his acts man works for the redemption of the world. Indeed, he works for the redemption of God Himself; for, through the supreme concentration and tension of his deed, and for an unfathomable instant's period of grace, he can cause the exiled glory of God[12] to draw closer to its source. Thus, the deed is here endowed with as vast a power and sublimity as appears, though in a wholly different aspect, only in ancient Indian religiosity, where man, concentrating on his intention, makes the world of the gods, the world of Brahma, tremble.

Now the free deed can confront the law as, to use a term employed by early Christianity, the perfect law of freedom. For Hasidism, therefore, man's final objective is this: to become, himself, a law, a Torah. And just as early Christianity had not wanted to abolish the law, so Hasidism too did not want to abolish it, only to fulfill it; that means, it wanted to raise it from the conditioned to the unconditioned, and at the same time to transform it from the rigidity of a formula into the fluidity of the immediate.

It did not succeed, because, having flourished, it soon began to disintegrate and to degenerate, for reasons not to be discussed here. In the absolute life of the Jewish people, it betokens the greatest triumph of the deed-idea achieved so far; in their relative life, Hasidism, too, remained only an episode. It was followed by a decline in which the struggle between law and deed reached its lowest level. I am referring to the bickering, devoid of ideas and spirit, between the Orthodox and the Reformers. It may well be the most bitter irony of our fate that the Reformers of this era are allowed to pose as the proponents of the deed-idea of prophetic Judaism. We must restore the greatness to the struggle for the deed-idea if we want Judaism to be great once again. If there are once more men who experience all the pride and all the magnificence of Judaism, they must demand that the striving of the people's spirit for the deed be renewed, and that it be given new form, in accord with our own new attitude toward the world.

The third tendency in Judaism is the idea of the future. This national trait stems from the fact that the Jew's sense of time is much more strongly developed than his sense of space: the descriptive epithets of the Bible speak—in contrast, for instance, to those of Homer —not of form or color but of sound and movement. The artistic form of expression most satisfying to the Jew is the art whose specific element is time: music. And the interrelatedness of the generations is a stronger life-principle for him than the enjoyment of the present. His consciousness of peoplehood and of God is, essentially, nourished by his historical memory and his historical hope, the hope being the intrinsically positive and constructive element. And just as each of the three tendencies has its vulgar as well as its sublime aspect, just as the unity-idea produced the conceptual constructs of rabbinism as well as the people's great yearning for God, and the deed-tendency led to a soulless panritualism as well as to a holy will to unconditionality, so is it also with the future-tendency.

On the one hand, it drives the Jew into a bustling activity with diverse objectives, and spurs on his urge for acquisition; this urge is, however, directed not toward his own comfort but toward the happiness of the next generation. The next generation, even before it becomes conscious of itself, is in turn charged with the task of taking care of still another generation, so that all reality of existence is dissolved in the care for the future. On the other hand, this tendency awakens Messianism in the Jew, the idea of an absolute future that transcends all reality of past and present as the true and perfect life.

Messianism is Judaism's most profoundly original idea. Think about it: in the future, in the eternally remote, eternally imminent sphere, as receding yet stationary as the horizon, in the realm of the future into which as a rule only playful, wavering, substanceless dreams venture, the Jew dared to build a house for mankind, the house of true life. Whatever yearning, hope, desire for a future crept into the consciousness of other peoples was wholly relative; its advent, either imminent or remote, might manifest itself in such and such a manner, but also in another manner. One wished for, dreamed about, its coming, but who knew whether it would indeed come? Who dared to believe in it when the cold, clear day shone through one's window? But here, in Messianism, something fundamentally different was at work. Here it was not a question of whether the future might come; it had to come: every moment guaranteed it, one's blood guaranteed it—and so did God. Nor was the coming to take place either imminently or at some remote time; it was to take place at the end of time, in the fullness of time, at the end of days: in the absolute future. And though very often what was expected to come was something relative—the liberation of a tortured people and its ingathering around God's sanctuary—on the summit it was the absolute, the redemption of the human spirit and the salvation of the world, where the relative was considered the means toward this absolute. Here, for the first time and with full force, the absolute was proclaimed as the goal, a goal to be realized in and through mankind.

At the same time, Messianism prepared, as it were, the ground for the final and complete realization of Judaism's two other tendencies, the unity-idea and the deed-idea. But just as an incessant battle had been waged around those ideas, so here, too, a battle raged; and we frequently find, at one and the same time, the most exalted concept of the Messianic ideal next to the vulgar notions of future comforts. Hence, the Messianic movements are a mixture of the most holy and most profane, of a future-oriented purpose and lack of restraint, of love of God and avid curiosity. Here, too, the people's bents resist spiritualization, and tarnish the purity of fulfillment.

It should be noted that early Christianity also was distinguished by the idea of an absolute future, the "end of days," a redemption of the world not yet accomplished but still to come. Here, also, a conflict flared up, the conflict between the Messianic ideal and the transference of Messianic concepts to the person of the leader and master.

Still another significant phenomenon calls for a closer

look. As is true of Spinoza's philosophy in the realm of
the unity-idea, this phenomenon, though part of the absolute life of Judaism, transcends its relative life and has
therefore not entered the people's consciousness. I am
speaking of socialism. Modern socialism has two psychological wellsprings: (1) critical insight into the nature of
man's coexistence with man, into the nature of the community and of society; (2) longing for a purer, truer, more
beautiful life, for a pure, a true coexistence of man with
man, for a human community built on love, mutual understanding, and mutual help.

The first wellspring, though it probably did not originate there, has nevertheless received its strength from
the wisdom of the West. Plato is the master whose image
hovers over the first swelling of its waters. The second
spring originated in Judaism, and steadily received a new
influx from it. The prophets were the first to proclaim its
message; the Essenes the first community to attempt to
live accordingly, in unconditionality. Clear at one time,
dim at another, the longing was never wholly extinguished. And when the Jews left the ghetto and entered
the life of the nations, both springs flowed in them, to
become the tenet and the apostolate of modern socialism. This modern socialism is a diminution, a narrowing, a finitizing of the Messianic ideal, though sustained
and nurtured by the same force, the future-idea. But the
future-idea will rise above socialism, to enter once again
the infinite, the absolute. We can only sense its future
shape, but our sensing it is in itself a sign that this idea of
Judaism, too, lives on—a mute, underground life, awaiting its day, the day of renewal.

It is only now that we can see what renewal of Judaism
means. The great spiritual process whose outlines I have
depicted has come to a standstill. If Judaism is not to continue its sham existence, if it is to be resurrected to true

life, its spirit must be renewed and its spiritual process
start anew. The true life of Judaism, like the true life of
any creative people, is that which I have called its absolute life. Only such a life can create not merely an aggres-
sive or defensive but a positive consciousness of peoplehood, the consciousness of the people's immortal substance. At the present time, the Jewish people knows only
a relative life; it must regain its absolute life, it must regain living Judaism.

In a hasidic legend it is told how a departed spirit wanders, in eternity, from gate to gate, from power to power.
But suddenly, unable to go on, he stops. Before him, he
sees an old man who asks: "Why do you stand here?"
"I cannot go on," the spirit answers. Whereupon the old
man replies: "This is not a good thing. For if you linger
here without going on and on, you may lose the life of the
spirit, and remain in this place like a mute rock."

This is the danger threatening the Jewish people:
that it may lose the life of the spirit. We cannot comfort
ourselves that the danger has passed by pointing to the
flourishing of a new literature or to any other values we
are accustomed to calling "Jewish Renaisssance," an
expression of hope rather than reality. I have pointed
out these beginnings so often that I need not fear to be
misunderstood when I say that all this still does not in any
way signify a renewal of Judaism. A renewal must originate in deeper regions of the people's spirit, where the
great tendencies of Judaism were once born. The battle
for fulfillment must begin anew.

But this alone is not enough. For now we know the
innermost sickness of the uprooted people, and its abys-
mal fate. We know that its absolute and its relative life
are sundered; that what constitutes the summit and the
eternal for the absolute life is wholly, or almost wholly,
unperceived by the relative life, or is at best looked upon

as a quickly-to-be-forgotten episode. Hence, renewal must
also mean this: that the battle for fulfillment encompass
the entire people; that the ideas penetrate the day's reality; that the spirit enter life. Only when Judaism once
again reaches out, like a hand, grasping each Jew by the
hair of his head and carrying him, in the tempest raging
between heaven and earth, toward Jerusalem, as the hand
of the Lord once grasped and carried Ezekiel, the priest,
in the land of the Chaldeans[13]—only then will the Jewish
people be ready to build a new destiny for itself where
the old one once broke into fragments. The bricks may
be, indeed must be, assembled now; but the house can be
built only when the people have once more become build-
ers.

Nor is it enough for only single ideas to be renewed,
whether it be one or another, or even the one and the
other. For Judaism cannot be renewed in bits and pieces.
Renewal must be all of one piece. And since we who have
undertaken to discern the meaning of past times and the
meaning of our time know all this, we should be allowed
to state what we sense will be the substance of the renewal
of Judaism: a creative synthesis of Judaism's three ideas,
in accord with the attitude toward the world of men yet to
come.

I have already said that these ideas are not abstract
concepts, rigid and finished, but that they are, on the contrary, innate tendencies of the people's spirit striving for
an ever purer shape, an ever more valid form, an ever
more perfect realization. They can, and must, find a new
shape, a new form, a new realization all merging in a new
attitude toward the world.

In a new attitude toward the world. I mean the attitude that is beginning to germinate in us, the men of today, the men who lead the way and pass on, and that will
sprout in the men of some future generation. This human

attitude is still unexpressed today. The molding of it and
the renewal of Judaism are two sides of one process. "For
salvation comes from the Jews" [14]: Judaism's basic tendencies constitute the elements out of which, recurrently, a
new universal conception of the world is created. Thus,
the most deep-seated humanity of our soul and its most
deep-seated Judaism mean and desire the same thing.

But what the nature of this future synthesis will be,
how it will be born, of this no word can be said. We
know that it will come; we do not know how it will come.
We can only be prepared.

To be prepared, however, does not mean to wait im-
movably. It means to educate oneself and others to the consciousness of Judaism, the consciousness in which the spiritual process of Judaism becomes manifest in all its magnitude, in the fullness of its substance, in the manifold
transmutations of its historical revelation, and in the nameless mystery of its latent forces.

To be prepared means even more. It means to realize Judaism's great tendencies in our personal lives: the
tendency toward unity, by molding our soul into a single
entity, in order to enable it to conceive unity; the tendency toward the deed, by filling our soul with unconditionality, in order to enable it to realize the deed; the tendency toward the future, by unbinding our soul from the
utilitarian bustle and directing it toward the goal, in order
to enable it to serve the future.

We read in Isaiah: "The voice cries: In the wilderness prepare the path of the Lord!" (40:3). To be prepared means to prepare.

IV

The Spirit of the Orient and Judaism

I.

AT THE END of the eighteenth and beginning of the nineteenth century, Herder and Goethe, Novalis[1] and Goerres,[2] were aware of the fact that the Orient is a single unit. Though they knew the diversity of its peoples—which, in fact, had been really discovered by Europe only then, through their historical and literary documents—these men looked through the shell of diversity and saw its unified spiritual core. To them, the Orient was no poetic trope but an undivided, efficacious reality whose touch they experienced and of whose greatness they had a first, awe-inspiring inkling. This insight remained alive until it was challenged by the widely successful racial theory of our age. What the application of the method of the natural sciences attempted to do to psychology, it here attempted to do to history: to corrode the noblest possession of cognitive man—totality. The ratio between the degrees of stimulus and reaction may be calculable, but this calculation cannot testify to the reality of psychic processes. No matter how precisely ascertainable racial differences may be, the supraracial structures—nations and complexes of nations—remain a spiritual reality, inaccessible to such investigation. The great complex of Oriental nations can be shown to be one entity, an organism whose members, no matter how functionally different, have a similar structure and a similar vitality; and, as such, the Orient holds a position in its own right vis-à-vis the Occident.

At certain times the Oriental was looked upon as representing a primitive developmental stage, as, so to speak, arrested man—a narrow, generalizing view. But one may well point out that the time that molded his spiritual character and determined his creative power, the hour of his decisive plasticity, came during an earlier epoch of world history than the European's formative hour. We can have only a faint inkling of the shaping forces experienced by China and India, Egypt and Asia Minor, during the prodigious third pre-Christian millennium, forces disclosed in the preserved remnants of the towering creations they produced in this and the following millennium —the Shi-Ching and the Vedas, the Pyramid manuscript and the Gilgamesh epos. What took place at that time becomes a little clearer to us when we include the men who arose in the Orient during the period of the Golden Age of Greece: men of restoration and regeneration, proclaimers of return and recovery—the Jewish prophets as well as the thinkers of the Upanishads, Zoroaster, and Lao-tse. It can then be understood why it must be asserted that, like Egypt's, the Orient's plastic art at the beginning of the third millennium is at once primitive and perfect.

I would define the Oriental type of human being, recognizable in the documents of Asia's antiquity as well as in the Chinese or Indian or Jew of today, as a man of pronounced motor faculties, in contrast to the Occidental type, represented by, say, the Greek of the Periclean period, the Italian of the Trecento, or the contemporary German, whose sensory faculties are greater than his motor. My calling them motor or sensory types is predi-

cated on the processes central to the psychic life of the
one or the other; in doing so, I well realize that I am sim-
plifying matters: in order to point out the essential, I
present what is mixed as pure, and what is in flux as
frozen.

The basic psychic act of the motor-type man is cen-
trifugal: an impulse emanates from his soul and becomes
motion. The basic psychic act of the sensory-type man
is centripetal: an impression is made on his soul and becomes an image. Both are perceiving, both acting, men;
but the one perceives in motions, the other acts in images.
The first, perceiving, has the experience of action; the
second, acting, has the experience of shape. Both think;
but the thinking of the first means doing, the thinking of
the other, form.

I said: the motor-type man perceives in motions; he
acts, as it were, his perception. It does not grow in him, but
strikes through him; it does not nest, in isolation, in his
brain, but, linked to all other senses, spreads throughout
his agitated body. The senses of this type of man are
closely connected with each other and with the dark life
of the organism; an impression made upon any one of his
senses passes like a shock through all of them, and their
specific qualities pale before the force of the general impact. In the sensory-type man, the senses are separated
from each other and from the undifferentiated base of
organic life; they are under the preponderant influence
of the most detached, most independent, most objective
among them: the sense of sight. The triumph of the
Greeks in the creative sphere of pure form and shape is
the work of this hegemony.

In the motor-type man, the sense of sight is not sovereign. It serves only as mediation between the motion
of the world and the latent motion of his own body, which
is capable of perceiving and experiencing the former

along with the latter. It is the motion of the world that he perceives with his sense of sight as well as with his other senses, an impression that spreads all through him. He is aware less of the multifarious existence of things in repose than of their processes and relationships, of their mutuality and their community; less aware of outline than of countenance; less of proximity than of sequence; less of space than of time. This contrast still prevails even in the most inward experiences of the mind. Plato envisions the ideas as being forever in repose; what the Indian mystic envisions is not repose but a cessation of motion. When Plato envisions something, there is nothing but the vision; the Jewish prophet envisions God only in order to hear His word. Plato calls the essence of things *eidos:* that means form; the Chinese philosopher calls the essence of things *Tao:* that means the way.

The Oriental's world-image is determined by his psychological nature. To sensory man, guided by the most objective sense, sight, the world appears objectified, as a multiplicity of things which is spread before his eyes and to which he himself and his body belong. To motor-type man, the world appears as limitless motion, flowing through him. Though he perceives individual things, he does not perceive them as separate entities, each reposing and complete in itself, but only as an aggregate of nodal points for an infinite motion, which flows through him as well. In this sense only can the Oriental justifiably be called a subject-oriented man. He views the world, naturally and primarily, as something happening to him; he senses rather than perceives it, for he is gripped by and permeated with this world, which, detachedly, confronts the Occidental.

The Occidental's comprehension of his sensations originates in the world; the Oriental's comprehension of the world originates in his sensations. The Occidental's world-image begins with the objective concreteness of the world, even if from there he proceeds to the highest abstractions, or delves into the deepest mysteries of the soul; the Oriental begins with the inwardness of the world, which he experiences in his own inwardness. But this inwardness of his, in which his body's and his soul's every motion is grounded, is itself not motion; he perceives it as lying in repose within him, invulnerable and invariable, primevally exempt from all multiplicity and all contrast, perceiving the womb giving birth to and devouring all multiplicity and all contrast, the nameless essence and meaning. And just as he comprehends the motion through his sensations, so are the essence and meaning of the world disclosed to him through his comprehension of the essence and meaning of his life; the one is revealed to him through the other, and, ultimately, the two are one.

The creative power of the Orient is rooted in this identification. The Occidental progresses, step by step, from the world's appearance to its truth, or he penetrates to this truth by a flash of intuition; the Oriental carries this truth in the essence of his being, finding it in the world by giving it to the world. This simultaneous giving and finding is the religious act of the Oriental. Every world-image, in conformity with its character as an image, is, of course, a simplification and standardization of the world; but the Greek, it may be said, simplifies it by classifying its phenomena according to universal categories; the Asiatic, by building a unified world out of his own inwardness, out of his undivided spirit. His unitary instinct is the more elemental of the two.

But—and this is where all great Asiatic religions and ideologies meet—the unified world must not only be conceived, it must be realized. It is not merely given to man, it is given to him as a task; he is charged with making the true world an actual world. Here the motor character of the Oriental is evidenced in its highest sublimation: as the pathos of command. The command may be answered by a wholly inward act; this is what the Indian of the Vedanta means when, tearing the web of appearance and recognizing his self as identical with the self of the world, he realizes the true, the unified world in the all-encompassing solitude of his soul. Or the command may be directed toward the total activity of a given world-view, an activity, say, that protects the becoming of the inner world within the external one from the encroachment of violent extremes. This is what is meant by the Taoist Chinese, in whose ancient world-image the world's happenings flow from the counteraction of two principles, the light and the dark, but who perceives Tao, the way, as the single, primal principle in which both are grounded. This is the Tao which the wise man realizes on earth through his life, not by interfering with but by actualizing in this world the cosmic intent of oneness through the significance of both his action and his non-action. Or the command may be directed toward an activity that, by opposing the obstructive, evil principle, serves the breaking-through of unity into the divided world. This is what is meant by the Persian of the Avesta, who is concerned not with maintaining a balance between light and darkness but with unreserved championing of light, whose war he will wage until darkness is completely annihilated and the world unified under the exclusive rule of light.

But whatever its guise, there is always the same inspirited demand for the good life, the fulfilling life, for the "way." Knowledge of the nature of the world, on which the Occidental who wants to master it depends, is forever subservient to the knowledge of the *way*. What is said of Buddha may be said of all Oriental teaching: he did not lecture on whether the world is eternal or temporal; he taught only the way. Socrates, too, desired to teach the way rather than merely transmit information; but

here a sense of life's ultimate truth is lacking: that the
world's inner destiny is, to an unfathomable degree, dependent upon the deed of the doer. It is this truth that
the "way" of Oriental teaching connotes: the truth of the
word, "One thing above all is needed." ³

The Orient perceives that the full manifestation and
disclosure of the world's inner substance is thwarted; that
the primally intended unity is split and distorted; that the
world needs human spirit in order to become redeemed
and unified; and that this alone constitutes the meaning
and the power of man's existence in the world. Being is in
the state of duality: the duality of yea and nay, as the
Chinese formulation expresses it; of good and evil, as
the Persian puts it; and of the real and the illusory world,
as given in the Indian formulation. Man is called upon to
change being from duality to unity. The world is waiting
for man, to be unified by him. The paths leading to this
work are many, but there is only one way: *he hodos tou
theou* (Mark 12:14), God's way in the world.

But the Orient's timeless greatness and its timeless
import for mankind reside in the fact that this perception
is wholly turned toward life: whether it is to be realized
in solitude or in communion, in tranquillity or in battle,
its essence is its demand for realization. As perception
it is merely an intention. Accomplishment is only in the
deed. To the Orient, the contemplated idea is a project
that becomes reality only in the lived idea. This alone,
the lived idea, *is*.

II.

The fundamental tenet of the Orient that I have described unfolded in all of its peoples who built their own
spiritual edifice. But in one among them, in the smallest

and youngest, settled along the spatial divide between
Orient and Occident, and blossoming forth at the temporal
divide between the flowering of the Orient and the flowering of the Occident, this tenet underwent a change that
has determined mankind's fate up to our time.

The Jews are the Orient's latecomers. They appear
long after the era of the great Oriental nations' plasticity,
their determining and molding experiences. The Jews'
creative power begins to manifest itself only long after
those nations have communicated theirs in widespread
civilizations. Two of these civilizations, referred to in the
biblical documents of Israel's earliest wanderings, the
Babylonian and the Egyptian, culturally enriched the
young Jewish nation. A group of scholars thought it
could be deduced from this fact that the Jewish mind is
unoriginal and unproductive. But all their efforts were
founded on a basically false premise: that it is inherent
in the nature of an individual's or a people's substantive
productivity not to take over from others any matter for
their creations. The opposite is true: to create means to
gather within oneself all elements, and to fuse them
into a single structure; there is no true creative independence except that of giving form. Not where one finds a
"motif" but what one does with it is historically decisive.
When an Egyptian priest of the second millennium
prophesies that a famine will stalk the land but that later
a king will appear who will restore the former prosperity,
a "schema" may have been transmitted, but it lacks content and is barren. But when, a thousand years later, the
prophet Amos of Tekoa takes up this schema and infuses
it with life by his inner fervor, when he proclaims that the
Lord God will sift Israel among all the nations, yet no
grain will fall upon the ground, and that He will raise up
David's fallen tabernacle,[4] then here and not there is
creation, here and not there a beginning.

We arrive at the same conclusion when we compare a Babylonian with a Jewish psalm of penitence. The first is a worshipper's protestation that he ate but unknowingly what is an abomination unto his god; the second, a supplication: "Renew within me a steadfast spirit" (Psalm 51:12). What does it matter how much may have been taken over, compared to the ineffable process of internalization? Internalization: we may be permitted to distinguish by this term what the Jewish people did with the Orient's spiritual creations that came into their possession. I do not, however, mean to designate by it anything general, but rather something that is unique.

All that I have said about the Oriental is especially true of the Jew. He represents the human type with the most distinctly pronounced motor faculties. Doing is more essential to him than apperception, or, more accurately, his essential, lived, experience consists of his doing. Like the Oriental in general, the Jew especially is more acutely aware of the countenance than of the outline of things, of sequence more than of proximity, of time more than of space. He experiences the world less in the separate, diverse, isolated existence of things than in their amalgamation, in their common and communal characteristics. For the Greek, the concept is the end of a psychic process; for the Jew, it is the beginning. But much more deeply rooted in him is the Oriental's elemental drive toward unity, which in him, as I have already said, has taken a memorable turn.

The Jew, too, perceives that the world's inwardness cannot fully manifest itself or be revealed, and that the primevally intended unity is split and distorted; he, too, is aware of the world's state of duality. But he experiences this duality not merely as something made known to him in the world, as does the Chinese, or in the relation be-

tween world and cognitive subject, as does the Indian, or
in the relation between world and acting subject, as does
the Persian. Rather, and above all else, he experiences it
in his inmost self, as the duality of his I. The unified world
—yet to be built—exists within man himself, intended
and projected as the "will of God"; but, also within man
himself, it is opposed by a resistant, reluctant element.
Man feels called to the former, but is held back by the
latter; he perceives himself as a battleground of prodigious
contradictions. A Jew who in this respect is representative,
Paul, expressed this perception in movingly simple words:
"For I do not that good which I will, but the evil which I
hate that I do." [5] When man is so beset, he is in a state of
bondage of duality, of conditionality, of division, of "sin";
for sin means nothing more than a divided, unfree existence. He is the bearer of the world's division, he experiences within himself the fate of the world which has fallen
from freedom into bondage, from unity into duality. But
it is within his power to be as well the bearer of the
world's unification. Just as the Indian brings the world to
unity by his insight, so the Jew brings the world to unity
by his decision. On the surface, both actions seem to be a
process taking place only within individual man; in actuality, the process takes place within the essence of the
world.

It is the essence of the world that is brought to its own
fulfillment, to its unity and its wholeness, by the insight
of the Indian and the decision of the Jew. This insight
and this decision are not merely an individual's revelation
that his spirit is at one with the spirit of the world; it is
through them that the unity of being is accomplished. In
man's decision, the divided world decides for unity. In
the act of decision, man knows nothing more than that he
must choose, and even this he does not know with his

reasoning faculties but with his being; when, however, he chooses "with all his soul," [6] the mystery is consummated, and the spirit of God hovers over the waters.[7]

"With all his soul." He who decides with all his soul decides for God; for all wholeness is God's image, shining from within with His own light. In that true, unifying decision in which dualism is abolished, the primal intent of the world is fulfilled, in eternal renewal. Of this, a Jewish saying declares: "The world was created for the sake of the choice of him who chooses."

The man confronted with making a decision perceives his own duality as a duality of good and evil, that is, of a sense of direction and powerful impulses. Only a soul incapable of assembling its forces into a whole chooses evil: it lets its directionless impulses take over. In the soul whose decision stems from its unity, impulse and sense of direction—the undiminished force of passionate drives and the unswerving directness of intent—are one. In the realm entrusted to him, such a man perfects the work of creation. And the perfection of any matter, the highest or lowest, touches on the Divine.

From this point it can be seen that of all the Orientals the Jew is the most obvious antithesis of the Greek. The Greek wants to master the world, the Jew, to perfect it. For the Greek the world exists; for the Jew, it becomes. The Greek confronts it; the Jew is involved with it. The Greek apprehends it under the aspect of measure, the Jew as intent. For the Greek the deed is in the world, for the Jew the world is in the deed.

The supreme sublimation of the Oriental's motor character, the pathos of a divine command, attained its greatest intensity in Judaism. His perception of the world's duality within himself as his own duality imparts an overwhelming impulsion to the Jew's longing for unity. He has not merely discerned the world's anxiety, he has suffered it. In his will to unification pulsates the yearning of the world; and a deeply hidden bond links what, liberating and uniting, he accomplishes for himself and for the creatures and things that are entrusted to him or that he encounters, to what he effects in the world. Every event reveals to him the Orient's ultimate, vital truth of which I have spoken: that the world's inner destiny depends, to an unfathomable degree, on the doer's deed. It is Judaism's basic tenet that the deed as an act of decision is an absolute value. On the surface it may seem that the deed is inescapably set into the unyielding structure of causality, whose rules determine its impact; in fact, however, it affects deeply the world's destiny, and when it remembers its divine goal, unity, when it extricates itself from all conditionality and walks by its own light—that is, the light of God—it is free and powerful, in covenant with the deed of God.

Of all the spiritual creations of mankind, Judaism alone endows man's decision with such centrality in all that comes to pass, and such meaningfulness.

Teshuvah, return, is the name given to the act of decision in its ultimate intensification; it denotes the decisive turning point in a man's life, the renewing, total reversal in the midst of the normal course of his existence. When in the midst of "sin," that is, in decisionlessness, the will to decision awakens, the cover of routine life bursts open, and primal forces break through, storming heavenward. In the man who returns, creation begins anew; in his renewal the substance of the world is renewed. It is told that before the world was created there was nothing, only God, and His name. Then it occurred to God to create the world, and He drew a sketch of it for Himself; but He perceived that the world could not endure, because it had no lasting foundation—whereupon he created the act of return.[8]

Through the fervor of its demand for return, and the fervor of its belief in the power and the glory of return, through its new magic, the magic of decision, Judaism won the Occident for the teaching of the Orient. By means of this teaching Judaism became the representative of the Orient at its best.

III.

None of the great religious teachings originated in the Occident. The Occident received and spiritually reworked what the Orient had to offer, assimilating it to its own forms of thought and sensibility and altering it to fit their pattern. At times, it succeeded in developing further what the Orient had to offer; but it was never able to oppose a symbol of its own to the towering symbols of Asia. Europe has ideologies of incomparable purity, certitude, and inner cohesion, but none of them possesses the elemental force of the great teachings; it has poetic works of sacred and powerful imagery, but none of them knows those metaphors of the nameless which constitute the language of the great teachings; it has religious geniuses of the greatest authenticity, but none of them has, by himself alone, raised the mystery out of the abyss and set it down in the world of man. All of them have received, supported, and proclaimed it, and even the greatest of them, Eckhart,[9] is but a late emissary of the Oriental master.

What is it that Europe lacks, of which it is forever in need and which it can never generate out of its own resources? It has the most comprehensive and highly developed knowledge, yet cannot of itself find meaning; it has the strictest and purest discipline, yet cannot of itself find the way; it has the richest and freest art, yet cannot of itself find the portent; it has the most deep-seated and unswerving beliefs, yet cannot of itself find God. It is surely not the unifying faculty that it lacks, since all its thinking is rooted in it; nor the symbolizing faculty, since all its imagery originates from there; nor creative vigor. What it lacks is the pristine knowledge of the meaning of authentic life, the innate certitude that "One thing above all is needed." It is this that is creatively enduring in the great Oriental teachings, and in them alone. They posit authentic life as the fundamental metaphysical principle, not derived from nor reducible to anything else; they proclaim the way. There is, so they say, no meaning and no truth for man anywhere except in that authentic life which unifies and liberates the world. He who walks on the way, walks in the footsteps of God.

Of the great spiritual systems of the Orient, the one destined to have a decisive effect on Occidental man had to be the system whose proclamation of the way of authentic life challenged every individual directly, the system that was not the privilege of the sage or the chosen but equally accessible to all, and that appealed especially and most powerfully to the man who had lost his way or who lacked direction, to the "sinner": the Jewish teaching of decision and return. Other teachings influenced the sages and the chosen; the Jewish teaching influenced the nations, the peoples of the West. The tenet that the gates of God's kingdom are open to all who embrace justice, and that the man who yearns for the consolation of the unconditioned need only choose the unconditioned and act upon it, impelled both the wise and the simple-minded into one community. This total openness was the greatest and most persuasive characteristic of the Jewish teaching; the second was its orientation toward the positive deed. It did not want—as, for instance, Buddhism did—to lead away from this world, but into its very heart; it did not ask active man to renounce action, but to learn to act justly; it did not kill the vital force of passion; indeed, it wished to intensify it by its prodigious demand. Both principles of the teaching merge in the solemn words of the book *Tanna debe Eliyahu*: "I call heaven and earth to be my witnesses that the Holy Spirit may indeed dwell upon heathens and Jews, upon man and woman, upon man-servant and maid-servant, depending solely upon the human deed." [10] And both sustained the early Christian movement, through whose development the Jewish teaching shaped the spiritual destiny of the West.

This movement did not, it is true, conquer the West by its original essence, but by a syncretistic mixture; it is also true that it took over from Hellenism more than images and words. But what remained enduringly creative in Christianity had originally been Judaism's prime possession. It is significant that the first word of Jesus' sermon in the Synoptics, which repeats the Johannine sermon, is the fundamental word of the prophets: "return," a word whose meaning can be understood only from the traditional teaching of *teshuvah*. The motive power of Jesus' message is the ancient Jewish demand for the unconditioned decision, a decision that transforms man and lifts him into the divine realm. And this demand continued to be the motive power of Christianity, re-called into play whenever it wanted to renew itself, no matter how de-Judaized it imagined itself to be.

IV.

The early Christian movement was no isolated phenomenon in Judaism. Having originated in the womb of ancient Jewish communal societies, it was, even in its own time, only one of the manifestations of a new spiritual flowering, of which our literature has transmitted to us significant, though only fragmentary, evidence. In the middle of this era of great productivity a fateful disaster overtook the Jews: the downfall of their state. At what apex of its vitality this people was broken was evidenced, six decades after the destruction of Jerusalem, by Bar-Kokhba's great rebellion,[11] which proved so powerful that Rome feared for all her Oriental possessions. And when, in the fourth year of incessant efforts by her best commanders and troops, she succeeded in subduing the small Judean nation, Hadrian, in his victory message to the Senate, omitted the usual formula: "I and my army are well." We can have only a faint inkling of the depth of the tragedy that befell Judaism at that time; the account of Jews sold for the price of a horse in the marketplace of Hebron, at the site of Abraham's terebinth, seems like a monstrous portent. And thus they came to the West.

This event split Judaism's history in two, in a manner that probably never happened before or since to any other people. By being torn out of its Oriental soil, it was also torn from the continuity of its spiritual development. This can be understood by looking at two factors: the attachment of the Jew of antiquity to his land, and the genesis of his spiritual productivity.

Some learned students of the psychology of Judaism maintain, with axiomatic certainty, that Israel has been and continues to be a nomadic people, and deduce from this all sorts of Jewish character traits, real or alleged. They seek to confirm this view by pointing out that in biblical books, in most of the Prophets, we find images and metaphors from pastoral life, whereas images and metaphors from agricultural life are exceedingly rare. This is not true of any of the books; indeed, in the older prophetic books—the First Isaiah, for instance—whose authors had the closest contact with the natural life of the people, there is hardly a single image from animal husbandry for every twenty from field, garden, or vineyard. Actually, we have too little reliable knowledge of the era preceding the conquest of Canaan to venture the assertion that at that time the Jews were an exclusively nomadic people; and insofar as we are at all justified in regarding the biblical tales as source material, we may in fact read them quite differently. Isaac's blessing for Jacob is the blessing of a tiller of the soil, and Joseph's dream of the tying of the sheaves is the dream of a tiller of the soil.[12] All the literature of the Palestinian period attests so great a love of the soil and exaltation of its cultivation as is found in but a few other nations. The object of divine threats as well as of divine promises is almost always the soil, and Ben Sira expresses the feeling of centuries when he declares that the plowman preserves the substance of eternal creation.[13] Seldom has there been another people so self-contained and so glorying in its rootedness. And the whole spiritual and religious life of ancient Judaism was closely bound up with the life of the soil, the life of this familiar earth. God was the lord of the field; His festivals were agrarian festivals, his law an agrarian law. However high a peak of universalism prophecy attained, it remained forever rooted in this nature-bound life, and its command was to be fulfilled in this same nature-bound life; its spirit at all times wanted to be clothed in a body of this particular Canaanite soil.

Jewish religion did not teach (and non-Pauline early Christianity remained faithful to this) a carrying-forth of the message to the nations, as Pauline Christianity did, nor a conquering of the world for the faith, as Islam did; it taught rootedness in one's native land, observance of the good life within narrow confines, and the building of a model human community on the scanty Canaanite soil.

And Judaism's most profoundly original creation, Messianism, is but the same idea, conceived as supreme fulfillment and projected into the absolute future when the Lord will prepare, on Mount Zion and for all nations, "a meal of pure wine, in which there is no yeast" (Isaiah 25:6). All creative work took its strength and its form from its organic ties to the soil. And now these ties were sundered, and, with them, the inner cohesion of the Jewish spirit. God, the lord of the soil, became the patron of piety; His festivals, once agrarian, became synagogue festivals; His law, once agrarian, became a ritual law. The spirit became detached from its roots. It was then that the Jews did indeed become a nomadic people.

There was still another contributing factor. The Oriental peoples' spiritual life, in which the perilous traits of the motor-type individual are combined with his most sublime potential, and in which both the self's abandonment to the world's frenzy and its contemplation of its own and the world's unalterable inwardness are nurtured by the same roots, tended to develop in the form of a struggle: the struggle of creative minds, of leaders and redeemers, against the aimlessness of the people's drives. This struggle was especially intense and fecund in ancient Judaism. The cognizance of inner duality and the immanent demand for decision—that is, of the soul's unification—divided the people into two psychologically distinct factions: one consisted of men who choose, who make decisions, who are impelled toward unconditionality and are dedicated to their goal; the other of laissez-faire men, decisionless men, men who remain indolently inert in their conditionality, and whose aim is self-aggrandizement and self-satisfaction—or, in biblical terms, men who are servants of God, and men who are servants of Baal. It should be remembered, however, that those men do not by any means decide for Baal and against God, but that,

as stated by Elijah, they "hobble along on two tree-
limbs" (I Kings 18:21). In the struggle against them, the
specific genius of the prophets and teachers of Israel is repeatedly set afire; theirs is a fighting genius, and Jewish
creativity is a fighting creativity, for the sake of the
spirit. [. . .]

With the destruction of the Jewish Commonwealth,
the creativity of the fight for the sake of the spirit was
diminished. All spiritual strength was now concentrated on
preserving the substance of nationhood against external
influences; on closely fencing in one's own realm in order
to keep out the influx of alien tendencies; on the codifi-
cation of all values in order to prevent any displacements;
and on an unequivocal, not-to-be-misconstrued—that is,
an invariably rational—formulation of religion. Increasingly, the God-permeated, commanding, creative element
was being replaced by the rigid, merely preserving, merely
continuing, merely defensive element of official Judaism.
Indeed, turning more and more against the creative element, which supposedly endangered the continued existence of nationhood by its boldness and liberality, official
Judaism charged men with heresy and became hostile to
life. In the sterile atmosphere of this conflict there developed a detached intellectuality that, as out of touch
with the fundamental roots of natural life as with the
functions of a genuine fight for the sake of the spirit, was
neutral, devoid of substance, and dialectical. This intellectuality dedicated itself to every sort of subject, even the
most trivial, analyzing or juxtaposing them; but it would
not commit itself to any one of them in a truly intuitive-
instinctive way. The broken creative force, robbed of
its natural context, the power of unconditionality, lived on
only in heretics, who as a rule remained powerless and
amorphous, perishing in the dark; occasionally they broke
through the fence, as the great Spinoza did, and addressed

the world, so that it fell silent, listening. It lived on also in the Messianic movements, which rose in the swirling flames of an ecstatic faith, and collapsed; and in the world of Jewish mysticism which, subterraneously, tended the sacred fire of the ancient bond with God, permitting it to flare up, and outward to the people, only once: in the rise of the great religious movement of Hasidism, which gripped Polish Jewry in the eighteenth century and revealed anew the limitless power of Oriental man. But inhibited by anxieties about preserving Judaism's special character, Hasidism did not dare touch the fence, and consequently it was incapable of taking over the functions of a genuine fight for the sake of the spirit.

Thus it could happen that in the nineteenth century, when the emancipation led Judaism to a high mountain peak and showed it the world's realms and their magnificence, the fence was broken and trampled down not by an elemental force pressing forward toward new creation but by a pale, feeble attempt at reform, which derived its thinking and its patterns from the catalogues of European enlightenment and the so-called progressive religions. We live in the uncertain state that followed these attempts: the last old structure of the Oriental spirit within Judaism appears to be shaken, with no foundation laid for a new one.

Nevertheless, this foundation exists, and continues to exist, unshaken. It is the Jew's own soul. For the Jew has remained an Oriental. He was driven out of his land and dispersed throughout the lands of the Occident; he was forced to dwell under a sky he did not know, and on a soil he did not till; he has suffered martyrdom and, worse than martyrdom, a life of degradation; the ways of the nations among which he has lived have affected him, and he has spoken their languages; yet, despite all this, he has remained an Oriental. He has preserved within himself the limitless motor faculties that are inherent in his nature, and their attendant phenomena, a dominant sense of time and a capacity for quick conceptualization. He has also preserved within himself, sometimes buried but never completely crushed, his elemental unitary drive and the motif of demand. One can detect all this in the most assimilated Jew, if one knows how to gain access to his soul; and even those who have eradicated the last vestiges of Judaism from the content of their thinking still, and ineradicably, carry Judaism with them in the pattern of their thought. But all these traits still live, and can be recognized from afar, in Eastern Europe's Jewish masses, who are poor in the skills of civilization but, despite encroaching corruption and corrosion, rich in the power of an original ethos and a spirit of immediacy.

We need only to look at the decadent yet still wondrous Hasid of our days; to watch him as he prays to his God, shaken by his fervor, expressing with his whole body what his lips are saying—a sight both grotesque and sublime; to observe him at the close of the Sabbath as he partakes, with kingly gestures and in concentrated dedication, of the sacred meal to which cling the mysteries of the world's redemption, and we will feel: here, stunted and distorted yet unmistakable, is Asiatic strength and Asiatic inwardness.

On this manifest or latent Orientalism, this base of the Jew's soul that has endured underneath all influences, I build my faith in a new spiritual-religious creation by Judaism. In the detachment and dissolution of its Western existence it can succeed only in parts. One may undertake bold spiritual ventures, or coin strong spiritual expressions; religious excitement may flash from the storm-heavy darkness of the people's fate; but a great creation that fuses all this into a single synthesis, re-establishes the continuity of Jewish becoming, and once more gives full expression to the immortal Jewish unitary drive—this will come into being only after the continuity of life in Palestine, where the great concepts of this unitary drive once originated, has been re-established. The Jew is not the same person he once was; he has passed through every heaven and hell of the Occident, and his soul has come to grief. But his original strength has remained unimpaired; indeed, it has been purified. Once it comes into contact with its maternal soil, it will once more become creative. The Jew can truly fulfill his vocation among the nations only when he begins anew, and, with his whole, undiminished, purified original strength, translates into reality what his religion taught him in antiquity: rootedness in his native land; leading the good life within narrow confines; and building a model community on the scanty Canaanite soil.

V.

Our age will one day be designated as the era of the Asiatic crisis. The dominant nations of the Orient have surrendered partly to the external power of Europe, partly to its internally-overpowering influences. They have not preserved their most sacred possessions, their great spiritual traditions; at times they even relinquished them voluntarily. The subjugation of India, the self-Europeanization of Japan, the debilitation of Persia, and, lastly, the ravaging of China where the ancient Oriental spirit seemed to dwell in inviolable security, are some of the phases of this process. The soul of Asia is being murdered, and is itself participating in this murder. The world is about to lose something irreplaceably precious, yet it does not care; instead, it applauds the nations that destroy it. We need a searching of our souls, a turning inward, a return. Eu-

rope must dare to promote a new era, in which the Orient
will be preserved and an understanding between East and
West established for their mutual benefit and for the hu-
manitarian work they must share. In this era, Asia will not
be overpowered by Europe but will be developed from
within, by its own inner resources; and Europe will not be
threatened by Asia but will be led by it toward the great
vital truths.

For this world-historical mission, Europe has at its
disposal a mediating people that has acquired all the wisdom and all the skills of the Occident without losing its
original Oriental character, a people called to link Orient
and Occident in fruitful reciprocity, just as it is perhaps
called to fuse the spirit of the East and the West in a new
teaching. How this will come about cannot as yet be outlined. But this much can be said: that Jerusalem still is—
and today more than ever—what it was considered to be
in antiquity: the gateway of the nations. Here is the timeless passageway between Orient and Occident. It was
here that ancient Asia came when it marched, conquering, toward the West, under Nebuchadnezzar and Cyrus,[14]
here Alexander's Europe and Rome's came when they
planned to subdue the Orient. Under the onslaught of
East on West, the First Jewish Commonwealth broke
down, as did the Second Commonwealth under the onslaught of West on East.[15] Since then, Palestine's importance for the world has increased and deepened. Today
Jerusalem is the gateway of the nations in an even more
profound, broader, more threatening and more promising
sense than before. It is up to us to seek its salvation, which
is the salvation of the nations.

V

Jewish Religiosity

JEWISH RELIGIOSITY is not, as many people think, a matter of admittedly special dignity but otherwise negligible moment for the so-called "solution of the Jewish question." It is rather, now as always, the only matter of unconditional moment for Judaism—motive power of its fate, guidepost to its destiny, a force whose upsurging blaze would restore it to new life and whose total extinction would deliver it to death. Renewal of Judaism means in reality renewal of Jewish religiosity. One may, unconcerned with Jewish religiosity, want, demand, and proclaim the dissolution of Judaism; or one may, still so unconcerned, want, demand, and proclaim its "preservation," that is, the imperceptible dissolution of Judaism —but not its renewal. Whoever longs for such a renewal wants a Judaism that is once more alive with all its senses, active with all its forces, joined together as a holy community; he has recognized that the only way that will take him there, out of the present Jewish existence, leads through renunciation and a new beginning. The more acutely man yearns for a renewal of Judaism, longing for it with all his powers of volition and recognition, the greater will be his certainty that such a renewal means a renewal of Jewish religiosity.

I say and mean: religiosity. I do not say and do not mean: religion. Religiosity is man's sense of wonder and adoration, an ever anew becoming, an ever anew articulation and formulation of his feeling that, transcending his conditioned being yet bursting from its very core, there is something that is unconditioned. Religiosity is his longing to establish a living communion with the unconditioned, his will to realize the unconditioned through his action, transposing it into the world of man. Religion is the sum total of the customs and teachings articulated and formulated by the religiosity of a certain epoch in a people's life; its prescriptions and dogmas are rigidly determined and handed down as unalterably binding to all future generations, without regard for their newly developed religiosity, which seeks new forms. Religion is true so long as it is creative; but it is creative only so long as religiosity, accepting the yoke of the laws and doctrines, is able (often without even noticing it) to imbue them with new and incandescent meaning, so that they will seem to have been revealed to every generation anew, revealed today, thus answering men's very own needs, needs alien to their fathers. But once religious rites and dogmas have become so rigid that religiosity cannot move them or no longer wants to comply with them, religion becomes uncreative and therefore untrue. Thus religiosity is the creative, religion the organizing, principle. Religiosity starts anew with every young person, shaken to his very core by the mystery; religion wants to force him into a system stabilized for all time. Religiosity means activity—the elemental entering-into-relation with the absolute; religion means passivity—an acceptance of the handed-down command. Religiosity has only one goal; religion several. Religiosity induces sons, who want to find their own God, to rebel against their fathers; religion induces fathers to reject their sons, who will not let their fathers' God be forced upon them. Religion means preservation; religiosity, renewal.

But whatever the way another people may find its salvation, to the Jewish people it will be disclosed only in the living force to which its peoplehood was ever bound, and through which it had its existence: not in its religion but in its religiosity. The Baal Shem[1] says: "We say 'God of Abraham, God of Isaac and God of Jacob'; we do not say 'God of Abraham, Isaac and Jacob,' so that you may be told: Isaac and Jacob did not rely on Abraham's tradition, but they themselves searched for the Divine." [2]

I shall try to extricate the unique character of Jewish religiosity from the rubble with which rabbinism and rationalism have covered it.

The act that Judaism has always considered the essence and foundation of all religiosity is the act of decision as realization of divine freedom and unconditionality on earth. The late-Jewish saying, "The world was created for the sake of the choice of him who chooses," is only the mature formulation of an idea that, though still unformulated, already existed and was basic in biblical times. Just as the sequence of Sinaitic laws opens with the call to an exclusive and unconditional decision for the One, so do Moses' greatest words serve to support the same demand: "Thou shalt be whole-hearted with the Lord thy God" (Deut. 18:13) and ". . . serve the Lord your God with all your heart and with all your soul" (Deut. 11:13). The prophets proclaim the same, beginning with Elijah, who speaks to the people: "How long will you continue to hobble along on two tree-limbs?" (I Kings 18:21). The idea is developed with increased poignancy in post-biblical literature. The Mishnah interprets the phrase "Thou shalt love God with all thy heart" to mean: with both your inclinations, the "good" as well as the "evil" [3]; that is, with and by your decision, so that the ardor of passion is converted and enters into the unified deed with all its strength. For no inclination is evil in itself; it is made evil by man when he surrenders to it instead of controlling it. The Midrash has God say to man, "You turned passion which was given into your hand into evil." [4] [. . .]

And it is stated with still greater emphasis: "Only when you are undivided" (that is, when you have overcome your inner dualism by your decision) "will you have a share in the Lord your God." [5] On the other hand, inertia and indecisiveness are called the root of all evil; sin is basically nothing more than inertia. The man who has fallen prey to it but later, by a wrenching decision, extricates himself from it; who has sunk into the abyss of duality but later hews his way out of it to unity; and who, taking himself into his own hands, like an inert earthen clod, kneads that self into a human being—that man above all is dearest to God. Or, in the words of the Talmud: "Even the perfectly righteous may not stand in the place where those who have returned are standing." [6] The great decision is the supreme moment in the life of man, indeed, in the life of the entire world. "One hour of return in this world," it is stated in the Sayings of the Fathers, "is better than the entire life in the world to come." [7] For the latter is merely being, whereas the former is the great becoming. Sin means to live not in freedom, that is, decision-making, but in bondage, that is, being acted upon, conditioned. The man who "returns" rises to freedom; he rises from conditionality into unconditionality; he is, as the Zohar calls it, "alive all around, at one with the tree of life."

No man knows the abyss of inner dualism so well as the Jew, but neither does anyone know so well the miracle of unification, which cannot be accepted on faith but must be experienced. Therefore, nothing already realized can ever suffice, but only the act that starts anew with every human being: realization. This is the intent of the teach-

ing of return: that everyone, alone and from his own
depth, must strive for divine freedom and unconditionality; no mediator can help him, nothing already accomplished by another can facilitate his own deed, for all depends on the shattering force of his own action, which can
only be weakened by any kind of help from outside. That
is why the early Christian movement became barren for
the Jew when it converted Jesus' truly Jewish proclamation that every man could become a son of God by living unconditionally into the doctrine that nothing except
belief in the only begotten son of God could win eternity
for man. And that is why Hasidism had to lose its renewing
effect upon the people when it replaced with the mediation
of the Zaddik[8] its former wondrous self-liberation, that
immediate relationship to God in which man "reaches
the root of all teaching and all commandment, God's I,
the simple unity and boundlessness in which commandments and laws fold their wings," because he has risen
above all of them through his unconditionality. To say of
this basic view of religiosity that it is an outpouring of the
Holy Spirit into the man who purifies and sanctifies himself [9] is no exaggeration, but only the strongest way of expressing it.

   The meaning of the act of decision in Judaism is falsi-
fied if it is viewed as merely an ethical act. It is a religious
act, or, rather, it is the religious act; for it is God's realization through man.

   Three distinct strata underlie this concept of realization
in Jewish religiosity. Their sequence reveals the development of the subterranean Judaism which, secret and suppressed, remains authentic and bears witness, in contradistinction to an official, sham Judaism whose power and
public representation have neither authority nor legitimacy.

   On the first, earliest, stratum, the act of decision is

conceived as meaning God's realization through imitation, an *imitatio Dei*. God is man's goal, the primal being
whose image he ought to strive to become, "for God created man to be His image" (Genesis 1:27), that is, so
that he may *become* His image. Fundamental to this concept is the text from Leviticus, "Ye shall be holy, for I,
your God, am holy" (19:2). This is interpreted to mean:
"As I am set apart," that is, determined by nothing, removed from all conditionality, "so you, too, shall be set
apart." [10] And further: "As God is one and only, so your
service be one." God is One; therefore man shall overcome
his duality and become one. God is unconditioned; therefore man shall extricate himself from the shackles of his
conditionality and become unconditional. The simplest
and most convincing expression of this view is given in
the words of Abba Shaul.[11] Explaining a verse of Moses'
song at the Sea of Reeds (Exodus 15:2), he said, "This
is my God—I and He; that is: I want to become like
Him." [12] That there is no other way to this goal but the
way of decision and of unconditionality is shown by the
myth of the Fall: man had the audacity to "be like
God" (Genesis 3:5) and thus to frustrate life's meaning
which lies in *becoming* like God; therefore he obtained
nothing more than an awareness of the dualism of the
Divine and the human, the "knowledge of good and evil."

On the second stratum, the act of decision is conceived
as meaning God's realization through an intensification
of His reality. The more man realizes God in the world,
the greater His reality. This seemingly paradoxical formulation of the idea is instantly grasped when the words
" 'Ye are My witnesses,' saith the Lord" (Isaiah 43:10)
are complemented by the interpretation given them by
Rabbi Simeon bar Yohai[13]: "If you are my witnesses, I am
the Lord, and if you are not my witnesses, I am not the
Lord." [14] God is man's goal; therefore, the force of all hu-

man decision flows into the sea of divine power. In the
same spirit, the words of the psalm, "Ascribe ye strength
unto God" (68:35), are explained by the statement that
the righteous increase the power of the upper dominion.[15]
Later writings, especially kabbalistic literature, greatly
enlarged the idea that the man who acts unconditionally
is God's partner and helper in the eternal work of creation. Thus a pillar rises for the righteous, reaching from
earth to heaven, supporting the universe. In the same
vein, the Zohar explains the words of the psalm, "The
works of His hands . . . are faithfulness and justice"
(111:7), as meaning that man who acts faithfully and
justly influences the becoming of the world; and the passage "God had not yet caused it to rain upon the earth,
and there was no man to till the ground" (Genesis 2:5)
is interpreted to mean that no action emanated from above
because no deed emanated from below. Then, however,
"there went up a mist from the earth, and watered the
whole face of the ground" (Genesis 2:6), which means
that action below effected action above.

Lastly, on the third stratum, which first appears in
the Kabbalah, the concept of God's realization through
man is expanded by the notion that man's deed affects
God's destiny on earth. His *shekhinah* has fallen into the
world of the conditioned; it is, like Israel, in dispersion, in
galut; like Israel, it wanders and strays, tossed into the
realm of things; like Israel, it wants to be redeemed, to
be reunited with the divine Being. But this consummation
can be effected only through him who, within himself, lifts
the conditioned to the unconditioned: thereby the world,
that is, the *shekhinah,* will be lifted. That is why a hasidic
adage declares that those who return redeem God. And
just as, with the entrance of the soul into the human body,
the king, God, is lovingly inclined toward the queen, the
shekhinah, so the queen, in the overcoming of the con-

ditioned by means of the returning soul, lovingly raises
herself up to the king. By such loving union, being is eternally renewed. "Thus life grows from above and from
below, the primal source fills eternally, eternally fills the
sea, and there is sustenance for all."

All three strata have in common a concept that is innate in Jewish religiosity: the concept of the absolute
value of man's deed, a value that cannot be judged by
our meager knowledge of the causes and effects of this
world. Something infinite flows into a deed of a man; something infinite flows from it. The doer cannot apprehend
who the powers are whose emissary and acting agent
he is; he must nevertheless be aware that the fullness of
the world's destiny, namelessly interwoven, passes through
his hands. It is said in the Mishnah, "Every man shall say:
'It is for me that the world was created.' "[16] And again,
"Every man shall say: 'The world rests on me,' " which
is corroborated by the hasidic text: "Yes, he is the only
one in the world, and its continued existence depends on
his deed."

In the unconditionality of his deed man experiences
his communion with God. God is an unknown Being beyond this world only for the indolent, the decisionless,
the lethargic, the man enmeshed in his own designs; for the
one who chooses, who decides, who is aflame with his goal,
who is unconditioned, God is the closest, the most familiar
Being, whom man, through his own action, realizes ever
anew, experiencing thereby the mystery of mysteries.
Whether God is "transcendent" or "immanent" does not
depend on Him; it depends on man. The Zohar remarks,
in connection with the tale in Genesis of the three men
who came to Abraham "in the heat of the day" (18:1):
"When the world below is ablaze with desire for the world
above, the upper world will descend to the lower, and
both will unite and permeate each other in man." A simi-

lar interpretation may be given to the words of the psalm:
"The Lord is close unto all them that call upon Him, to all
that call upon Him in truth" (145:18). That means, in
the truth they *do*.

In the truth they do. This truth is not a What but a
How. Not the matter of a deed determines its truth but the
manner in which it is carried out: in human conditionality, or in divine unconditionality. Whether a deed will
peter out in the outer courtyard, in the realm of things, or
whether it will penetrate into the Holy of Holies is determined not by its content but by the power of decision
which brought it about, and by the sanctity of intent that
dwells in it. Every deed, even one numbered among the
most profane, is holy when it is performed in holiness,
in unconditionality.

Unconditionality is the specific religious content of
Judaism. Jewish religiosity is built neither on doctrine nor
on an ethical prescription, but on a fundamental perception that gives meaning to man: that one thing above all is
needed. This perception is transformed into a demand
(*Forderung*) wherever religiosity is community-forming
and religion-founding, wherever it moves from the life of
individual man into the life of the community. The founding of the Jewish religion and all its essential revolts are
marked by this demand and the struggle for it.

The founding of the Jewish religion was consummated
in demand and struggle. When Moses, his eyes ablaze with
the fire of the burning bush, steps before the elders of
Israel, one can already anticipate all that is going to happen. I know of no greater, more awful event in world
history or world myth. The people had broken away from
the One whom it could not yet grasp, and the sons of Levi,
at Moses' command, walk through the camp, slaying three
thousand of their brothers.[17] The exodus generation cannot
withstand the tribulations of the desert; it must die out in

the desert. In the annihilation of everything that is half-hearted and inadequate, the proclaimed God reveals Himself as the consuming fire of unconditionality.

Here the two dominant human types who wage the struggle of Judaism's internal history are already juxtaposed to each other: the prophet and the priest. Moses is the man of demand who listens only to the voice, acknowledges only the deed. Aaron is the mediator, as accessible to the voices as to the voice, who destroys the people's discipline by his directionless and subservient formalism. The prophet wants truth; the priest, power. They are eternal types in the history of Judaism.

In the struggle, Jewish religiosity turned from the spirit of Moses to religion. Still struggling, it must repeatedly renew itself from within religion, whose formalism threatens to choke it; must endeavor, again and again, to recast, by its fervid demand, the solidified mass. It never succeeds in wresting dominance from official Judaism; but, overtly or covertly, it always has profound effect on the development of the people's spirit. At times religion rises to a new, higher life. At other times it breaks out of the communal structure. And occasionally, after a brief flowering, it decays. The history of Judaism furnishes representative examples of all these possibilities.

Israel's sacrificial cult may have originated in the primitive need for a living communion with God through some sacramental act, such as a communal meal; undoubtedly, this was soon complemented by a quite different feeling: the need for a sacrificial offering that could symbolize, as well as proffer, the intrinsically desired and intended self-sacrifice. Under the leadership of the priest, however, the symbol became a substitute. The sacrificial cult was so elaborated and codified that in every phase of his life, at every moment of his destiny, man had at his disposal a prescribed sacrifice for establishing a communion

with God; but this communion no longer consisted of anything but the sacrifice. It was now no longer necessary,
when gripped by suffering or terrified by one's sin, to commit oneself to God in struggle and surrender, in a storm
of decision, until the creature's cry was stilled before
the secret voice. One offered a sacrifice, one acted according to regulations, and God was appeased. To be sure,
this sacrificial cult with its claim to truth opposed the
promiscuous idol-worship among the people, and Elijah
did not yet know how to phrase his protestations except
to say that he was fighting for God and against Baal.[18]
But whether worship-service serves idols or serves God
depends not on the name by which one calls one's God
but on the way in which one serves Him. This is the great
insight manifested by the later prophets, who began to
address the people a century after Elijah. With imperious
passion, Amos and Micah, Isaiah and Jeremiah repudiated
the "abomination" of the sacrificial cult, demanding true
service of God: "justice," that is, living unconditionally
with God and with men. The prophetic message shares
its substance and its ethical norms with the teachings of
other nations; what is unique in it and specifically Jewish
is the breath of unconditionality that pulsates in it from
beginning to end, the postulate of decision that resounds
in all its words and in the very rhythm of its demands: its
religiosity. Every construct of a "pure ethics" of Judaism
misses this basic point. Wherever the unconditioned deed
reveals the hidden divine countenance, there is the core of
Judaism.

The prophets wanted to demolish a sacrificial cult
devoid of intention. They were unable to lessen its dominion; leadership remained in the hands of the priest.
Nevertheless, they renewed Jewish religiosity, and the
people's soul; thus, imperceptibly, are victories of the
spirit consummated.

In the Second Commonwealth a new religious institution became central: the Scriptures. These were gradually canonized as the fixed expression of the state religion. Corps of compilers, subordinate to the priesthood, sifted from the wealth of material whatever seemed to them mythical or suspect. Thus came into being the one Book that encompassed all the writings henceforth considered valid. This Book became so all-embracing that all writings not included in the canon disappeared. But it triumphed not only over all other writings; it triumphed also over life. Henceforth Scripture was truth; one could reach God only by adhering to it in every detail. But it was not viewed, either by the priest or later by the originally more liberal-minded scholar, as a proclamation to be meaningfully adapted to life and given new significance for life. It was viewed as a statute, a sum of prescriptions, formalistically circumscribed by the priest, dialectically spun out by the scholar, and always directed toward the narrow, the rigid, the unfree—thwarting instead of promoting living religiosity.

This tendency of official Judaism engendered two counteractions: one was the more moderate counteraction, developed within its own camp, whose late literary deposit we find in the Aggadah[19]; the other, the more radical, counteraction developed within the self-segregating Essene community and in the movement surging around it that eventually flowed into early Christianity. What is said of the Therapeutae[20] holds true for the attitude of both counteractions to Scripture: they viewed all legislation as a living being whose body was composed of words, its soul of a hidden meaning in which the human soul beholds its own self. Conscious of the externalization that had been inflicted upon Scripture, both pointed to its inwardness. And just as the prophets had not turned against the sacrificial cult as such, so the early Christian

movement did not turn against Scripture but against a
perversion of its meaning from the unconditioned to the
conditioned; it wanted to restore the ardor of the demand.
But none of these movements succeeded in renewing Jewish religion. The Aggadah did not succeed because its
influence had been only fragmentary and because it did
not consolidate its forces. Essenism did not succeed because it succumbed to a sterile separation and did not
reach out to the people. And early Christianity was lost
as a source of renewal for Judaism when it became untrue
to itself, narrowing the great idea that had carried it aloft,
the idea of the God-winning "turning," to a communion
by grace with the Christ; at that point it won the nations,
and abandoned Judaism by sundering the structure of its
community. From then on Christianity rose to dominion
over the nations, and Judaism sank into rigidness, humiliation, and degradation; but its core unshakably maintained its claim to be the true ecclesia, the ever faithful
community of divine immediacy.

Ever since the destruction of the Temple, tradition
has been at the center of Judaism's religious life. A fence
was thrown around the law in order to keep at a distance
everything alien or dangerous; but very often it kept at a
distance living religiosity as well. To be sure, to manifest
itself in a community of men, to establish and maintain a
community, indeed, to exist as a religion, religiosity needs
forms; for a continuous religious community, perpetuated
from generation to generation, is possible only where a
common way of life is maintained. But when, instead of
uniting them for freedom in God, religion keeps men tied
to an immutable law and damns their demand for freedom; when, instead of viewing its forms as an obligation
upon whose foundation genuine freedom can build, it
views them as an obligation to exclude all freedom; when,
instead of keeping its elemental sweep inviolate, it trans-

forms the law into a heap of petty formulas and allows
man's decision for right or wrong action to degenerate into
hairsplitting casuistry—then religion no longer shapes
but enslaves religiosity.

This process characterizes the history of Jewish tradition. Religiosity's counteraction assumes a twofold
shape. One is the sporadic flare-ups of the heretical rebellions, often tied to powerful Messianic movements, which
arouse all the people. The other is the steady, constructive activity of Jewish mysticism, which strives to revive
the ossified rites through the notion of *kavanah,* intention,
and to endow every religious act with a hidden significance
directed toward God's destiny and the redemption of
the world. In the older Kabbalah this tendency was still
imbued with an inherently theologico-allegorizing element that prevented it from becoming popular. It is only
in the later Lurianic Kabbalah[21] that this tendency acquired a dimension of intuitiveness and immediacy. In
Hasidism it developed into a great folk-movement. Hasidism had no desire to diminish the law; it wanted to restore it to life, to raise it once again from the conditioned
to the unconditioned: every man, by living authentically,
shall himself become a Torah, a law. Out of Hasidism
could have come, as never before, a renewal of Jewish
religiosity. But, charged with heresy, slandered, denounced
by official Judaism, and degenerating because of the
weakness of the people, which was not yet equal to the
decisiveness of its teachings, Hasidism deteriorated before
it had done its work.

All three movements—the prophetic, the Essenic-
early Christian, and the kabbalistic-hasidic—share a re-
solve to make man's life not easier but more difficult, while
at the same time inspiriting and exalting it. All have in
common the impetus to restore decision as the determining motive power of all religiosity. Through ossification

of the sacrificial cult, of Scripture and tradition, man's free
decision has been suppressed. It is no longer the deed,
born of decision and drawing breath in unconditionality,
that is viewed as the way to God, but compliance with
rules and regulations. Prophecy, early Christianity, and
Hasidism, on the other hand, call for decision, remem-
bering that this is the soul of Jewish religiosity. The timeless meaning these movements have for Judaism and their
importance for us in the work of renewal is to be found
not in how they ended but whence they came; not in their
forms but in their forces. These are the forces that never
assumed adequate form, never won dominion in Judaism,
and have always been suppressed by official Judaism, that
is, by its ever-dominant dearth of vitality. They are not
the forces that belong to specific periods in the people's
life or to specific segments of the people, nor are they the
forces of insurrection and sectarianism. They are the forces
that fight living Judaism's spiritual battle against bondage;
they are the eternal forces. Only from them can come
the religious inner shock without which no renewal of
Jewish peoplehood can succeed.

Religiosity is, as I have said, man's urge to establish a
living communion with the unconditioned; it is man's will
to realize the unconditioned through his deed, and to establish it in his world. Genuine religiosity, therefore, has
nothing in common with the fancies of romantic hearts,
or with the self-pleasure of aestheticizing souls, or with
the clever mental exercises of a practiced intellectuality.
Genuine religiosity is *doing*. It wants to sculpt the unconditioned out of the matter of this world. The countenance
of God reposes, invisible, in an earthen block; it must be
wrought, carved, out of it. To engage in this work means
to be religious—nothing else.

Men's life, open to our influence as is no other thing
in this world, is the task apportioned to us in its most in-

ward immediacy. Here, as nowhere else, multiplicity is given into our hands, to be transformed into unity; a vast, formless mass, to be in-formed by us with the Divine. The community of men is as yet only a projected opus that is waiting for us, a chaos we must put in order, a Diaspora we must gather in, a conflict to which we must bring reconciliation. But this we can accomplish only if, in the natural context of a life shared with others, every one of us, each in his own place, will perform the just, the unifying, the in-forming deed. For God does not want to be believed in, to be debated and defended by us, but simply to be realized through us.

VI

Myth in Judaism

I.

To CLARIFY our own understanding of the concept "myth" we can do no better than to start with Plato's interpretation of this term: a narrative of some divine event described as corporeal reality. Consequently, an attempt to describe a divine event as a transcendent or psychic experience should not be called "myth"; a theological statement, whatever its evangelical simplicity and grandeur, or an account of ecstatic visions, however profoundly affecting, is outside the realm of the properly mythical.

This original content of the linguistic tradition is so profoundly and enduringly justified that it is easy to see why the view had to evolve that the myth-making capacity is a trait characteristic only of those peoples who perceived the Divine as a corporeal substance, and who, therefore, apprehended the actions and passions of the Divine as correlations of purely physical events. One went still further, juxtaposing polytheistic peoples as myth-making, and monotheistic peoples as mythless. The Jews were counted among the latter, the mythless people, and as such were either glorified or held in contempt. They were glorified when the one who pronounced judgment viewed myth as a low, preliminary stage of religion, and held in contempt when one saw in myth a summit of humanity, which rose above all religion as an inherent and eternal metaphysics of the human soul.

Such attempts—usually effective—to evaluate rather than comprehend the character of peoples are always foolish and useless, especially when they are based, as they are here, on ignorance or distortion of historical reality. Truly, ignorance and distortion are the main bases of the modern, racio-psychological treatment of Judaism. For instance: someone detects a rationalistic or utilitarian feature in certain declarations or customs of official Judaism, whereupon he asserts that he has proved Judaism's rationalism or utilitarianism; he does not, nor does he wish to, suspect that these are but small, though consequential, falterings in the great yet humble flow of ardent, dedicated Jewish folk-religiosity, which transcends mere expediency. On the other hand, the Jewish apologists—whose wretched zeal is bent on demonstrating that there is nothing at all special about Judaism, that it is simply pure humanism—do the same, in their own fashion, for they themselves are prone to the corruption of rationalism and utilitarianism.

Consequently, and for a long time, both sides denied the existence of myth in Judaism. This was not at all difficult. The true nature of post-biblical literature long remained unknown: the Aggadah was regarded as an idle play of fancy or a fictional composition of shallow parables, the Midrash as a collection of hairsplitting and uncreative commentaries, the Kabbalah as an absurd and grotesque numbers game; and Hasidism was barely known by name, or was disdainfully shrugged off as an unhealthy daydream.

And it may well have seemed even to genuine scholarship that anything mythical was alien to the Bible. For the Bible was given the form in which it has come down to us by a body of men who, imbued with the spirit of

official, late-Jewish priesthood, regarded myth, the nurturing source of all genuine religiosity, as the arch-enemy
of religion as they conceived and wanted religion to be;
they therefore excluded from the wealth of transmitted
writings whatever, to the best of their knowledge, was
mythical. Fortunately, their knowledge was not perfect,
and much with whose original character they were no
longer familiar escaped them.

Thus, scattered veins of the precious ore can be
found in all the books of the Bible. When these veins
were discovered by new research, the existence of Jewish
myth could no longer be denied; now, however, one dis-
puted its originality. Whenever a similar mythic motif was
found in the literature of some other people of Asia
Minor, that motif was designated the original one and the
Jewish motif was called a poor imitation; and if none was
found, it was simply assumed that the original had been
lost. It is not necessary to pursue these details here (which
originated in the deeply rooted yet hopeless desire of the
present-day Occidental to de-Judaize his Christianity,
which he cannot renounce); much more important than
refuting them one by one is realizing that the whole concept of history that made them possible in the first place
is a monstrous fallacy. To attempt to judge so immense
an asset as a people's heritage of myths from the woefully
ephemeral viewpoint of "originality" is a perverted and
presumptuous undertaking. When we are confronted
with the world of the mind, it is not originality that matters but reality; and the creations of the mind are not
meant to be dissected by us in order to assay the findings
of our analysis, that is, whether these creations appear
here for the first time. This "for the first time" can be the
concern only of a mole's stunted intellect, incapable of
discerning the mind's never-ending history with its eternally new creations carved out of the eternally same mat-

ter. The creations of the mind are meant to be perceived, experienced, and revered as a molded entity, a cohesive structure, a reality.

And whatever Jewish myth we are able to reconstruct, despite all Jewish and anti-Jewish attacks, is such a reality. It may have all sorts of "motifs" in common with other peoples' myths; and it will never be possible to really ascertain which of them stem from migration from people to people—an experience that, with its give and take, is, after all, undergone by *all* peoples, the so-called productive as well as the so-called receptive—and which stem from innate traits shared, then as now, by the Jews and those other peoples: common forms of experience and of expressing this experience; and, further, a common soil and common destiny, that is, the substance of this experience. This, I maintain, will probably never be fully ascertained. But for us, the descendants of these Jews, this is not essential. What is essential is the purity and greatness of a creative humanity that throws all these factors into the smelting furnace—as Cellini[1] did with his household utensils—to create out of them the immortal form.

Simultaneously with the Bible, though not to the same degree, late-Jewish literature became an object of the new research. And though, like the Bible, this literature is obviously influenced and circumscribed in its utterances by elements hostile to myths, by the rigorism of the law and by rabbinic dialectics, one could not help discovering a wealth of mythical material in it. What had been viewed as an arbitrary commentary on biblical passages proved to be a shaping and remolding of the most ancient folk-heritage. Ancient legendary material which the compilers of the canon had tried to suppress flourished here in primal profusion. Just as the anti-Jewish race-theoreticians could no longer maintain the fiction that

there was no Jewish myth, after it became a well-known
fact that the Bible contained mythical elements, so the
rationalistic Jewish apologists could no longer maintain
the same fiction after it became a well-known fact that
post-biblical literature contained mythical elements. The
apologists therefore used a new approach: they now distinguished between a negative mythological and a positive monotheistic Judaism; they rejected the former as a
retarding and beclouding element and glorified the latter
as the true doctrine. They sanctioned rabbinism's fight
against the concept of myth as a progressive purification
of a significant ideological complex and more or less
joined this fight.

A noted Jewish scholar, David Neumark,[2] though
aiming at larger goals than apologetics, formulated this
view in the declaration: "The history of the development
of Jewish religion is really the history of the battles of liberation fought against both its own and alien mytholo-
gies, against a time-honored mythology as well as a newly
constituted one." This declaration contains a truth, but a
truth obfuscated by the partisan manner in which it is expressed. Let us elucidate it by giving it a fairer formulation: The history of the development of Jewish religion
is really the history of the struggles between the natural
structure of a mythical-monotheistic folk-religion and
the intellectual structure of a rational-monotheistic rabbinic religion. I said, "a mythical-monotheistic folk-religion"; for it is not at all true that monotheism and myth
are mutually exclusive and that a monotheistically-in-
clined people must therefore be devoid of a myth-making
capacity. To the contrary, every living monotheism is
filled with the mythical element and remains alive only so
long as it is filled with it. To be sure, rabbinism, in its
blind zeal to build a fence around Judaism, endeavored
to restore a faith in God that was "purified" of myth; but

the result of this endeavor was a miserable homunculus.
And this homunculus was the eternal exilarch: it held
sway over the *galut* generations; under its tyranny the living force of Jewish God-consciousness, myth, had to lock
itself in the tower of the Kabbalah, or hide behind the
women's distaff, or flee from the walls of the ghetto into
the world. It was tolerated as an esoteric doctrine, or
scorned as superstition, or banished as heresy, until Hasidism established it on a throne, a throne of a short day's
duration, from which it was pushed down to slink around,
like a beggar, in our melancholy dreams.

Nevertheless, it is to myth that Judaism owed its inmost cohesiveness in times of danger. Not Joseph Karo[3]
but Isaac Luria in the sixteenth century, and not the
Gaon of Vilna[4] but the Baal Shem in the eighteenth century, truly consolidated and demarcated Judaism by raising a folk-religion to a power in Israel and renewing the
people's personality from the roots of its myth. And if
the Jews of our generation find it so difficult to fuse their
human religiosity and their Judaism into one, it is the
fault of rabbinism, which has emasculated the Jewish
ideal. But if, in spite of that, the road to unity is still open
to us; if, along with the perfecting of our humanity, it is
granted to us to gain our peoplehood; and if, worshipping
the Divine in conformity with our sensitivity, we hear
the wings of the Jewish spirit stir above our heads—all
this has been brought about by the exalted power of our
myth.

II.

If we want to comprehend the nature of the monotheistic Jewish myth and at the same time learn to grasp, in
depth, the nature of myth itself, we must study the origin

of Jewish monotheism as it is manifested in the Bible. We
shall then discover three clearly distinguishable strata.
The first of these three religio-historical strata—which
are not to be mistaken for the textual-historical strata of
modern biblical criticism—is characterized by its use of
the name Elohim, the second by the use of the name
YHVH, and the third by its use of both names, to indicate a
truly nameless divine Being's twofold manifestation as
universal God and national God. Each of these strata
—from which Jewish myth evolves—has its specific mythology.

The name Elohim appears usually as a singular in the
Bible, but it was originally unmistakably a plural, meaning, approximately, "the powers." There are several
traces of this plural divinity, a divinity not differentiated
into separate, individually existing beings, each with its
own nature and own life, but representing, as it were, a
plurality of cosmic forces, distinguished in their nature,
united in action—an aggregate of creating, sustaining,
and destroying powers, a God-cloud moving above the
earth, deliberating within itself, and following its own
counsel.

One can point to related phenomena among other
peoples. But there they are all secondary deities, auxil-
iary deities; there is nothing comparable to the monumen-
tal monopluralism of the Elohim-myth. Its further development is also unique. Out of the plurality of the Elohim
emerges a single dominating force, a single name-bear-
ing, overruling being that seizes more and more power and
finally detaches itself as an autonomous sovereign,
adorned with the mythical insignia of an old tribal god:
YHVH. Though one still sings, "Who is like unto Thee
among the gods?" (Exodus 15:11), this being soon carries along with it the powers that were once its companions as attendant host with which it also augments its

name: YHVH of the Hosts (YHVH *Zebaot*). Finally,
the Elohim sinks to the level of a mere attribute: YHVH
Elohim is called the One; but the erstwhile polydemon-
ism may yet echo in its other names, in, for instance, *Shad-
dai*. And much later still, when he has already been elevated to the noncorporeal realm, he occasionally speaks
as if he were still addressing the primeval plural divinity.

YHVH is the divine hero of His people, and the ancient hymns—which, like an echo from an earlier geo-
logical period, have been preserved for us scattered
in the prophetic writings, in Job and the psalms—
praise His triumphant deeds, every one of which is a genuine myth: how He crushed the monster of Chaos, and
how, accompanied by the jubilation of the morning stars,
He sank the pillars of the earth into the deep.[5]

And now Judaism's predominant characteristic, its
tendency not to be content with any one unit, but to go
on from there to a higher, more perfect unity, sets to
work, expanding the cosmic-national YHVH into the God
of the universe, the God of mankind, the God of the soul.
But the God of the universe may no longer walk to and
fro, of an evening, under the trees of His paradise; nor
may the God of mankind wrestle with Jacob until day-
break; and the God of the soul may no longer burn in the
unconsumed bush.[6] The YHVH of the Prophets is no
longer a corporeal reality; and the old mythical images in
which He is glorified are now only metaphors for His
ineffability. Thus, the rationalists seem to be vindicated
after all, with the Jewish myth apparently ended. But
this is not true, for, even millennia later, the people have
still not truly accepted the idea of an incorporeal God.
Above all, however, this is untrue because the rationalists' definition of the concept of myth is too narrow and
too petty.

We began by defining myth as a narrative of a divine

event described as corporeal reality. But neither Plato nor our own sense of language understands this definition to mean what the rationalists say it means: that only a tale of the actions and passions of a god who is presented as a physical substance may properly be called a myth. This, rather, is what the definition means: that we must designate as myth every tale of a corporeally real event that is perceived and presented as a divine, an absolute, event.

For a full and clear understanding of this concept, we must re-examine the general problem and reinvestigate the origin of myth.

III.

Civilized man's understanding of the world is based on his comprehension of the functioning of causality, his perception of the processes of the universe in an empirical context of cause and effect. Only through an understanding of this functioning can man orient himself, find his way, in the infinite multiplicity of events; at the same time, however, the significance of the personal experience is diminished, because it is grasped only in its relation to other experiences, and not wholly from within itself. Primitive man's comprehension of the functioning of causality is still rather poorly developed. It is practically nonexistent in his approach to such phenomena as dreams or death, which for him denote a realm he is powerless to penetrate by investigation, duplication, or verification. It is also nonexistent in his relations with such men as sorcerers or heroes, who intervene in his life with a peremptory, demoniacal power that he is unable to interpret by analogy with his own faculties. He does not set these phenomena within a causal relationship, as he sets the small incidents of his day; does not link the actions of these men, as he links his own actions and the actions of men he knows, to the chain of all happenings; does not register them with the equanimity of experience, as he registers the familiar and the comprehensible. Instead, unimpeded by a sense of causal operations, he absorbs, with all the tension and fervor of his soul, these events in their singularity, relating them not to causes and effects but to their own meaning-content, to their significance as expressions of the unutterable, unthinkable meaning of the world that becomes manifest in them alone.

As a result primitive man lacks the necessary empiricism and sense of purpose to cope with such elemental experiences; but at the same time he has a heightened awareness of the nonrational aspect of the single experience, an aspect that cannot be grasped within the context of other events but is to be perceived within the experience itself; of the significance of the experience as a signum of a hidden, supracausal connection; of the manifestness of the absolute. He assigns these events to the world of the absolute, the Divine: he mythicizes them. His account of them is a tale of a corporeally real event, conceived and represented as a divine, an absolute event: a myth.

This myth-making faculty is preserved in later man, despite his more fully developed awareness of causal functioning. In times of high tension and intense experience the shackles of this awareness fall off man: he perceives the world's processes as being supracausally meaningful, as the manifestation of a central intent, which cannot, however, be grasped by the mind but only by the wide-awake power of the senses, the ardent vibrations of one's entire being—as palpable, multifaceted reality. And this, more or less, is how the man who is truly alive still relates to the power and the fate of a hero; though capable of placing him within causality, he nevertheless

mythicizes him, because the mythical approach discloses
to him a deeper, fuller truth than the causal, and by so
doing first reveals to him the very being of the beloved,
beatific figure.

Myth, then, is an eternal function of the soul.

Now, it is strange and significant to note how closely
this function approximates the fundamental view of Jewish religiosity, while at the same time it encounters there
a basically different element which transforms it. It is
equally strange and significant that, though by its very
nature the Jewish myth represents, so to speak, a historical
continuity, it is at the same time endowed with a special
character that is alien to other myths, particularly the
Occidental.

It is fundamental to Jewish religiosity, and central to
Jewish monotheism—which is so widely misunderstood
and so cruelly rationalized—to view all things as utterances of God and all events as manifestations of the absolute. Whereas to the other great monotheist of the Orient,
the Indian sage as he is represented in the Upanishads,
corporeal reality is an illusion, which one must shed if he
is to enter the world of truth, to the Jew corporeal reality
is a revelation of the divine spirit and will. Consequently,
all myth is for the Indian sage, as later for the Platonist, a
metaphor, whereas for the Jew it is a true account of God's
manifestation on earth. The Jew of antiquity cannot tell
a story in any other way than mythically, for to him an
event is worth telling only when it has been grasped in
its divine significance. All story-telling books of the
Bible have but one subject matter: the account of YHVH's
encounters with His people. And even later, when from
the visibility of the pillar of fire and the audibility of the
thunder over Sinai He passed into the darkness and the silence of the noncorporeal realm, the continuity of mythic
story-telling is not broken; true, YHVH Himself can no

longer be perceived, but all His manifestations in nature
and in history can be so perceived. And it is of these that
the inexhaustible subject matter of post-biblical myth is
composed.

From what I have said it should be clear what this
something is that I have called the special character of
Jewish myth. Jewish myth does not dispense with causality; it merely replaces an empirical causality with a metaphysical one, with a causal relationship between experienced events and the divine Being. This is not, however,
to be understood as meaning solely that these events have
been wrought by God. Instead, and ever more strongly,
a more profound and more creative reverse concept is
evolved: the concept of the influence man and his deed
have upon God's destiny. This view, which earlier assumed a form at once artless and mystical, finds its ultimate expression in Hasidism, and teaches that the Divine is
dormant in all things, and that it can be awakened only
by him who, in sanctification, conceives these things and
consecrates himself through them. Corporeal reality is
divine, but it must be realized in its divinity by him who
truly lives it. The *shekhinah* is banished into conceal-
ment; it lies, tied, at the bottom of every thing, and is redeemed in every thing by man, who, by his own vision
or his deed, liberates the thing's soul. Thus, every man is
called to determine, by his own life, God's destiny; and
every living being is deeply rooted in the living myth.

There is a correspondence between these two concepts and the two basic forms in which the Jewish myth
developed: the tale of YHVH's deeds and the legend of
man who lives from his very core, in perfect realization.
The first basic form follows the course of the Bible, forming, so to speak, a second Bible of legends, scattered in
innumerable writings, around the nucleus of Scripture.
The other basic form first relates the stories of certain

biblical personalities, especially the mysterious figures
neglected by the canonical text (such as Enoch, who was
transformed from flesh into fire and from a mortal to
Metatron, "prince of the divine countenance" [7]); then
it recounts, in cosmic proportions, the lives of the holy
men who dominated the inner world. The first form represents, as it were, eternal continuity; the second, eternal renewal. The first teaches us that we are conditioned
beings; the second, that we can become unconditioned
beings. The first is the myth of world-preservation; the
second, the myth of world-redemption.

VII

The Holy Way: A Word to the Jews and to the Nations

IN MEMORY OF MY FRIEND
GUSTAV LANDAUER[1]

FACED WITH the need of measuring Judaism's reality against its truth, we must start with an accusation. For whatever is to be learned here about the hidden relationship of metal and dross cannot be recognized from the outside; it will be disclosed only to him who throws himself into the testing fire. By this crucial test, then, we shall perceive that we Jews, all of us, are renegades. Not because another people's landscape, language, and culture have permeated our soul and our life; even if our own landscape, our own language, our own culture were given back to us, we could not regain that inmost Judaism to which we have become unfaithful. Nor because many of us have renounced the norms of Jewish tradition and the system of rules imposed by this tradition; those of us who have kept these norms and rules inviolate in their yea and nay have not preserved this inmost Judaism any more than those who renounced them. All that is customarily referred to as assimilation is harmlessly superficial compared to the fateful assimilation I have in mind: the assimilation to the Occidental dualism that sanctions the splitting of man's being into two realms, each existing in its own right

and independent of the other—the truth of the spirit and
the reality of life—an assimilation to the mentality of
compromise. All renunciation of the treasures of national
culture or religious tradition is trifling compared to the
fatal renunciation of the most precious heritage of classical Judaism: its disposition toward realization.

This disposition means that true human life is conceived to be a life lived in the presence of God. For Judaism, God is not a Kantian idea but an elementally present spiritual reality—neither something conceived by pure
reason nor something postulated by practical reason, but
emanating from the immediacy of existence as such,
which religious man steadfastly confronts and nonreli-
gious man evades. He is the sun of mankind. However, it
is not the man who turns his back on the world of things,
staring into the sun in self-oblivion, who will remain steadfast and live in the presence of God, but only the man
who breathes, walks, and bathes his self and all things in
the sun's light. He who turns his back on the world comprehends God solely as an idea, and not as a reality; he is
aware of Him in some experiences in life (*Erlebnis*), but
he is unaware of Him in life itself.

But even he who turns toward the world and desires
to see God in all things does not truly live in His presence.
God may be seen seminally within all things, but He
must be realized between them. Just as the sun's substance has its being among the stars yet beams its light
into the earthly realm, so it is granted to human creatures
to behold in their midst the radiance of the ineffable's
glory. It glows dimly in all human beings, every one of
them; but it does not shine in its full brightness within
them—only between them. In every human being there
is present the beginning of universal being (*Allsein*); but
it can unfold only in his relatedness to universal being, in
the pure immediacy of his giving and taking, which sur-

rounds him like a sphere of light, merging him with the oneness of the world. The Divine may come to life in individual man, may reveal itself from within individual man; but it attains its earthly fullness only where, having awakened to an awareness of their universal being, individual beings open themselves to one another, disclose themselves to one another, help one another; where immediacy is established between one human being and another; where the sublime stronghold of the individual is unbolted, and man breaks free to meet other man. Where this takes place, where the eternal rises in the Between, the seemingly empty space: that true place of realization is community, and true community is that relationship in which the Divine comes to its realization between man and man.

These are fundamentals of the teaching in which Judaism's vocation is grounded. In Judaism, however, the precepts that I have here tried to formulate in the spirit and language of the man of today existed not as dicta but as a living tendency, and words have always served this tendency merely as tools, and not as final expression. These precepts were not a theory that hovered above life but a determining force, an integral part of life. The teaching of realization was already confirmed in the manner in which it manifested itself. Judaism's task is not the intellectual grasping of the spiritual, nor the artistically creative expression of it, but its realization.

It is characteristic of Judaism that it can be content neither with truth as idea nor with truth as shape or form, neither with the truth of a philosophical theorem nor with the truth of a work of art. Its goal is truth as deed, and the striving toward this truth is its meaning and lasting significance. It is imbued with the will to create the true community on earth. Its longing for God is the longing to prepare a place for Him in the true community; its consciousness of Israel is the consciousness that out of it the true community will emerge; its wait for the Messiah is the wait for the true community. Judaism therefore is not concerned with a God who lives in the beyond, for its God is content to reside in the realm between one earthly being and the other, as if they were cherubim on the Holy Ark; nor is it concerned with a God who dwells in things, for it is not in the being of things that He abides but only in their perfection. Hence Judaism must not liken itself to other nations, for it knows that, being the first-born, realization is incumbent upon it; but neither must it consider itself superior to them, for it has fallen so far short of the ideal image set before it that it is at times barely able still to distinguish it. So long, therefore, as the kingdom of God has not come, Judaism will not recognize any man as the true Messiah, yet it will never cease to expect redemption to come from man, for it is man's task to establish God's power on earth.

Thus the special character of Judaism resides in neither the religious nor the ethical realm but in the unity of both realms. Their unity, not their junction; the two realms are but two aspects of the same basic state. To do the good deed is to fill the world with God; to serve God in truth is to draw Him into life. In genuine Judaism ethics and faith are no separate spheres; its ideal, holiness, is true community with God and true community with human beings, both in one. The distorted images of a divided state of mind—holiness-through-works and holiness-by-grace—are alien to it.

And by the same token it does not view the national and the social principles as separate entities: the national principle denotes the substance; the social, the task. Both are united in the idea that the people must be molded into a true human community, a holy congregation. Nationalism as an isolated view of life and socialism as another isolated view of life are equally alien to Judaism. Modern thinking in which these spheres, the ethical and the religious, the national and the social, have become separated and differentiated from each other, with each following its own rules, each indifferent to the other, is totally un-Jewish. And so is a world in which one performs charitable acts without sanctifying one's soul through them, and without becoming aware of God's presence in one's deed; in which one participates in religious services without hearing the message commanding him to go out into the world and—despite resistance and repulsion, indeed even at the price of perishing—to hammer God's intent out of the unmalleable stuff of life, human life as well as national. So too is a world in which love of one's people means lust for power, and the will to establish a community means splitting into parties. Men who consider themselves members of either the Jewish faith or the Jewish nation, who worship the idols of this world and observe its commandments, usurp the name of Jew, whether they wear the ceremonial fringes under their coats, or the Zionist button on them.

The world of true Judaism is the world of a unified life on earth; a unity not of being but of becoming, and not alone a becoming, but a becoming informed by spirit —the human spirit chosen by the divine spirit to be, as the exalted Jewish words proclaim, God's "partner in the work of creation," [2] to finish the work begun on the sixth day, and to realize the unconditional where it has not yet assumed definite shape: in the all-embracing and all-determining sphere of community.

Realization—this is the awesomeness of the covenant between God and man, presented in the threefold tale of the Scriptures: the first covenant with the lump of clay which the Creator, kneading, and by the breath of His mouth, imbues with His own likeness,[3] so that it might

unfold in man's life and thus reveal that not being but becoming is man's task; the second covenant with the chosen
patriarch, the covenant that begins with the parting from
home and kin and concludes with the demand for the
sacrifice of the son,[4] so that it might be revealed that realization demands the ultimate stake and unconditional
dedication; the third covenant, in the Sinai desert, with the
people whose first command is "Ye shall be unto Me a
priestly realm, a holy people," [5] so that it may be revealed that realization of the Divine on earth is fulfilled
not within man but between man and man, and that,
though it does indeed have its beginning in the life of
individual man, it is consummated only in the life of true
community.

And of the covenant the Talmud says: "In the hour
when Israel spoke: 'We will do and we will hear' (Exodus
24:7)—first doing and then hearing—a heavenly voice
went forth, addressing them: 'Who disclosed to My children the mystery performed by My ministering angels?'
As it is said: 'Bless the Lord, ye angels of His . . . that
fulfill His word, hearing unto the voice of His word'
(Psalm 103:20)—first the doing and then the hearing." [6]
This talmudic saying may be interpreted as meaning
that revelation resides within the deed itself; from within
his own deed, man as well as nation hears the voice of
God.

I repeat: not truth as idea nor truth as shape or form
but truth as deed is Judaism's task; its goal is not the creation of a philosophical theorem or a work of art but the
establishment of true community. Herein is grounded
the grandeur, but also the paradox, of Jewish existence.
For idea and shape or form are ends in themselves. Whoever has been endowed with the ability to create a perfect
philosophical theorem or work of art has added a sublime

structure to the colonnades of the spirit; he has known fulfillment, even though his restless soul may already, painfully, be attempting to carve out a new block. Pure and undefilable, the *eidolon,* form as truth, shines upon the world.

Not so the deed. It is its nature to point beyond itself. No matter how free its intention, how pure its manifestation, it is at the mercy of its own consequences; and even the most sublime deed, which does not waste so much as a glance at the lowlands of causality, is dragged into the mud as soon as it enters the world and becomes visible. And the deed concerned with the growth of true community especially has everything lined up against it: the rigorism of the habitual traditionalists and the indolence of the slaves of the moment, yet equally a rash doctrinairism and irresponsible disputatiousness; miserly egotism and untractable vanity, yet also hysterical self-effacement and disoriented flurry; the cult of the so-called pure idea, hand in hand with the cult of so-called *Realpolitik.* In addition, it is opposed by all the established forces that do not wish to be disturbed in the exercise of their power. All these forces rage in a clouded and beclouding whirlwind around the lonely and dedicated individual who boldly assumes the task of building a true community—and with what materials! There is no undefilable perfection here; everywhere the impure challenges the pure, dragging it down and distorting it; all about him gloating derision apprises the heroic victim of his futility, and the abyss pronounces its inexorable sentence on the dying to whom victory is denied.

The paradox of Judaism, as well as of those of its leaders in whom Judaism's vigor and teaching were concentrated and manifested, is rooted in this fateful attempt to mold a community. The internal history of Judaism's classical age is easily understood from this paradox: legisla-

tion that was never fully put into effect, and prophetic
admonitions that were never wholly listened to; a people
that repeatedly grumbled on its trek through the wilderness, and in its own land repeatedly retrogressed into the
service of Baal; an internal struggle raging even at the
hour of extreme danger and bitterest resistance against
enemies; attempts at restoration, and deterioration; Messianic fervor, and a penchant for assimilation. All these
manifestations, in their positive as well as negative aspects, are expressions of the paradox that, with tragic
logic, resulted from the conflict between the dominant
tendency toward realization of the Divine within the
community and the natural resistance of the substance
that was to be the instrument of this realization. I say "natural resistance." By this I do not mean the special nature
of this people, whom its leaders so emphatically accused
of being stiff-necked and recalcitrant, important though
this may be; I am speaking of human nature in general,
the universal human nature of the stubborn mass that resists with all its active and latent energy the commanding
will to mold it, pulling the deed down into its destructive
vortex; the mass that does not merely impede all transformation, but—and this is much worse—pollutes, distorts,
and corrodes whatever transformation might have already begun.

The measure of ancient Judaism's commanding will
to create the true community becomes especially evident
when we compare it with antiquity's most beautiful creation, the Greek *polis*. Here is a rigidly structured unit, a
community in which dwells an *eidolon,* as it dwells in the
philosophical theorem or in the work of art—a pure construct. But it is based upon a class differentiation, which
not infrequently reserved even the designation "virtuous"
solely for the aristocrats, that is, the well-to-do. And its

social ideologies, such as Plato's, are only a refinement, an intellectual reformulation, of this radical inequality, and not a counterdemand for an all-embracing community life. Demos, the "great beast," is allotted only the task of procuring, by its labor, freedom and sovereignty for the higher classes. This order of fundamental inequality, which was only occasionally and temporarily, superficially and imperfectly, revoked by force through political upheavals, is opposed in early Jewish legislation by the idea of rhythmic adjustment, of a social rhythm that, like the natural rhythm of the year, constantly restores the equilibrium of development and permits a new start. Thus, legal statics in the *polis*, interrupted only by occasional crises, are, in Judaism, opposed by legal dynamics. Inequality of property is not abolished, but it loses its static character; in the seventh year all debts are to be canceled and slaves freed; in the fiftieth year, all land property is to be restored, and every man come into his own. "And the land shall not be sold in perpetuity; for the land is Mine; for ye are strangers and settlers with Me" (Leviticus 25:23).

This idea of God as the sole owner of all land, incomprehensible to a Greek, is the cornerstone of the Jewish social concept. It corresponds to the idea, in the political sphere, of the sovereignty of God, that is, of God as the sole sovereign of the community. Though at times abused by a power-hungry priesthood, this concept appears in unconditional purity in Jewish legislation. From Moses to Samuel, the leaders are merely deputies of God, and the people, though already repeatedly falling into apostasy and idol-worship, are God's immediate congregation.

The concept is expressed most clearly in the memorable scene with which one era ends and another begins: the scene between Samuel and the elders who ask him to set a king above them.[7] (I am not concerned here with

the question of whether the written account of this event
and its presuppositions are historical fact, or whether they
bear the imprint of a later period and point of view; their
inner truth is unmistakable.) The immediate impetus
for the scene is Samuel's own violation of the true meaning
of community. Up to that time every judge had been
called by God. Their mandate and their office were attested by such manifestations as God's spirit coming over
Othniel, God's awakening of Ehud to be His helper, His
bestowal of the gift of prophecy upon Deborah, His taking Gideon away from the winepress, His choosing Samson in his mother's womb, and His revealing Himself to
Samuel in a dream.[8] To put it in the language of today:
it was always the best man, the one most capable of ren-
dering aid, who judged in the name of God. Samuel, however, appointed his unworthy sons as judges; with this he
introduced an alien principle into the community: heredi-
tary leadership. Now the community wanted to appropriate the principle in its entirety, and demanded a king such
as all nations had. And the multitude knew only one answer to the admonitions and warnings of the elders: "We
also may be like all the nations" (I Samuel 8:20). God,
however, spoke to Samuel: "Hearken unto the voice of
the people . . . for they have not rejected thee, but they
have rejected Me that I should not be king over them"
(I Samuel 8:7).

This moment is the true turning point of Jewish history. Though realized only imperfectly, there had been
up to that time a unified community, a living unity of the
temporal and spiritual realms, a community permeated
by the guiding presence of the Divine: God's immediate
congregation. Now the temporal state began, and with it,
division. Kings, it is true, were still called and deposed by
God, and God's spirit still came over them when they
were called (and here the concept has a greater mean-

ing than the medieval theory of the divine right of kings;
it signifies transformation, a renewal of man's being),
but the original unity of life was sundered, and the nation's gradual disintegration into two Commonwealths
seems to us a symbolic portent.

The great succession of prophets who were to lead
the cause of God and of His realization against the king
had already begun when David ruled. The most outstanding were Nathan, pitted against David, Ahijah against
Jeroboam, Elijah against Ahab, Amos against the second
Jeroboam, and Jeremiah against Jehoahaz, Jehoiakim,
Jeconiah, and Zedekiah.[9] The significance of these con-
frontations is most evident in the last, when Jeremiah in-
veighs against Zedekiah for his failure to observe the law
of the release year, the seventh year when all slaves were
to be freed.[10] This law, we learn from the prophet's words,
had not been observed for a long time; but even after
the people reassumed the obligation, they soon reversed
their course again, desecrating the divine name anew.
And the people's inner tragedy is once more revealed to
us when, just prior to the fall of the Commonwealth and
the Babylonian exile, the commanding will to create community and the stiff-necked people's inertia oppose each
other in relentless clarity. The spirit that wants to infuse
the unmalleable material of communal life with a sense
of the Divine chastises with ardent words the state which,
in its desire to adjust communal life to the demands of the
established powers, now falls prey in turn to a more powerful state.

The magnitude of this prophetic attitude must be perceived in the right light. The prophets do not fight the
state as state, even though it has dislodged the form of
community that was conceived as God's immediate congregation; they fight a state that lacks a divine, a spiritual,
element. Faithful to the Jewish concept, they cannot deny

the world as it exists, cannot turn away from it; they must endeavor to permeate it with spirit, the spirit of true community. Over and over, they experience this world's intense resistance against the spiritual; exposed to every kind of torment and humiliation, they personally experience the impact of this world's superior power. But they do not give up. Compromise with the status quo is inconceivable to them; but escape from it into the realm of a contemplative life is equally inconceivable. Through torment and humiliation, their impassioned words storm against the rich, the powerful, the princes. They have neither a home in the world nor a shelter in the desert; inexorably, the hand of the Lord has set them their hopeless task. They know, with the last spark of their energy, that the ultimate is at stake; they do not shrink from rejecting the achievements of civilization where the comforts these bring impede righteous living, and where inner communication between man and man is destroyed for the sake of facilitating superficial communications. Indeed, where necessary, they do not even shrink from sacrificing the independence of their state, if the sacrifice rescues a remnant of the people from utter destruction and preserves it as a nucleus for a future new community. But the prophets never differentiate between the spiritual and the temporal, between the realm of God and the realm of man. For them, the realm of God is nothing more than the realm of man as it is to be. Forced to despair of fulfillment in the present, they project the image of their truth into an absolute future; the elaboration of Messianism is the creative expression of this despair. But neither does Messianism signify an antithesis to this human world in which we live; it signifies, instead, its purification and completion; not a community of detached spirits but a community of men, that is, a true community of true men; "a new heaven and a new earth" (Isaiah

65:17), but founded on the renewal of the human being.
It is this that is the legacy of the Jewish prophets.

The history of the First Commonwealth is permeated
with the conflict between the idea of true divine rule and
a state increasingly alienated from this idea. In the history
of the Second Commonwealth, a distorted image of the
idea of divine rule is realized. This development, determined by the political situation, begins as early as Ezra.[11]
Since the outlines of the temporal order are drawn by the
Persian Empire, the leaders' tendency to build a society
imbued with the spirit of the Divine is weakened; the
only realm left to them is of the spiritual order. Moreover,
the situation-induced striving for safeguarding the race
and the national ethos against the dangers of the Diaspora
also pushes the preoccupation with the creation of the
true community into the background. Ritualism and nationalism join ranks against this yearning. And finally,
when at times even these conservative forces go into a
decline, the so-called theocracy that develops in a community robbed of all the vitality of free communal life
finds its ultimate embodiment in the caricature-like figure of the Hellenistic high priest.[12] This figure, it is true,
is wiped out by the Maccabean uprising; but the Hasmonean rulers too know only how to misuse religious hopes
for political intrigues and how to amalgamate religious and
political power; that political life should be informed by a
religious spirit is a concept wholly alien to these typically
Oriental despots. And the spirit itself seems paralyzed; no
leaders toward the deed arise; the active Messianism that
wants to prepare the world to be God's kingdom is followed by a passive Messianism that waits for God to build
His kingdom for Himself. The age of a prophecy that
fought for divine rule knew the resistance of the element
that frustrates all transformation; the age of false the-

ocracy encountered the debasing influence of the element
that pollutes, distorts, and corrodes all transformation.

An innovation that on the surface seemed contrary
to the reaching for realization but in fact only gave it a
new shape in response to the needs of the age must be
understood in the light of this profound disillusionment—
the innovation that developed in secrecy and has apparently
remained hidden from the people's sight until today:
Essenism. Its beginnings are shrouded in darkness, but
we have reason to assume that it had its roots in a group
of "Hasidim" who actively participated in the Maccabean
uprising but did not wish to participate in the Hasmonean
expansionist rule, and who apparently observed special
ancient traditions. Only to a cursory glance would the
meager accounts that have been preserved seem to point
to an esoteric sect. Though not always in accord, they do
indeed tell us that the Essenes lived apart from the cities,
to avoid the irremediable contamination of its polluted
air, as Philo puts it.[13] But they were devoted neither to
meditation nor to an out-of-the-way cult in their self-segregation; instead, their day was organized around austere
work, especially in the fields, and around this work's natural interruptions. They also engaged in several handi-
crafts, except the making of weapons; but they abstained
from trading, replacing it by barter and free gifts. Property was held in common, amassing of possessions was
unknown, and all social life breathed a quiet good will.
Cleanliness and purity, intimately related, permeated life
with their radiance; for the body, though mortal, was val-
ued scarcely less highly than the soul. Meals were sacred,
and so was linen; most sacred of all was the light of the
sun. Celibacy was observed by individual groups but was
not generally obligatory. They obeyed unconditionally the
orders of their chosen leaders, but rejected man's rule over
man as "unjust and godless."

The Essenes were more than a sect or an order; they were a total, living community with economic autarchy and social consistency. The desire for realization was not suddenly reversed here; it merely turned, as it were, inward. Responding to the need and disillusionment of their age, the Essenes began with realization in their own midst. This does not imply renunciation of hope for the state's transformation; it does signify, however, abandonment of the attempt to achieve such a transformation by words alone. It signifies a desire to build that does not wait for God to make a start but surmises that by building it will become aware of God, its fellow builder. It signifies a will to create the true community by starting where alone a start can be made: here and now. It signifies the Messianism of determined men to whom their own undivided life seems just good enough to become a tiny seed of the Messianic kingdom. And it signifies a vital sense of purity and unity that, in the waste and confusion of a disintegrating society, endeavors to take seriously at once God and the community, God as being in the community. [. . .] "Begin to be Jews"—this is the secret legacy of the Essenes, meant for the ear of a later century.

I cannot today trace history step by step. But I must mention a man, a Jew to the core, in whom the Jewish desire for realization was concentrated and in whom it came to a breakthrough. His is the original Jewish spirit of true community when he teaches that two who become one on this earth can gain everything from God, and that he who has put his hand to the plow and looks back is not fit for the kingdom of God. What he calls the kingdom of God—no matter how tinged with a sense of the world's end and of miraculous transformation it may be—is no other-world consolation, no vague heavenly bliss. Nor is it an ecclesiastical or cultic association, a church. It is the perfect life of man with man, true community, and, as such, God's immediate realm, His *basileia,* His earthly kingdom. (Even the Johannean words of the kingdom that is not of this world[14] are still rooted in Judaism's linguistic usage, which juxtaposed "this" world not with a world beyond but with the world "to come." The kingdom of God is the community to come in which all who hunger and thirst for righteousness will be satisfied; it will come not by divine grace alone but only out of the collaboration of divine grace with the human will and the mysterious union of the two.

Whatever else may separate him from traditional teaching, Jesus did not want to abolish society; he wanted to perfect it, as did Israel's prophets. And like the Essenes, he did not want to flee the worldly community but to build out of it the true, the spiritual, community. This knowledge—that God wants to be realized within the world and its worldliness through their purification and perfection; that the world is a devastated house that must be restored for the spirit; and that so long as this remains unaccomplished, the spirit has no dwelling place—is Jesus' most deep-seated Judaism. And yet tradition has transmitted a declaration of his that seemingly expresses the very opposite—his answer to those who ask whether one should pay tribute to the emperor: "Render unto Caesar what is Caesar's, and unto God what is God's." [15]

This answer apparently implies a separation between world and spirit, between the corrupt and monstrous actuality whose existence one must accept and the pure ideality through which one may be delivered from this actuality. Outer life must pay tribute to the first, but the inward life belongs to the second.

But this only appears to be a separation. The state Jesus confronted was no longer a state that one could attempt to recast in its totality by looking its ruler straight in the eye, as the prophet had done with Judea's or Israel's kings; it was not a state that could be conquered by an idea. This was Rome; it was the state pure and simple, which neither knew nor acknowledged anything superior to itself, which tolerated even the gods only as guardians of its power and its law, unless it preferred to set up the emperor himself as a god. This state was a forced union that had supplanted all natural communion; it was legitimized arbitrariness, sanctioned sacrilege, a mechanism wearing the mask of an organism, an organism wearing the mask of the spirit.

Arrayed against this massive power-structure stood, resurrected in new strength and greatness, the Jewish will for realization, the will for a pure community, assuming a threefold pattern: 1) stepping aside in order to rescue the teaching and preserve the divine mandate enclosed in it for a more auspicious time—a pattern embodied by Yohanan ben Zakkai,[16] who, in the year of Jerusalem's destruction and with the emperor's permission, founded the Academy in Jabneh; 2) fighting a war of liberation, one of the most heroic in world history (for it was fought against superior weapons and despite utter hopelessness) to heroic defeat—a pattern embodied by the great rebels, beginning with the leaders of the Jewish war and ending with Bar-Kokhba[17]; 3) and founding a new community that wished to grow in the monster's body and to burst it open—a pattern embodied by Jesus. He who declared "No one can serve two masters" [18] did not mean that one could serve God as well as Rome. He meant that uprisings and revolutions are futile and bound to be self-destructive so long as a new structure of genuinely communal human life is not born out of the soul's renewal, a structure that, in gaining strength, will jolt the loathsome old system. Another of his sayings, "Do not resist evil!" [19] means: resist evil by doing good; do not attack the reign of evil but

unhesitatingly band together for the reign of the good—
and the time will come when evil can no longer resist
you, not because you have conquered it, but because you
have redeemed it. Jesus wished to build the temple of true
community out of Judaism, a community whose mere
sight would cause the despotic state's walls to crumble.

But it is not thus that later generations understood
him. Two millennia of the West's history of ideas are
filled with massive misinterpretations of his teaching. The
Jewish consciousness of a unified world, tarnished and
confused but redeemable by man's struggling will, is replaced by an acceptance of the principle of fundamental
and unbridgeable dualism: human will and divine grace.
Replaced too is the genuinely Jewish awareness that, in
becoming, man's will raises itself up to God's will, that
His image is thus perfected. The human will, admittedly
prone to falling into apostasy yet capable also of experiencing the awesomeness of "return," can no longer hope
for the infinite power of salvation or the call to an infinite
work of salvation; it is instead unconditionally evil and
incapable of rising up again by its own power. Not the will,
in all its contradiction and all its potential, is the way to
God, but faith and trustful waiting for the touch of grace.
Evil is no longer the "shell" that must be broken; it is an
elemental power opposing good as its great adversary.
The state is no longer a contraction of a strayed will to
community and therefore capable of being permeated and
redeemed by the right kind of will; it is either, as in Au-
gustine, the realm of the eternally damned, and therefore
a realm from which the chosen must forever stay apart,
or, as it is for Thomas Aquinas, a preliminary stage and
preliminary training school for the true, the ecclesiastical community. True community is no longer to be realized in the totality of men's life with one another, in hallowed worldliness; it is to be realized in the Church,

which as community of the spirit is separated from the
community of the world, and as community of grace is
separated from the community of nature.

Nor did Protestantism transcend this separation. For
it, too, life is split into two separate realms, the realm of
works and the realm of faith. Protestantism desires a coexistence of church and state, not a merging of the two
into a higher unit, into true community. The perception
of undivided being and consciousness of the conditionality of evil and the unconditionality of the human soul live
on only in mysticism. But mysticism is wanting in the element of activity in the state of unconditionality, the tendency to realize undivided life in the world of man, in the
world of being with one another.

Thus, though the peoples of the West took over Jewish teaching when they took over the teaching of Jesus,
they did not take over its essence; the bent for realization did not become part of the spiritual foundations of
these peoples' lives. Its flame did indeed flare up repeatedly in the passion of heretic and sectarian communities
that wanted to initiate the kingdom of God; but it was just
as repeatedly extinguished by the air in which nations
breathe, the atmosphere of acquiescence in dualism. This
atmosphere, which still obtains in our time, is an atmosphere of dualisms of truth and reality, idea and fact, morals and politics. It is the atmosphere in which Christianity rendered unto the Roman emperor what was Caesar's
for so long a time that it had nothing left to deny him; the
atmosphere in which Christianity did not oppose evil for
so long a time that, when it finally did attempt to resist its
most devastating excesses, it was forced to realize that it
had become incapable of doing so.

We must not forget, however, that the man who, in
transmitting Judaism to the peoples, brought about its
breakup was also a Jew, a representative Jew. To fully

understand this violator of the spirit, one must seek out in
him that primal experience of the Jew from which the
reaching for realization is generated, eternally anew.
This primal experience is an elemental perception of
inner duality, inherent, to some degree, in all men but
especially in Jews; it is also the desire to overcome this
duality by realization of unity.

Saul, the man from Tarsus, expressed the duality he
found within him more unequivocally and more force-
fully than any other man in the fateful words that ushered
in the Christian era: "For that which I work, I understand not. For I do not that good which I will; but the
evil which I hate, that I do." [20] To Paul, however, this terrible and paradoxical insight does not signify what it had
once signified to the Jew and what it must once again
signify to him: an overpoweringly strong incitement to
dare the assault, no matter how impossible it seems; to
break open the shell; and to realize God's will in the
unification of one's own will. [. . .]

This man summarizes the great disappointments Judaism's reaching for realization was forced to suffer up to
his own day. Adding up the national, as well as mankind's total, he declares that we ourselves can achieve
nothing; that is, nothing by our own efforts but only by
the grace of God or—and to him it is the same thing—by
faithful adherence to the one in whom grace had visibly
resided, the one who, as it is said, "knew no sin." [21]

The fact that at the time there was apparently no
longer any reliable knowledge of Jesus' first thirty years,
that even in the legend only the emblem of his threefold
temptation[22] bears witness to the period of his struggles
and his victories, so that the harmony of his spirit is, os-
tensibly, manifested without there having been any previous discord—this fact made it easier for Paul to develop
his ideology. He transmitted Jesus' teaching, transformed

by this ideology, to the nations, handing them the sweet poison of faith, a faith that was to disdain works, exempt the faithful from realization, and establish dualism in the world. It is the Pauline era whose death agonies we today are watching with transfixed eyes.

While the peoples of the West thus assimilated and nullified Jewish teaching, the Jewish people walked in their midst, face veiled, as an exile—cut off not only from its land and from its natural ties but also from its task. For, however inadequately the Mosaic legislation may once have been fulfilled, the obstacles to its fulfillment had lain solely in the people itself, which, in moments of deep contemplation, had felt that it would be able to remove these obstacles by an act of inner realization. But now it was subject to alien laws, dispersed among alien legislations, and able to retain only the most superficial aspect of its own legislation in the ghetto's surface catacombs, until all this too sank into the whirlpool of the emancipations. No matter how often the prophets' calls to a life of truth had been ignored through indolence or been outshouted by a lie, they had, nevertheless, also repeatedly, reached the ears of free men who undertook the task of establishing the law in their land. But now something new had arisen, more paralyzing than indolence or falsehoods: the power of an alien world, a power that constrained every man to exhaust his energies half in adaptation, half in setting up safeguards, in continuous adjustment, positive or negative, to the alien world. And so the people were forced to realize that in fact not only they alone but also the *shekhinah,* the divine Presence dwelling within the human element, had gone into exile. For the *shekhinah* is at home only where there dwells a potent will for a covenant with God and an equally potent striv-

ing for realization of such a covenant, only where man endeavors to live within the sight of the unconditional. When
the covenant is relaxed, when the striving slackens and
man loses sight of the unconditional, the *shekhinah* is in
exile. But matters came to such a pass that the Jew
learned quite well how to be tolerably at home even with
his back turned to the unconditional. And this is more sinis-
ter than the bloodbaths of the Crusaders or the tortures of
the Inquisition, more heinous than pogroms.

Dependence upon an alien world's power that one
cannot attempt to shake off by wars of liberation, as was
the case here, has to lead to adjustment, a twofold adjustment to the alien world: the establishment of safeguards,
and adaptation. I do not mean, insofar as Judaism is concerned, the petty, modern, vulgarized form of either, but
the great adjustments made throughout the millennia.
By adjustment through setting up safeguards I mean the
development of a pure ritualism which was intended to
prevent, and did prevent, the influx of alien teachings
and customs, but which at the same time led to atrophy of
the inner life of Jewish religiosity, of its striving for realization. For how can the desire for a covenant with God
established through actualization of living in true community arise? It can arise in full force only where man does
not believe that this covenant is already fulfilled by his
observance of certain prescribed forms. And by adjustment through adaptation I mean the development of a
monetary system that was meant to enable the people to
continue to exist, even under the most extreme pressure,
but which wrecked realization's true realm, a life lived
with men and things. For wherever money is transformed
from a symbol of exchange between man and man into a
divisive and corrosive substance, there can be no immediacy between man and man. And when things are per-

ceived not according to their living intrinsic worth but in the distorting mirror of their pecuniary value, divine power cannot come to fruition in them.

Wherever these two adjustments coincide, wherever the religious forms are so alienated from their primal basis that they can live compatibly with capitalism's most degenerate forms, there modern Judaism has reached its lowest point. To me, the most repulsive of men is the oily war-profiteer, who does not cheat any God, for he knows none. And the Jewish profiteer is more repugnant than the non-Jewish, for he has fallen lower. But my deepest revulsion is incited by still another man, the man who cheats the God he knows, the man who discusses his business prospects while wearing his *tephillin*.²³ A tale tells of the *tephillin* God Himself puts on,²⁴ *tephillin* in which is encapsuled the saying "Who is like Thy people Israel, a people one in the earth?"²⁵ And a legend relates that Rabbi Levi Yitzhak of Berdychev called to God, "Your *tephillin* have fallen to the ground!" The fall of the people Israel—God's *tephillin* had fallen to the ground—that is the message proclaimed to us by the sight of the profiteer putting on his *tephillin*. He is the man of the double pact, a pact with God and a pact with Satan, and both are in accord. But this is only the crassest aspect of the matter; from there, a step-by-step progression leads to the most subtle rationalizations. And who among us dares to deny his own part in this guilt?

Legend has it that another hasidic rabbi was able to tell, merely by looking at the Jews before him, whether their soul's origin went back to Abraham's seed or to the "motley rabble" that had run along as Israel came out of Egypt.²⁶ Since the days of this rabbi the "motley rabble" has apparently become terrifyingly rampant. This is most clearly evident in the development of Hasidism itself.

Hasidism came into being in the late period of the Diaspora, as a bold endeavor to establish, in the midst of its confusion, a true community, and to create a brotherly union out of all the people bent under the yoke of an alien environment and threatened by degeneration. It was to be a pure abode for God's realization, so long as some spark of the folk spirit still lived among the people. This true community was to grow out of individual communities in which a path was to be broken to the unconditional by the intimate association of the Zaddik with his Hasidim, and by the Hasidim's association with one another, an association of mutual physical and spiritual help.

The fundamental view that gave rise to this structure is expressed in a hasidic book: "We may say of this generation that it possesses knowledge; but everybody desires only his own perfection and is not concerned with the community. Salvation, however, hinges upon one's desire for the perfection of the world." No single individual can reach the bird's nest—as the Zohar calls the abode of the Messiah—but a hundred men together can do so, if, each climbing upon the other's shoulders, they form a ladder that will reach to heaven.

What is intimated here began to take shape in the first creative period of Hasidism. But it lasted only a short time. A hundred years later the effects of the psychological pressures of alien environments and of the need for safeguards and adaptation proved their superior might. The ritualism that the first Hasidim had purified by endowing it with a new soul and new inwardness, and by adding to the traditional matter of prayers and customs an intent directed toward divine destiny, soon degenerated again; the depth of intention was schematized into vulgar magic formulas and letter-manipulations. The mammon-

ism that had been overcome by the precept and the deed
of unconditional mutual help once again intruded everywhere with its corrosive ways, even upon the sacred relationship between leader and community, undermining
the righteousness of the Zaddik and with it the justification of his authority. But the ruinous consequences of
safeguards and adaptation were most shockingly demon-
strated by the manner in which late Hasidism related itself to the realities of public life, by its politics. To secure for itself noninterference with and freedom for its
religious practices, late Hasidism renounced all manifestations of the Jewish ethos to the outside world, selling itself to the authorities of the day—a repellent example of
safeguarding by adaptation. Here, under the influence
of the *galut* situation, the Jewish spirit sank from the high
venture of a pure will to realization, into the disgrace of
the lowest finagling of pacts. And this is more than a mere
verbal description: it is a demonstration of what *galut*
means.

It is told of Rabbi Yaakov Yitzhak of Pzhysha (who
is commonly referred to simply as "the Yehudi," the
Jew[27]) that one night he did not sleep at all but sighed incessantly. Asked for an explanation by his favorite student, he said, "I must think of the fact that Moses was
followed by the Judges and the Judges by the Prophets;
then came the men of the Great Assembly, then the Tan-
naim and Amoraim, and after these the exhorters; and
when this, too, failed, and the number of false exhorters
increased, the Zaddikim arose. And this is what I am sigh-
ing about, seeing that this, too, will fail. What will Israel
do?"

We who live a hundred years after the Yehudi's
death, and today are looking back upon the history of the
Jewish will to realization, know no longer how to sigh.
We ask: "What *shall* Israel do?"

What shall Israel do? What shall it do to redeem itself
from the ghostlike unreality of its present, and to achieve
its realization, the realization of truth?

Three ways are pointed out to us as possible answers:
the way of humanitarianism, the way of formal nationalism, and the way of religious conservatism. Let us examine them.

The humanitarians—I choose the best among them
—say: "Go out into the world, children of Israel, and
bring about the realization of the spirit among men. Your
sin was that, in your longing for a life of true community,
you kept yourselves separate; now you must atone by
giving unreservedly of yourselves. Fling the torch of your
longing into the world! Stir the hearts, burst open the
gates of the will, storm the Bastille of the spirit! Fight for
a new mankind! Off with you to the barricades, children of Israel! Did you not know how to die at the stake
when the issue was separation? Know, then, how to die
even more gloriously now that the issue is union, union
of the peoples!"

To this we answer: "Speak more softly. You shout
like people who have awakened during an earthquake.
We, however, have seen many a world fall into ruins and
have forgotten nothing. You speak of our yearning with
unclean lips; you know nothing about it. Our longing is
older than yours, whether yours be one year old, or four,
or ten. Ours is thousands of years old. It may be assumed
that it has learned how to wait; yet it is more impatient
than yours, for it knows it must die if forced to go on bearing this unreal, ghostlike existence. It is more impatient,
for it will not be content with proclaiming man's rights—
or will they be called 'people's rights' this time?—only to
have its proclamation followed by such an era as the most
recent one. It will not be content with storming the Bas-
tilles of the spirit only to have the liberated spirit become

as homeless as it is today. Our longing wants to build a
solid home for the spirit, the abode of community. But
where can that be built if not where a people with a sense
of national cohesion and national community is already
in existence, where an ancient bond of heritage and destiny has already provided the foundations for community?

"Nor can Judaism build its home on the foundations of
other nations. The Jew can participate in the speeches
on the tribunes, he can fight with others on the barricades, but when it comes to building on foreign soil he
usually fails. He is foremost in developing political theories and in their promotion; but when it comes to their
practical application it becomes evident that he knows
only a sketch for the planned building but not its already
existing foundations to which he would have to adapt it.
He neither is aware of, nor does he honor or take into
consideration, the special beginnings of a true community
that may exist specifically in any one of the peoples; he is
not aware of its soul, life, history. It is this unawareness
that has in our day engendered the tragic conflict between
political doctrine and national character that is the initial
product of the Russian Revolution. We need our own materials and our own soil for our building. We do not wish
to build as individuals but as a people. Individual Jews
will still have much to give that is essential to the Western
world, especially as teachers. But the Jewish people's
longing to build points somewhere else: to its own land."

But now the dogmatizers of nationalism speak to us:
"Well put! The Jewish people must, at last, take its destiny into its own hands. It will serve mankind best by
freely developing its own talents. Therefore, let us create the preconditions for such an unhampered development. But have no preconceived notions about it. Do not
prescribe to the people the path it should take. Leave it

to them to clear the right path for themselves and to find
the right forms, as any other people does if its energies
are given free play. Today, we cannot as yet know what
Israel will have to do; but once we loosen its shackles it
will surely do its part. And why should our people be burdened with the task of building the true community? Why
do you want to make the difficult work of its restoration
still harder by saddling it with this load? We do not have
to realize ourselves in any way that is different from the
way of other peoples; we need only the unhampered development of our special character. Let us be like all the
nations, O House of Israel!" [28]

To this we answer: "Not the men who would let us
serve the true God in an alien land are the assimilation-
ists, but you who would readily approve any idol-worship
in our homeland if only the idols bear Jewish names!
You are assimilated to the dominant dogma of the century, the unholy dogma of the sovereignty of nations.
Every nation, so teaches this dogma, is its own master
and its own judge, obligated only to itself and answerable
only to itself. Whatever it does for the sake of its own ad-
vantage is well done; whatever it adopts as its own cause
is a good cause. Its needs are sufficient justification of its
actions, its special character sufficient justification of its
ethos, its drive to power sufficient justification of its right.
Today this dogma triumphs in many different ways; wherever it appears, naked or in all kinds of guises, it is regarded as final authority, and whatever political factor
may be loath to submit to its arbitration must at least pre-
tend to do so.

"We want to be understood correctly: recognition of
the nation as a fundamental reality in the life of mankind
can no longer be eradicated from man's consciousness,
nor should it be. But this recognition must, and will, be
augmented by another: that no people on earth is sover-

eign; only the spirit is. But the spirit—whatever the perverted relativism of a spirit-forsaken generation may have
to say against it—the spirit, which gives shape to the nations that are but lumps of clay, is one and indivisible. So
long as the nations continue to evade its command and
live out of sight of the unconditional, they will devour
each other. The more a people rejects love of the spirit,
preferring success, the more void will it be in the face of
eternity. But the people that, ready to extricate itself from
the whirling frenzy, humbles itself before the spirit will
receive its guidance.

"Our words are directed to the Jewish people, the
worldly people of the spirit, to keep faith with it and not
fall prey to assimiliation to dogma. It will not be easy;
but then we do not mean to make it easy for the Jewish
people. Nor do we intend to leave it to its own devices.
Its legitimate leaders have never done so. They did not
ask road directions of the people's 'special character'—
it had many a special character-trait against which they
lashed out with fiery tongues; they asked only the one,
the indivisible, spirit revealed to them and within them.
And thus it will continue to be. We must be willing to subordinate ourselves to the spirit in order that through our
means it may become reality. Only so long as we are of
the spirit do we carry within us the seed of true life; on
the day we become like all the nations, we shall indeed
deserve to be no more than that."

But now the dogmatists of the law take up the matter: "You speak truly. But what is this spirit that you profess, and what is its command that you proclaim? It remains a shadow, and its command an empty sound, unless
you infuse it with life and consciousness drawn from the
only source from which such can be drawn, the wellspring of Jewish tradition. If not so drawn, you proffer directions prompted not by need but by arbitrariness. You

want true community—but where else can you hear its
law if not in the word God spoke to His people? And how
can you distinguish between what in God's word seems
to you to be still fresh and applicable and what antiquated
and spent? There is no other way: if you want to be
Jews and to realize Judaism, you must return to pious
submission to God and His law. Only within the law,
within the one and only communal Jewish form, can
you become an organic part of the people once more and
regain solid ground under your feet."

To this we answer: "Oh, you who are safe and secure,
you who take refuge behind the bulwark of the law in order to avoid looking into God's abyss! Yes, you have solid,
well-trodden ground under your feet, whereas we hang
suspended over the infinite deep, looking about us. Oh,
you heirs and heirs of heirs who have but to exchange the
ancient golden coins into crisp new bills, while we, lonely
beggars, sit at the street corner and wait for the coming of
the One who will help us. Yet we would not want to exchange our giddy insecurity and our untrammeled pov-
erty for your confidence and your riches. For to you God
is the One who created once, and then no more; but to us
He is the One of whom people profess that He 'renews the
work of creation each day.' [29] And He truly does renew it,
within us and through us, desiring to enter by our means
into a new reality. Just as He restricted and contracted
Himself for the sake of the creation of the world,[30] so does
He restrict and contract Himself within us for the sake of
the work of mankind. To you God is Being who revealed
Himself once and never again. But to us He speaks out
of the burning bush of the present, and out of the *Urim*
and *Tummim*[31] of our innermost hearts.

"We honor the law, the armor of our peoplehood that
was forged by venerable forces. We salute the men who,
unmediatedly certain that God put it, just as it is, on the

people with His own hand, ride with us into the field unimpeded by the weight of the armor. But we commiser-
ate with those who wear it without this certainty, with the
men whose limbs it makes so rigid and so stiff that they
cannot go forth to perform their work, for the venerable
armor hangs on their bodies like a costume in a historical
parade. But we shall resist those who, invoking the authority of the already existing law, want to keep us from receiving new weapons from the hands of the living God.
For we can tolerate nothing that comes between us and
the realization of God.

"To be sure, you can say about God: 'He commanded this or that, and we fully understand all He wants
of us.' We who are still on the watch, we beggars know
as yet only the eternal aspect of His will. The temporal
aspect we must prescribe ourselves; ever anew, we must
set the stamp of the eternal's command upon the stuff
of reality. Because you possess the forms you think that
you no longer need to search the infinite for the right content, for it is enclosed within the forms; we, however, let
our souls reach out into the infinite, there to receive anew
the content for which a new form is to be created. For
you, the road is mapped out in books, and you know
your way; but we must feel around for it with our hands
in the beclouded chaos of the present. We are, however,
guided not by arbitrariness but by the most profound
need, for we are guided by the voice. It bids us work for
what is most profoundly Jewish, more Jewish than all
forms and all norms: realization, reconstruction of God's
community, and a new beginning. 'Break ground for yourselves,' says the voice, 'sow not among thorns' (Jeremiah
4:3). We want to obey this voice. We want to walk on the
road to Zion, that is, on the way to lived truth. It is not,
as you suggest, by receiving a law from the hands of the
people rather than from the hands of God that we shall

become an organic part of our people, but by sharing in the work of realization, of reconstruction, of a new beginning. Then, too, the hour will come when what was wordless will be defined by words, by a new word. A word that will reveal itself to us in the true life between man and man. First we shall do, and only then shall we hear it[32]: out of our own deed. True community is the Sinai of the future."

In examining the ways offered us in answer to the question of what Israel should do, we have, by a process of testing and elimination, arrived at the right way, the only one. It is the way leading, through Zion, to the renewal of human community.

In the Messianic dreams and outbreaks of the *galut*, national and human elements have always been merged, namely, a longing for liberation and for redemption, a striving for our own land and for true community. They promised fulfillment equally to the Jew in Israel and to the man in Israel. They were the refuge of the will to realization. When modern Zionism made the desire for a Jewish Palestine the center of a political movement, it defined this desire in predominantly national terms. Zionism wanted to be an essentially national movement—of which the West has an overabundance—though with the addition of a special colonizational intent. Its leaders, it is true, painted a picture of a "more just society" and favored modern ideas of settlement; but the unmistakably deeper pathos, unmistakably stronger color, of this picture came to light when its basic outlines were shown to be those of a national renaissance, a new national culture. Here undoubtedly was the movement's spiritual center of gravity. But a genuine renaissance has never emerged from purely national tendencies; specific forms have never been its goal. Rather it has always been based on a passionate reaching out for renewed human content, on "humanism"; it has developed new forms because the impact of this content burst open the traditional forms. Thus, Europe's national language cultures came into being because a new intellectual world urgently strove for expression. Thus, too, not Hebraism but Hebrew humanism—understood in the great historical meaning of this term—will have to be at the core of a Jewish movement for regeneration. This means that we must reach out passionately to grasp and renew Judaism's great human content. Or, to put it more precisely, we must grasp its greatest, its original content, the reach for realization, and live it anew; then the great national form will take shape by itself. Culture is neither a people's productivity nor the sum total of the works it produces; culture flourishes only where mutually shared work flows from a mutually shared spirit and life. Hence the fact that the Jewish will to realization is beginning to have a hold on Zionism means not a weakening but a strengthening of its national character; it means that its national idea is acquiring substance —that Zionism is beginning to change from a national movement into a national reality. Only when the national human elements, the longing both for liberation and for redemption, the striving both for a land of one's own and for true community, will all have been welded into a new shape—only then will the regeneration of the Jewish people be achieved.

Let us, in passing, address a word of warning to those who are exclusively political-minded. A Jewish Commonwealth is to be built in Palestine. It must not become just another of the numberless small states that are devoid of spiritual substance, a place like any other in today's Western world where spirit and people are separated, with both languishing: the one as intellectualism remote from life, the other as the masses remote from ideas. It

must not become a community where possessing replaces
being, and mutual exploitation replaces mutual help, a
place where men do not annihilate one another only because they fear and need each other. If the Jewish Commonwealth to be established in Palestine joined in the
war of all against all it would be crushed in the machin-
ery of its own intrigues, even if it declared itself "neutral" a thousand times over. Only if it becomes a spiritual force will it endure. A spiritual force does not mean
intellectual standards or cultural achievements. It means
rather realization of the spirit which—though alive
within the nations in the form of suffering, bitterness, in-
dignation, longing, or wishful dream—cannot assume a
concrete shape, because it is suppressed by the evil reign-
ing all about and within the nations. It means an espousal
of spirit and people, and their interpenetration. It means
an overcoming of the dualisms of truth and reality, idea
and fact, morals and politics. It means the substitution
of concord for total war that is tempered only by convention. It means religion, the religion of communal living,
of God's revelation in the community: lived religion. At
this turning point of our age, no other spiritual force but
lived religion can withstand the impact of our times, as
Moses once withstood the confrontation with Pharaoh.
The land that first saw the realization of the wishful
dream will become the nations' new sanctuary, and the
people that once led in this realization will become, forever, its inviolable priest.

    And what other people could take the lead in this
enterprise if not the one that is not burdened with the bal-
last of any single constitution, yet has endured and amply
suffered from all of them, a people that bears the summons to true community—a thousand times polluted, a
thousand times betrayed, yet inalienably its own—in the
memory of its heritage and of its destiny? And in what

country could this enterprise be realized first if not in the
one that teems with awesome relics of a towering will and
striving, yet also offers virgin soil and new territory for
social reformation?

Total effectiveness of Western revolutions is impeded
by the fact that in the existing institutions both the de-
cayed roots of sovereign rule and the seeds of community that have been kept alive since primordial times are
intertwined. Consequently, either the revolution pulls
both out of the ground, which means that the healthy
growth in need of care is destroyed along with whatever
should be destroyed; and when this is the case, those
of the revolutionaries who know the irreplaceable worth
of organic continuity yield to the representatives of a self-
glorifying intellectualism, who now endeavor, in vain, to
build everything anew out of cerebral concepts. Or the
revolution bogs down in the chaos. Fearing either the
task of new creation or impairment of the young growth,
it shies away from setting to work on the decaying material. As a result, the latter again overtakes the former,
the symbols devoid of spirit are restored, forms devoid of
soul are given magic names, and the sacred living seeds of
the community continue to await their hour, uncared for
and uncultivated.

We may, however, hope for something different from
the revolutionary colonization which is our task. I say revolutionary colonization, for we do not have to rebuild an
already existing structure but are summoned to effect a
transformation, a reshaping, within and through the new
settlement we shall found. No established institutions that
will thwart our efforts are waiting for us; it is our task to
create for our Commonwealth forms conducive to its
growing into a truly communal structure and an ever
purer realization of its idea. But it is not out of the vacuum
of intellectualism that these forms materialize; pre-

served in our people's memory, in our internal history, we bear the exalted commandment to establish a genuinely communal, an as yet unrealized settlement. We must separate the pure and eternal aspects of this tradition from the impure and temporal, and set to work.

Given our spiritual heritage can we not succeed where institutions always fail—in the difficult task of separating what is alive, though suppressed, from what is dead, though still dominant? Our revolution, the revolutionary settlement through which we become a constructive element in mankind's beginning revolution, signifies the fulfillment of a task with which tradition has charged us; but it is an elective fulfillment. Selection, and consequently rejection, constitute its revolutionary character. But this selection, this choice, I repeat, is no arbitrary matter. Within our personal will a greater one is at work.

"A renewal of the whole person"—I cannot describe any more adequately today than I did nearly twenty years ago[33] the significance of the great process whose external aspects are manifest in some recent events, the emigration of a part of Jewry to Palestine and the establishment there of a more or less extensive self-government. But like all renewal in the life of individuals and of peoples, societies and precepts, this renewal does not mean that our soul is being equipped with a new power never known until now, or that it is given a new face, never seen before. It means rather that a buried ancient treasure is being uncovered, a forgotten direction found again, and a neglected human potential reactivated; it means a reactivation of something that ancient times had possessed, either as an acquired way of life or as an innate striving, but that has been lost since then. Yet through this process, in a new age and under new conditions, in a new psychological and historical situation, with a new wealth of material and under new creative tensions, something that is essentially new does take place after all. I spoke of an acquired way of life and of an innate striving. This acquired way of life wants to be taken up again and pursued anew, though under fundamentally changed conditions, and by a soul that has passed through many trials and tribulations. Such a reactivation would consist of regaining the early Hebrews' attachment to the soil, of work on the soil and joy in the soil. As for the innate striving [. . .] possessed in ancient times and lost or weakened since then, it can be truly reactivated only if this process is begun at once, amid the process of renewal. And it is a grievous misjudgment of the significance of such a "now" if one consoles oneself with the notion that this action could be made up for at some later time. Here, the revolutionary significance of our task to establish a new settlement is disclosed most clearly.

It is, however, evident to the man of vision and of will that both innate striving and acquired way of life are intimately connected; for in ancient Judaism that striving was intent exclusively upon the elevation, sanctification, and perfection of this way of life. Ancient Judaism did not want to realize the Divine in a purely spiritual life but in a natural life. Just as its religion was an agrarian religion, so its legislation was agrarian legislation. The humaneness demanded by its prophets was a humaneness rooted in the soil; and even Essenism still derived the notion of sacredness from the work of the plowman and the sower. The establishment of a true community cannot come about unless the agrarian life, a life that draws its strength from the soil, is elevated to a service of God and spreads to the other social classes, binding them, as it were, to God and to the soil. The laws of the spirit are the laws of the soil, correctly understood; they carry out the dictates of a nature that has become humanized and God-directed.

Our revolution, the revolutionary settlement, signifies the elective fulfillment of a task with which our tradition has charged us. We must choose in this tradition the elements that constitute closeness to the soil, hallowed worldliness, and absorption of the Divine in nature; and reject in this tradition the elements that constitute remoteness from the soil, detached rationality, and nature's banishment from the presence of God.

When we thus perceive our internal history, the memory of the Jewish will to realization, then the following principles present themselves to us:

community, as the realization of the Divine in the shared life of men;

soil, as the maternal element of such a shared life, bestowed by God on the community alone and not on any individual man;

work, as the continually renewed bond between man and soil, hallowed where it is performed with man's total earthly being of body and soul, as communal service freely offered, a divine service;

aid, mutual material and spiritual aid, as man's support, succor, and liberation of his fellow man for the work of realization, which through such aid is truly rendered unto God;

leadership, as the office of those most willing and most capable of helping, administered as a mandate from God, the one and only ruler; that is, leadership not by specialists in spiritual matters who descend upon earth but by ordinary worldly men who sanctify their lives by the spirit;

the community in its multifarious forms, as local community, cooperative society, fellowship, and brotherhood, as the cell-unit of every community in which the immedi-

ate relationship between man and man, the carrier of the
Divine, assumes lasting shape;

the commonwealth, as the association of communal
units that are full of vitality and the will to realization and
whose interrelationship is based on the same immediateness that is present in each of them individually—on mutually owned land, mutually distributed work, a system of
mutual help supported by the representative bodies of the
community; a commonwealth led by men who, within
this system, have proved to be the most dependable
helpers;

mankind, as an association of such commonwealths,
interrelated in the same immediateness;

spirit, as the prophetic teacher of faithfulness and
renewal; as admonisher of men to be faithful to the task
of realization and its laws and to hold fast to the institutions that serve the true community; but also as the
guardian of social dynamics out of which all institutions
and communal forms must renew themselves in an eternal
rhythm in order to avoid rigidity and to keep the dead
from dominating the living, as has thus far always been
the case in the world of man.

But looming above all is the name of the nameless,
all realization's goal; a grace open beyond any need for
words to all who are determined to start the work of realization, even if, having outgrown old terminologies, they
may imagine to have outgrown God; but woefully unfamiliar to those who are too indolent to be concerned with
realization, to men who mouth designations of God devoid of all meaning.

All these principles can be summed up in the watchword: from within! Nothing new can be established by
stripping an autocratic constitution off a country and super-
imposing on it a communist one instead when life between
man and man remains unchanged, and so too the methods

of government. To bring about a true transformation of society, a true renaissance, human relationships must undergo a change. Our hope is rooted in the belief that in the generation of Jews who are returning to their homeland at this moment of our history, after so great a shock and motivated by so great a decision, the preconditions for a transformation of relationships are raised to a power never known before.

It is not my task today to speak of the establishment of a true community in Zion beyond the general and internal aspects of the question. Nor is it up to us to impose structural schemes upon future developments whose specific structure will have to evolve from the creative conflicts of an age of beginning and sacrifice. The spirit must recognize the limitations within which it may impose itself upon life; beyond them, it must wait until, in new words and a new law, it can re-emerge from life. But within these self-recognized, self-drawn limitations the spirit must make a start, must determine, must command. And it will do so.

We are well aware that a struggle against immense odds is waiting for us. Nor have we forgotten that the deed concerned with the growth of community has everything lined up against it: the rigorism of the habitual traditionalists and the indolence of those enslaved by the moment; rash doctrinairism and irresponsible disputatiousness; miserly egotism and intractable vanity; hysterical self-effacement and disoriented agitation; the cult of the "pure idea" and the cult of *Realpolitik*. Neither have we forgotten the nature of the endless masses who resist with all their active and latent energies the challenge of the desire to in-form them, who pull the deed down into their destructive vortex. Nevertheless, we go on hoping and planning, and we are making a beginning. Indeed, we know the "motley rabble" only too well, compulsive compromisers who are hostile to the work of realization and who violate all pure becoming in Judaism. We do not know how far we shall succeed in keeping them out of the land where they probably will smell an opportunity for exploitation and profit. But far more profoundly, beyond all past and future disappointment, we are certain of Israel, and expectantly ready for God.

VIII

Herut: On Youth and Religion

"God's writing engraved on the
tablets"—read not *harut* (engraved)
but *herut* (freedom).
—Sayings of the Fathers VI, 2

AMONG ALL the problems of present-day Jewish life,
that of youth's attitude toward religion is probably most
in need of elucidation. But, one may ask, does youth
really have a special religious problem? Is youth, as such,
concerned with religion at all?

Is youth concerned with religion? This means: individually, young people may be religious or irreligious,
depending on their personal disposition, upbringing, or
environmental influences; but in what way does youth,
as youth, have a definite attitude toward religion? Are we
justified in demanding that it have one? Youth is the time
of total openness. With totally open senses, it absorbs the
world's variegated abundance; with a totally open will, it
gives itself to life's boundlessness. It has not yet sworn
allegiance to any one truth for whose sake it would have
to close its eyes to all other perspectives, has not yet
obligated itself to abide by any one norm that would silence all its other aspirations. Its quest for knowledge
knows no limits other than those set by its own experience, its vitality no responsibility other than the one to
the totality of its own life. Sooner or later it will have to
subordinate its own power of perception and volition to
the restrictive power of natural and moral laws, thus los-

ing its boundlessness. The decision of whether to submit
to religious or other theorems, to religious or other rules,
should therefore be left to youth itself. Whoever imposes
religion upon it closes all but one of the thousand windows
of the circular building in which youth dwells, all but one
of the thousand roads leading into the world.

This admonition would be justified if religion were
really, by nature, the dispenser of fixed orientations and
norms, or a sum of dogmas and rules. By nature, however,
it is neither. Dogmas and rules are merely the result, subject to change, of the human mind's endeavor to make
comprehensible, by a symbolic order of the knowable
and doable, the working of the unconditional it experiences within itself. Primary reality is constituted by the
unconditional's effect upon the human mind, which, sustained by the force of its own vision, unflinchingly faces
the Supreme Power. Man's mind thus experiences the
unconditional as that great something that is counterposed
against it, as the Thou as such. By creating symbols, the
mind comprehends what is in itself incomprehensible;
thus, in symbol and adage, the illimitable God reveals
Himself to the human mind, which gathers the flowing
universal currents into the receptacle of an affirmation
that declares the Lord reigns in this and in no other way.
Or man's mind captures a flash of the original source of
light in the mirror of some rule that declares the Lord
must be served in this and in no other way. But neither
symbol nor adage makes man unworthy or untrue; they
are rather forms the unconditional itself creates within
man's mind, which, at this particular time, has not yet
developed into a more effective tool. In mankind's great
ages, the Divine, in invisible becoming, outgrows old sym-
bolisms and blossoms forth in new ones. The symbol becomes ever more internalized, moves ever closer to the
heart, and is ever more deeply submerged in life itself.

[. . .] It is not God who changes, only theophany—the manifestation of the Divine in man's symbol-creating mind—until no symbol is adequate any longer, and none is needed; and life itself, in the miracle of man's being with man, becomes a symbol—until God is truly present when one man clasps the hand of another.

But such is the mysterious interconnection of the mind that, in this most essential of all human concerns, every human being comprises, potentially, all of mankind, and every human destiny, all of history. At some time or other, be it ever so fleeting and dim, every man is affected by the power of the unconditional. The time of life when this happens to all, we call youth. At that time, every man experiences the hour in which the infinite beckons him, testing whether, sustained by the power of his vision and the creation of symbols, by his dedication and response, he can unflinchingly confront it. In this most inward sense, every man is destined to be religious. Indeed, what the total openness of youth signifies is that its mind is open not merely to all, but to the All. But most men fail to fulfill their destiny. Whether they remain close to their ancestral religion or become alienated from it, whether they continue to believe in and to practice this religion and its symbolism or refuse to adhere to its command, they are unable to withstand the impact of the unconditional and therefore evade it. They do not approach it with the power of their vision and their work, with their dedicated and responsive deed; they turn away from it, and toward the conditional.

It should not, however, be assumed that by the conditional we mean secular things, not at all. We mean rather the things that have been stripped of their consecration and robbed of their bond with the unconditional. For the man who wholly gives himself to the unconditional—whatever he may call it—consecration re-

sides in all things; in his dealings with them the divine
Presence becomes manifest, and all is immortal. But the
man who denies himself to the unconditional lives out his
life amidst unholy conditionalities; he is ever surrounded
by turmoil, and fulfillment comes apart in his hands.

We are not concerned, then, with imposing religion
upon youth, or with forcing it into a system of the knowable and doable, but with awakening youth's own latent
religion; that means: its willingness to confront, unwaveringly, the impact of the unconditional. We must not preach
to youth that God's revelation becomes manifest in only
one, and in no other, way; rather, we must show it that
nothing is incapable of becoming a receptacle of revelation. We must not proclaim to youth that God can be
served by only one, and by no other, act, but we must
make it clear that every deed is hallowed if it radiates the
spirit of unity. We must not ask young people to avow as
exclusively binding in their lives only that which emanated
at some hour of the past, but we must affirm for them that
"every man has his hour" [1] when the gate opens for him
and the word becomes audible to him. We who stand in
awe of that which is unknowable do not want to transmit
to youth a knowledge of God's nature and work. We who
consider life as more divine than laws and rules do not
want to regulate the life of youth by laws and rules at-
tributed to God. We want to help youth not to bypass its
destiny, not to miss its metaphysical self-discovery by being asleep, and to respond when it senses within itself the
power of the unconditional. By so doing, we do not diminish the openness of youth but promote and affirm it;
do not curtain any of its windows, but let it absorb the all-
encompassing view; do not shut off any road, but make it
easier for youth to see that all roads, if walked in truth
and consecration, lead to the threshold of the Divine.

But one may ask: "If religion's basic significance lies not in the mores or institutions of a community united by precept and cult but rather in acts derived from an innate awareness common to all men, that is in 'universally human' acts, how then is it possible to speak of a specific kinship between Jewish youth and religion? Or, to put it more generally, how is it possible to speak of a specific kinship between the youth of any people and religion?"

For an answer, we must first look at the general aspect of this question, and then investigate whether some special elements, nonexistent in any other people, are not at work in Judaism and in its youth.

I have pointed out the error that threatens all young people and to which many fall prey: unable to withstand the impact of the unconditional, they evade it. But there exists still another, and more serious, error: the *pretense* of withstanding—a deception not only of others but of oneself. The unconditional affects a person when he lets his whole being be gripped by it, be utterly shaken and transformed by it, and when he responds to it with his whole being: with his mind, by perceiving the symbols of the Divine; with his soul, by his love of the All; with his will, by his standing the test of active life.

But it may happen, by some odd perversity, that an individual entertains the illusion that he has surrendered himself to the unconditional whereas in fact he has evaded it: he interprets the fact of having been affected by the unconditional. as having had an "experience" (*Erlebnis*). His being remains wholly unperturbed and unchanged, but he has savored his hour of exaltation. He does not know the response; he knows only a "mood" (*Stimmung*). He has psychologized God.

The first of these errors, evasion, was especially characteristic of an earlier generation, which inclined toward superficial rationalism; the second, a quasi-acceptance, is common to the new generation, which is given to no less superficial emotionalism. This latter error is by far the more serious one, for a quasi-affirmation is always more questionable than a negation. In some way, religiosity may possibly penetrate the evaders but never the pretenders. One can be a rationalist, a freethinker, or an atheist in a religious sense, but one cannot, in a religious sense, be a collector of "experiences," a boaster of moods, or a prattler about God. When the teeming swarms of the marketplace have scattered into the night, the stars shine over the new stillness as over a mountain silence; but no eternal light can penetrate the fumes of the chatter-filled public house.

But how can youth be saved from this error? Or rather, how can youth save itself from it? It has a great helper by its side: the living community of the people. Only the disengaged man, incapable of drawing upon any source deeper than that of his private existence, will degrade the unconditional's impact to an "experience" and respond with literary effusions to the music of the spheres. The man who is truly bound to his people cannot go wrong, not because he has at his disposal the symbols and forms that millennia of his people's existence have created for envisioning as well as for serving the unconditional, but because the faculty to create images and forms flows into him from this bond to his people. I said: the man who is truly bound to his people. Right here it must be pointed out that a declaration of solidarity with one's people does not yet mean that one is truly bound to it. It means, at best, only the desire for such a bond.

When bound to his people, man is aware that the living community of this people is composed of three elements. Preceding him, there is the people's sacred work, expressed in literature and history, the scroll of words and deeds whose letters tell the chronicle of this people's relation to its God. Around him, there is the present national body in which, no matter how degenerate it may be, the divine Presence continues to live, immured in the tragic darkness of the everyday, yet shedding upon it the radiance of its primordial fire. And within him, in his soul's innermost recesses, there is a silent, age-old memory from which, if he can but unlock it, truer knowledge pours forth for him than that from the shallow wavelets of his private experiences. But this deep wellspring can be unlocked only by him who has made his wholehearted decision for such a bond.

Three elements that compose his people's living community, a threefold source of strength for the young, a threefold anchorage for his relation to the unconditional!

It should be remembered that the unconditional's effect upon individual man represents, as it were, a foreshortening of its effect upon mankind's mind in general. How could an adequate response develop in individual man, how could he even conceive of an appropriate symbol, were he not part of the continuity of mankind's spiritual process? Response and symbol, however, are given to individual man directly only in the absolute, that is, the religiously creative, life of his people. Here mankind's wordless dialogue with God is condensed for him into the language of the soul, which he is not merely able to understand, but to which he himself can add new expressions, as yet unspoken. Without this language, he could do no more than stammer and falter. For even the founders of new religions, however new their words and deeds may seem to be, stand in fact within the continuity of their people's creation of symbols and images; and when they strike water out of the rock, this water was already flowing, invisibly and inaudibly, deep within the stone before their staff ever struck it. All religious found-

ing, all genuine personal religion is merely the discovery
and raising of an ancient treasure, the unveiling and freeing of a folk-religion that has grown beneath the surface.
Without a bond to his people, man remains amorphous
and adrift when God calls him; it is only from this bond
that he derives contour and substance, so that he can
dare to confront his Caller.

What I said about the young person's relation to the
religious life of his people is especially relevant to Judaism, for two reasons. The first is the autonomy of Judaism's religious development, an autonomy not experienced by Western peoples. Among them, the natural
growth of religious tendencies and forms was circumscribed and transformed by a spiritual principle imposed
from the outside, Christianity; and despite all the artful
attempts of the Church to incorporate into its doctrine
and its service the primal forces that had been at work
in pagan myth and magic and had stirred the peoples'
emotions, no perfect unity was achieved. Hence, in Christianity, the young person who wishes to derive sustenance
and support for his personal relation to the unconditional
from his association with his people must turn not so
much to religion proper as to the primal forces that live
on, covertly, in the faithful images of a people's life: its
customs and tales, songs and sayings. In Judaism, however, other influences notwithstanding, all religious development sprang exclusively from forces inherent in the
people's own soul, and foreign elements had no part in the
conflicts that accompanied this development. Here, therefore, the young person faces a unified realm, and when
the official outward forms of his religion do not provide
him with the help he needs, he need not turn away from
them to another sphere of his people's existence; he has
only to descend into their own depths, to those ramifica-

tions of Jewish religiosity that, not having become dominant, still continue to live beneath the surface.

But an even more essential reason is the fact that he
cannot turn to any other sphere of his people's existence,
for in the life of the Jewish people no sphere is uncon-
nected with the religious one. Not only is Judaism's specific productivity bound up with its relationship to the
unconditional, but so too is its specific vitality. Any distinction between different fields of endeavor, characteristic of most other peoples, is alien to the nature of Judaism; its extrareligious elements are either so peripheral
as to have no part in its creative expression, or they are,
in one way or another, determined by and dependent
upon religious factors. It is characteristic that even the
people's original defection from the God of biblical religion assumed a religious form: the defecting masses were
not content with surrendering themselves to their newly
freed instincts; they expressed their driving passion by
gathering together their valuables for the casting of an
idol. [2] The case of the modern Hebrew poet who, not
content with forswearing allegiance to the old God, wor-
shipped instead Apollo's statue,[3] exemplifies the same
characteristic. No matter what form religious creativity
may assume in Judaism, it never loses its basic character.
The greatest philosophical genius Judaism has given to
the world, Spinoza, is the only one of the great philoso-
phers for whom, in reality, God is the sole subject of
thought; and ancient Messianic dreams live on in the
ideologies of Jewish socialists.

I am well aware that ever since the demand for Jewish regeneration in our time became more insistent there
have been men who deplore the predominance of the religious element in Judaism, though they are far from hold-
ing any shallow enlightenment theories.[4] They see in this
predominance a narrowing of the people's life, a weaken-

ing of its vitality, and a divergence of its energies from
their natural tasks. These men demand a secularization
of Judaism, and, given the vegetating *galut* life in which
religious demands in their narrowest sense have so frequently stifled the people's vitality, I recognize that there
is justification for such a view. Nevertheless, it is based
on a fundamental error that mistakes the historical outward forms of its religion for Judaism's great religious
creativity. Religion is detrimental to an unfolding of the
people's energies only where it concentrates—as it has
indeed done to an ever-increasing degree in the Diaspora
—on the enlargement of the *thou shalt not,* on the minute
differentiation between the permitted and the forbidden.
When this is the case, it neglects its true task, which is
and remains: man's response to the Divine, the response
of the total human being; hence, the unity of the spiritual
and the worldly, the realization of the spirit, and the
spiritualization of the worldly; the sanctification of the
relationship to all things; that is, freedom in God. But
Hasidism, though still closely tied to the tradition of the
thou shalt not, already presents a great, though unsuccessful, attempt at a synthesis between the spiritual and the
worldly order, a fusion of fundamental religious consciousness with the unaffectedness and fullness of natural
life. And the future of creative Judaism lies not in a weed-
ing out of religiosity but in the direction of this synthesis.
The growing striving for this synthesis is youth's guarantee that it will not find decomposing rocks but the waters
of genuine life when it descends into the depths of Jewish
religion in search of help for its soul.

Intellectualization, in the making for centuries and accomplished within recent generations, has brought a
depressing loneliness to the youth of present-day Europe.
By intellectualization I mean the hypertrophy of intel-

lect that has broken out of the context of organic life
and become parasitic, in contradistinction to organic spirituality, into which life's totality is translated. Because the
bridge of immediate community, whether its name be
love, friendship, companionship, or fellowship, connects
only man with man, and hence spirit with spirit, but not
thinking apparatus with thinking apparatus, this intellectualization begets loneliness. Not the exultant loneliness
of the summit experienced by the first climbers who are
waiting, with silent hearts, for their companions who have
fallen behind, but the negative loneliness of the abyss experienced by the lost and the forlorn. Out of the anxiety
and depression of such a state of mind, modern Europe's
youth longs for community, longs for it so powerfully that
it is ready to surrender to any phantom of community,
as we have so abundantly experienced. But, owing to the
anomaly of *galut* life, intellectualization has progressed
still further, and the loneliness of Jewish youth has been
intensified. In addition, a large segment of Jewish youth,
especially in the Western world, is cut off from its
natural national existence and gradually loses the illusion
that it has organic ties to another one. And this too in-
tensifies its longing for community.

Only a genuine bond with the religiously creative
life of its people can still this longing of Jewish youth,
and overcome the loneliness of its intellectualization.

I have already indicated why youth needs this bond
for the building of its inner religious life: to enable it to
confront the unconditional not with the arbitrary mood
of the dreamer who has had an "experience" but with
the readiness of the fighter and worker who, despite
all personal freedom, binds himself to his people's creativity and pursues it in his own life. But youth needs this
bond no less for its inner national life. It must no longer
permit itself the illusion that it can establish a decisive

link to its people merely by reading Bialik's[5] poems or
by singing Yiddish folksongs; nor by the addition of a few
quasi-religious sentiments and lyricisms. It must realize
that something bigger is at stake: that one must join,
earnestly and ready for much struggle and work, in Judaism's intense creative process, with all its conflicts and
subsequent reconciliations; that one must recreate this
process from within, with reverence of soul and awareness
of mind; that one must participate in it not only with his
inwardness but with his total life, by affirming and trans-
lating into reality all one finds along the way; that what
needs to be done is to get ready for renewal. For the idea
of renewal must not—as so often happens to ideas in the
short-winded Jewish movement of our days—degenerate
into a comfortable slogan that would exempt us from the
effort of struggling, studying, and building, a slogan in
which the emotions may luxuriate and the mind go slack.
The idea of renewal must be the banner carried at the
head of the procession by those who put their beliefs into
practice. Renewal is in the making when Judaism's spiritual process, which is a process of religious struggle and
religious creativity, is restored to life, in word and deed,
by a generation earnestly resolved to translate its ideas
into reality.

But restoration demands something more creative
than mere joining-in, though it cannot be achieved without it. And here the basic question comes to the fore:
what should the nature and the object of this joining-in
be?

Depending on whether the essence of Jewish religion
is viewed as lying in its teaching or in its law, two ways
are advocated for today's youth to follow: to commit itself either to Jewish teaching or to Jewish law.

I shall begin with the first of these views. Its leading

proponents[6] sublimate the many-faceted and vital fullness of religion into a system of abstract concepts. But in
the process the nurturing, creative, inexplicable element
of religion, the awareness of its suprarationality, is lost.
Dogmas, primarily the dogma of God's oneness, and moral
commandments, primarily the commandment to love
one's neighbor, are singled out and summarized in formulations that as a rule are shaped to fit one or another
dominant philosophical school. Consequently, to anyone
unfamiliar with the suprarational wealth of Jewish religiosity, Judaism appears to be a curious, awkward detour to some modern philosophical theorems—as, for
instance, the idea of God as a postulate of practical reason, or the categorical imperative—a detour that historically was probably unavoidable, but that has now become
wholly superfluous.

The originators of such theories overlook the fact
that religious truth is not a conceptual abstraction but has
existential relevance; that is, that words can only point
the way, and that religious truth can be made adequately
manifest only in the individual's or the community's life
of religious actualization (*Bewährung*). Indeed, they
overlook the fact that a master's teachings lose their religious character as soon as they are taken out of the context of his own life and the life of his followers and transformed into a wholly non-personal, autonomous maxim,
recognizable and acknowledgeable as such. Frozen into a
declaration of what is or into a precept of what ought to
be, the words of religious teaching represent a more inspirited, but also a more primitive, variation of a metaphysical or ethical ideology. But viewed as part of the
utterances of a great life to which conceptualization cannot do justice, they are beyond the sphere of all ideologies
and not subject to their criteria; they are truth *sui generis*,
contingent upon no other: religious truth. Here, not the

words themselves are truth, but life as it has been, and will be, lived; and the words are truth only by virtue of this life. In Judaism, therefore, the truth of God's oneness encompasses not only the "I shall be there" [7] but also all of Moses' life; not only the "Hear, O Israel" [8] but also the death of the martyrs.

Furthermore, the authors of the aforementioned theories overlook the fact that religious truth is not static but dynamic; that is, it neither belongs to nor is finished with any single historical moment in time. Nor can it be taken out of the context of such a single moment. Instead, every moment of the past, no matter how rich in revelation, is one phase of this truth, as is in fact every religiously creative period. Thus, in Judaism, conjoined to the truth of God's oneness is its entire development and all its transformations: the multiplicity of God's biblical names in their gradation from a natural plurality to a spiritual singularity; and equally the separation of the *shekhinah,* in correspondence with the growing awareness of the empirical world's imperfection. The heavenly hosts who are asked to create man are part of it, and so are the *sephirot*[9] through which the Divine emanates into the world—all of which, instead of diminishing oneness, intensify it. Some subsequent developments are also part of it, and, I daresay, some that are yet to come.

Religious truth, in contradistinction to philosophical truth, is not a maxim but a way, not a thesis but a process. That God is merciful is an abstract statement; to penetrate the religious truth that lies beyond it, we must not shrink from opening the Bible to one of its most awful passages, the one where God rejects Saul, His anointed (upon whom, at election, He bestowed a new spirit), because he spared the life of Agag, the conquered king of the Amalekites.[10] Let us not resist the shudder that seizes us, but let us follow where it leads as the soul of the people struggled for an understanding of God. We shall then come to that wondrous passage in the Talmud where, according to an old biblical interpretation, God rejoices in Goliath's soul and answers the angels who remind Him of David: "It is incumbent upon Me to turn them into friends." [11] Here we see a religious truth.

Purity of soul is an ethical concept. Nevertheless, let us not recoil from reading, in the third Book of Moses, the paragraphs that describe purification by the blood of sheep and doves as well as the great purification through the scapegoat. And when our hearts tremble under the impact of the great, ancient, but also alien, symbol, let us follow the way the people's soul took as it struggled for its purity, a way leading beyond prophets and psalmists to Akiba's liberating cry: "God is the purifying bath of Israel!" [12] Only then will we become fully aware of the religious element in this concept of purity.

A bond between virtue and reward has become unacceptable to our own sensibility toward life and the world. But we must not read this attitude into the records of the ancient Jewish religion where, from God's covenant with the patriarchs, through Moses' blessing and curse, to the promises and threats of the prophets, the belief in reward and punishment constitutes a self-evident basis for the moral postulate, a belief perpetuated even in the abstraction of the Maimonidean articles of faith. At the same time we must not close our eyes to the struggle in which men of sacred will turned, with ever increasing determination, away from this belief. We can follow the progression of this from the lofty talmudic phrase "for the sake of the Torah itself" [13] to that hasidic tale in which the Baal Shem (who, owing to a transgression, is to be denied life in the world to come) gratefully rejoices, for only now will he be able to serve God wholly for His own sake.[14] Here, a religious truth unfolds for us.

We must therefore reject commitment to a claim that Jewish teaching is something finished and unequivocal. For us, it is neither. It is, rather, a gigantic process, still uncompleted, of spiritual creativity and creative response to the unconditional. It is in this process that we want to participate with our conscious, active life, in the hope that we, too, may not be denied a creative spark. But to achieve this participation, we must fully discern this process—discern not merely some of its isolated aspects or effects, not only maxims or theses, but, in earnest awareness, its whole development up to the present, recreating it in its entirety from within. Yet this is not enough. We must truly *will* this process, all of it, from its beginnings, through all its ups and downs, conflicts and reconciliations, up to ourselves—the lowly but God-inspired sons of a transitional generation, doing their share to the best of their abilities—and beyond our time.

The second of the two views I spoke of renders the word Torah not as "teaching" but as "law"; its proponents bid Jewish youth to commit itself to Jewish law. By the term "law" they mean the sum of all the statutes, preserved at first in unwritten form but later committed to writing, that God, according to tradition, gave to Moses on Mount Sinai, within the hearing of the assembled people of Israel. The tradition of this giving of the law, reinforced by the life and death of a long chain of generations, is so powerful and venerable that some of its power and venerability is imparted to every man who truly dwells within it; that is, to the man who with his total being adheres to its commandments and prohibitions, not because he was taught and conditioned to do so by his

parents or teachers, but because he feels certain in his
very soul that these 613 commandments and prohibitions[15] are the core and substance of God's word to Israel.
Samson Raphael Hirsch[16] is fully justified in assigning a
central position to this principle in his concept of the
Jewish law, a principle used by his antipode, Mendelssohn,[17] in his dispute with Lavater,[18] as the main argument for the validity of Judaism. Having pointed out the
fact that all of Israel had heard the Lord's voice, without
any intermediary, Hirsch continues: "By this fact, which
excludes any possibility of error, the Torah has been
established, immutably, for all generations and for all
times."

Genuine affirmation of the law must be anchored in
this certitude of the fact of revelation and that its content
has been faithfully preserved in the 613 *mitzvot* and their
framework. Indeed, such affirmation has religious value
only insofar as it is supported by this certitude. The legitimacy of the life of the man whose observance of the law
is grounded on this basis is unassailable, the legitimacy of
what, to him, is truth, irrefutable. He deserves our esteem
and approbation, especially when, for the sake of observing the law, he gladly assumes the burden of overcoming
the countless difficulties and temptations presented by our
society. But if he lacks this certitude, his sacrificial spirit,
whether a result of piety or of habit, loses its religious
import and hence its special sanctity.

Observance of commandments because one knows or
feels that this is the only way in which to live in the name
of God has a legitimacy all its own, essentially inaccessible
to all outside criticism, whose criteria it can reject. But
observance without this basic attitude means exposure
of oneself as well as the commandments to a test by criteria of a wholly different ethos. For relationship to the
unconditional is a commitment of the total man, whose

mind and soul are undivided; to divorce the actions indica-
tive of this commitment from the yea-saying of man's undivided soul, to sever them from their accord with man's
undivided mind, is to profane them. But it is such prof-
anation that is perpetrated by those blind followers of the
law who demand that it be accepted not out of certitude
of its divine origin but out of obedience to the authority of
the collective Jewish will. They declare that, first and foremost, the law must be observed; everything else will then
follow. The law, they say, restrains the will but leaves the
personality free.

We reject this dialectic completely. In the image
of man to which we aspire, conviction and volition, personality and performance, are one and indivisible. And
though it may yet take lengthy, indescribably difficult
battles against the enormous resistance of external and
internal forces before this unity is realized in all other
areas, there is one particular area in which there must be
no further delay: the area of religiosity. For this is the
true realm of unity, the realm where man, in every other
respect still divided, split apart, and torn by conflict, may
at any moment become whole and one. [. . .]

For those who have not been granted the certitude I
spoke of, this insight charts a course that is incompatible
with the acceptance of traditional law. And no one familiar with the new religious consciousness of a new youth—
this planet, still aglow and uncongealed, that is as yet
aware only of revolving around its own axis, with barely
a first inkling of an orbit around the unknown sun—no
one who has ever been close to the secret of this becoming
will think it could contain the belief in a one-time revelation, transmitted in its entirety and binding for all time.

It would seem, however, that the passionate will for
community that I spoke of is motivating Jewish youth to

commit itself to traditional teaching and law after all. It feels an ever-growing urge to truly find its way back to its people—not merely to this people's recorded past and dreamed-about future but also to its actual present—and to become an organic part of the people, to merge with it. And it seems to some of them that such a merging can be achieved only by acceptance of the special teachings and customs of the Jewish people, which constitute the teachings and customs of Jewish tradition. They are supported in this view by exhorters and zealots who, dissatisfied with their experience of Jewish nationalism—dissatisfied because, in their opinion, it is not Jewish enough; dissatisfied, in truth, because it is not human enough—now proclaim as the last and redeeming word a commitment to the law of their common tradition. But those who clutch at this belief are blind to the signs appearing, at this hour, on the firmament of our destiny and the destiny of the world. There is greatness in the national body, and its faithful adherence to the law is awe inspiring. Yet greater still is the working of the national spirit, and he who, in sensitive awareness, has opened his soul to it knows that something new will rise out of it.

But neither will this new element rise out of nothingness. It, too, will develop and transform already existing material; it, too, will be a discovery and raising of an ancient treasure, an unveiling and freeing of something that has grown beneath the surface. It behooves us, therefore, to grasp the old, with our hearts and minds, but not lose our hearts and minds to it. We want to remain faithful to the intent of that great spiritual movement which we call the Jewish movement, a movement that is not romanticism but a renascence. For, even though the admonishers and zealots may not concede it, it is always romanticism when the spirit, in its search for a people, submits and surrenders to the forms developed in that

people's past and transmitted, in word and custom, from
that past. And it is always a renascence when the spirit
brings to life the primal forces encapsuled in those forms,
calling them forth to new creation—when it encounters
a people and makes it creative.

In the light of this perception we shall try to find an
answer to the question occupying our mind. But first I
must explain to whom I refer by this "we," and to whom
I am united in question and answer. They are the people
for whom this address is intended. There are only a few
of them. They are those members of Jewish youth who
genuinely participate in the evolving religious awareness
of an evolving generation. By this I mean those young
men and women who are concerned not with acquiring
security in the chaos of our time by conforming to the
tested order of the knowable and doable but solely with
confronting, unwaveringly, the impact of the unconditional at this hour of twilight, an hour of death and birth.
A detached, ego-centered life cannot provide youth with
the contour and substance required for such a confrontation. To acquire such contour and substance, man must
commit himself totally to all the forces that have shaped
the human spirit up to now, and which are given to individual man directly only in the absolute, that is, the religiously creative, life of his people, whose spiritual process
he must restore to life in word and deed. To be sure, such
restoration requires something more creative than mere
commitment, but it cannot be achieved without it. We
asked ourselves what manner of commitment this should
be. We shall now try to find an answer to our question.

As we have seen, we cannot commit ourselves to an
acceptance of Jewish teaching if this teaching is conceived
as something finished and unequivocal; nor can we commit ourselves to Jewish law if this law is taken to mean

something closed and immutable. We can commit ourselves only to the primal forces, to the living religious
forces which, though active and manifest in all of Jewish
religion, in its teaching and its law, have not been fully
expressed by either. [. . .] They are the eternal forces
that do not permit one's relationship to the unconditional ever to wholly congeal into something merely accepted and executed on faith, the forces that, out of the
total of doctrines and regulations, consistently appeal for
freedom in God. Though religious teaching may assign
to the Divine a Beyond from where our world is enjoined, rewarded, and punished, the primal forces point
beyond this division (apparently without violating religious teaching) by permitting the birth of unity in the
free deed of the complete human being. And though the
law may proclaim a differentiation between the holy and
the profane, these primal forces overcome this differentiation (apparently without violating the law) by permitting
the hallowing of the profane in the free deed of the complete human being. Their task is to call forth man's response to the Divine, the response of the complete human being, and, hence, the unification of the spiritual
and the worldly: the realization of the spirit and the hallowing of the worldly, the sanctification of the relationship to all things, that is, freedom in God. God's writing
on the tablets constitutes freedom; the religious forces
persistently strive to rediscover those symbols of divine
freedom again. God's original tablets are broken. The
religious forces of eternal renewal persistently strive to
restore the blurred outlines of divine freedom on the
second tablets, the tablets of the teaching and the law.
The eternally renewed effort of these forces denotes the
endeavor to fuse, once again, fundamental religious consciousness with the unbiasedness and fullness of natural
life, as they had been fused on God's original tablets.

There are intimations of a new endeavor. We believe it will succeed; we have faith in the new element trying to emerge from the people's spirit. To help prepare this emergence of the new, a generation willing to put its ideals into practice and to restore Judaism's spiritual process to life, in word and deed, must commit itself to the primal forces. They are the treasure that must be uncovered and raised, the subterranean growth that must be brought to light and freed. We need their help in order to withstand the impact of the unconditional in this hour of death and birth.

Mankind's religious longing, awakening at this hour, is akin to Judaism's primal forces. Today, thinking men can at last no longer tolerate the dualism of spirit and "world," the antithesis between the soul's hypothetical independence from the world's deadening hustle and bustle and life's dependence on it. They no longer want to bear the yoke of this conflict sanctioned by the churches; they want to grasp the unity of spirit and world, realize it, and thus bring about true freedom, that is, freedom in God. Divided man is, of necessity, unfree; only unified man becomes free. Divided man can never effect anything but division; only unified man can establish unity. Unified, unifying, total man, free in God, is the goal of mankind's longing that is awakening at this hour, just as he is the meaning of Judaism's religious forces. Herein resides the power that alone can raise Judaism above degeneracy and torpidity, and by so doing enable it to once again write its message into the history of the world.

But comprehension of their fundamental tendencies hardly constitutes sufficient commitment to these forces. Such comprehension is only the gateway to full awareness of their entire course. We must, I repeat, participate from within in the mighty spiritual process with reverence and awareness of mind. Having thus joined in this process, we must, by our active participation in it, begin affirming and realizing all we have found there with the totality of our life.

But we cannot participate in this spiritual process, nor walk inwardly along the path of the primal forces, solely with our emotions. It must be done in reverent and unbiased knowledge, a knowledge that, though it will always owe to intuition its access to the heart of things, cannot dispense with the reliable tools of assembling, sifting, and examining the facts before it can ever find this access. Only the fusing of all that has been found will be the business of our freely creative emotions.

I say reverent and unbiased knowledge, for it is a painful failing of our youth to approach matters of Jewish religion partly without reverence and partly without freedom from bias. This lack of reverence is by no means characteristic only of those who have no religious inclinations; it is characteristic also of those who do have religious inclinations but, content with these inclinations, treat the great historical religious systems either as obsolete or irrelevant to their own religious emotions. If, instead of simply luxuriating in them, these young people would ask themselves whether their emotions are actually anything more than a mood, they would recognize their lack of substance. They would also perceive that, no matter how lofty they may appear to be, these emotions will remain sterile if they fail to derive nurture from the records and forms in which the effect of the unconditional upon the spirit of the people has become manifest during the four millennia of its path. Others, on the other hand, easily fall prey to the bias that views these records and forms, so long as they are sanctioned by official tradition, as an undivided whole in which no distinction may be made between living and dead forces, or between symbols of vital or of negligible import. But, though it is indeed possible to accept them without an unbiased, discerning view, it is not possible to choose from them— and it is this that is of decisive importance here.

Our religious literature must become the object of reverent and unbiased knowledge. The reader of the Bible must attempt to understand the spirit of its original language, the Hebrew—an understanding that is service (*dienendes Wissen*); he will approach it not as a work of literature but as the basic documentation of the unconditional's effect on the spirit of the Jewish people; whatever his knowledge of old as well as new exegesis, he will search beyond it for the original meaning of each passage. No matter how familiar he is with modern biblical criticism's distinction between sources, he will penetrate beyond this criticism to more profound distinctions and connections. Though unafraid of bringing to light the mythical element, no matter how initially alien it may be to him, he will not advance a mythical interpretation where there exists an adequate historical one. He will read the Bible with an appreciation of its poetic form, but also with an intuitive grasp of the suprapoetic element which transcends all form. To such a reader the Bible will reveal a hidden treasure and the operation of primal forces from which the seed of new religiosity can derive sustenance and substance. Such reading of the Bible should be followed by earnest study of later literature, without omitting the unwieldy and seemingly unpromising material.

Similarly, the Jewish masses and all their beliefs and customs must also become an object of reverent and unbiased understanding. We must come close to their inner life, submerging ourselves in its inwardness and ardor, which have not been diminished, and indeed cannot be diminished, by any misery; must perceive how the Jewish people's old religious fervor still endures among them, though in distorted and occasionally degraded form, and how there burns within it the desire, as yet unstilled, to hallow the earthly and to affirm the covenant with God in everyday life. We must discern, simultaneously, two things: that this people is in need of regeneration and that it is capable of achieving it, for, along with those of decadence, it carries within it the elements of purification and of redemption.

Together, these two undertakings, exploring the people's literature and probing the depths of its life, will enable a generation that possesses reverent and unbiased understanding to go step by step along the course of the primal forces as it leads up to its own time.

For us, even more distinctly than for other men, this is a time of doom as well as of liberation, of going astray as well as of returning. Whether the presently unfolding religious consciousness of a new generation will grow to full maturity, and whether this generation will then assume leadership, will be decisive for mankind's fate. As for Judaism's fate in particular, it will be decisive whether a generation at the turning will be capable of resuming the course of the primal forces; that is, whether it will be able to find once again within its own soul the readiness for struggle and the creativity of the forces whose original struggles and creativity they have discerned and experienced. Both fates, mankind's general and our particular one, are connected at their core. For mankind's religious longing, awakening at this hour, is akin to the primal forces of Judaism.

Walking along the pathway of the primal forces, the generation at the turning encounters its own self; it can encounter it solely along this pathway. But only when it finds that the forces it has discerned dwell also within its own self can it make a choice and give direction to its own innermost powers.

When the primal forces become truly alive within a new Jewish generation, and desirous of being reactivated, then, in close linkage to them, this generation must resume their work; must begin to prepare a new work site for them within its own community, on the soil where, under cinders and ashes, still glimmer sparks of the old forge.

We must create a community, cemented by joint labor and joint sacrifice, a community of men who, in the name of the nameless God, will journey to the Zion of His realization. The mystery within their hearts is swelling, beyond all confines of teaching and law, toward the still inexpressible, the still formless. Discernment of the primal forces has disclosed to them the power whereby the inexpressible and formless can undergo a new incarnation: the human response to the Divine, the unification of spirit and world. There is only one road that will deliver us from the doom of our time: the road leading to freedom in God. If we know this, not through concepts or "moods" but through genuine awareness of a life of decision, then, no matter how far removed from all tradition we may seem to an insensible glance, we will have committed ourselves to the great course of Judaism.

THE LATER ADDRESSES

1939-1951

Preface to the Later Addresses (1951)

BETWEEN 1909 and 1918 I delivered, in Prague, Vienna, and Berlin, seven addresses on Judaism which had a pronounced and disturbing effect.

In a changed world in which the external crisis of Judaism, previously only sensed, became manifest in the great holocaust, I spoke once again on Judaism. I delivered an address, first in Jerusalem, in 1939, then in London, in 1947, with some changes motivated by the events of the intervening years. This was the address that appears in the present volume under the title "The Spirit of Israel and the World of Today."

And in 1951, when, despite the seeming security of our renewed statehood, the internal crisis of Judaism was also coming to the fore, the other three addresses were delivered in Jerusalem, London, and New York.

These four addresses must be read as being directed, in these fateful hours, by a Jew to Jews. Yet what is said here is of concern to every man qua man.

I

The Spirit of Israel and the World of Today

FOR MANY years now, Jews all over the world have
been asking one another: "How is it all going to end? Are
we completely in the hands of Evil? Will the power of
wickedness continue to grow stronger? Or are we possibly
entitled to hope, to hope with a trembling heart, that the
spirit of Israel will prove victorious?"

When I am asked these questions, I respond with a
query of my own: "What is it you have in mind when you
speak of the spirit of Israel? Your own spirit? Or that
spirit which we have betrayed and which we continue to
betray day after day?" The reply to the question posed
by these various Jews turns on their reply to my question.
Everything, indeed, depends on their answer.

There is a Jewish tradition about seventy angels
known as "princes" who are set in charge of the seventy
nations of the world.[1] Each of these "princes" supervises
his own nation, acting as its spokesman before the throne
of glory. When their respective nations are embattled,
they too become involved against each other. The
"princes" are the real victors and the real vanquished;
and their wars, victories and defeats, their ascents and
descents on the mighty ladder, are what historians char-
acterize by the name of history. Each of them has a pur-

pose and function of his own; and so long as the "prince" does his part, so long as he accomplishes his purpose and fulfills his function, he is entrusted with power. But he is responsible to his Master, and is required to render an accounting to him. Therefore, when he becomes so intoxicated with power as to forget who he is and what his function is, arrogantly assuming himself to be the lord and master—then the hand of his Sovereign falls upon him: falling either in the form of lightning which flings him into the abyss of nothingness, or gradually as a steady rain, which carries him little by little down to the abyss of nothingness.

Now it is said that the Jewish people, too, have a "prince" appointed over them; but there are those who assert that the children of Israel refused to accept the yoke of any angel, rejecting all yokes except that of the kingdom of God. And it is this latter belief alone that is in accord with the fundamental biblical view of the relationship between Israel and the Divinity.

The source of the people of Israel is to be found not in that world of multiplicity where "princes" contend with one another, but rather in the world of the one truth which, indeed, reveals only a hint of its essence to human beings. But even that hint is adequate for man and nation to know that there is one truth above them; and that, furthermore, neither that people nor the "prince" of that people is the possessor of the truth, its sole possessor being the Prince of princes and the Lord of the world.

The typical individual of our times is no longer capable of believing in God, but he finds it impossible to believe even in his own substance—that substance which has neither pediment nor basis—and so he holds fast to his faith in his expanded ego, his nation, as being the highest authority within his reach. And since he has no genuine and vital relation to the truth that is above all the nations, to the truth that requires the nations to realize it, he transforms his nation into an idol, he sets up the personality of his people as God; he makes the "prince," who is a mere ministering angel, into a god. And since there is no level above that of the nations, since there is no court of appeal on high, the end must be that the nations and their "princes" wage war against each other, using every means they can and without balking at anything until they encompass their own destruction.

Those secret forces, the "princes," are nowadays nothing more than the various national ideologies, the various state myths used by the leaders and misleaders of the nations in order to fire their egoism with the illusions and deceits of an imaginary idealism. This is the hour when the princes forget who they are and what their function is, and vaunt their arrogance; each of them imagines that he is the supreme master. But the hand of their Master is over them.

But what of us Jews? We talk of the spirit of Israel and assume that we are not like unto all the nations because there is a spirit of Israel. But if the spirit of Israel is no more to us than the synthetic personality of our nation, no more than a fine justification for our collective egotism, no more than our prince transformed into an idol—after we had refused to accept any prince other than the Lord of the universe!—then we are indeed like unto all the nations; and we are drinking together with them from the cup that inebriates.

And when we grow drunk after their fashion, we become weaker than any other nation, and find ourselves entirely defenseless in their hands.

It is only if we do not really become like them, it is only if we refer by the term "spirit" not to ourselves but to the living truth, which is not in our possession, but by which we can be possessed, which is not dependent upon us, but we upon it, and which nonetheless needs us in order to become something that is of the lower realm, something concrete, something "historic"—it is then, and only then, that we have the ground of combat and victory beneath our feet.

But it may be that one of you is secretly asking me the question: "What then is this spirit of Israel of which you are speaking?"

It is the spirit of realization. Realization of what? Realization of the simple truth, that man has been created for a purpose. There is a purpose to creation; there is a purpose to the human race, one we have not made up ourselves, or agreed to among ourselves; we have not decided that henceforward this, that, or the other shall serve as the purpose of our existence. No. The purpose itself revealed its face to us and we have gazed upon it.

Again, this cannot be defined in terms of concepts; yet we can know and express the fact that unity, not division and separation, is the purpose of creation, and that the purpose is not an everlasting struggle to the death between sects or classes or nations. Our purpose is the great upbuilding of peace. And when the nations are all bound together in one association, to borrow a phrase from our sages, they atone for each other.[2] In other words, the world of humanity is meant to become a single body; but it is as yet nothing more than a heap of limbs, each of which is of the opinion that it constitutes an entire body. Furthermore, the human world is meant to become a single body through the actions of men themselves. We men are charged to perfect our own portion of the universe—the human world. There is one nation that once heard this charge so loudly and clearly that the charge penetrated to the very depths of its soul. That nation accepted the charge, not as an inchoate mass of individuals, but as a nation. As a nation it accepted the truth that calls for its realization by the human nation, the human race as a whole. And that is its spirit, the spirit of Israel.

The charge is not addressed to isolated individuals but to a nation. For only an entire nation, which comprehends peoples of all kinds, can demonstrate a life of unity and peace, of righteousness and justice to the human race, as a sort of example and beginning. A true humanity, that is, a nation composed of many nations, can only commence with a certain definite and true nation. The hearkening nation was charged to become a true nation. Only the realization of this truth in the relations between the various sections of this people, between its sects and classes, is capable of serving as a commencement of an international realization of the truth and of the development of a true fellowship of nations, a nation consisting of nations. Only nations each of which is a true nation living in the light of righteousness and justice are capable of entering into upright relations with one another. The people of Israel was charged to lead the way toward this realization.

From age to age the people of Israel has preserved its heritage, which is this charge. As long as it lived in its own land, it represented the charge to other nations. When it was exiled from its land, it introduced it to the other nations. The people of Israel proclaimed it in that confession to which it was faithful even unto martyrdom, and proclaimed it by its very indestructible existence: the existence of those who guard the heritage. But the Jewish nation did not meet the test. For untold generations the Jews observed the 613 commandments of the Torah; but the charge that is higher than every formulation of individual precepts was not fulfilled. The life of the nation as such never became one of justice. The people did not become a true nation taking the lead in the realization of the ideal.

Only one great attempt was made to create, under
the restricted and restrictive conditions of the Exile, a concrete social life, the fraternal life of sons of the One God
living together. That was the attempt of Hasidism, and
even it did not pierce to the vital, the essential problem,
but crumbled away after a time. The local community, too,
the sole social basis in the life of the Diaspora, lost more
and more of the originality of its form and content. But
how can the community of Israel continue to live in truth
when there are no longer any local communities that live
in truth?

And now that we have once again achieved, though
only for a section of our people, a chance to live in our
country and an authority of our own, what have we
done? Important social experiments, to be sure, have been
made. Independent forms of social association have been
born, particularly different varieties of communal settlements which will yet prove of the utmost importance in
the development of the new human society. But to what
extent has the communal settlement influenced the Jewish
community in Palestine? How much weight does it carry
in the emerging social form of that community? And has it
reached the level of genuine fraternity itself? [. . .]

Age after age the Jewish people believed in the Messianic tidings. They believed them and proclaimed them,
and occasionally even rose to the summons of false "mes-
siahs" and hastened to join them. But they did not realize
what is incumbent upon the individual and the nation: a
new beginning. Of course, it lies in the power of heaven
to introduce the kingdom of God; the preparation of the
world in readiness for that kingdom, the beginning of a
fulfillment of the truth, calls for men and a nation consisting of men. And now, after a proclamation without fulfillment, there has come some measure of fulfillment with-

out proclamation. But then what is the proclamation of a kingdom without a King?

The spirit of Israel is the spirit of realization. But where does it exist? For if it has not existence, it has no force at this hour. Not only do we have no realization of the truth to any adequate extent, but faith in the truth is growing steadily weaker even among ourselves. Day by day an increasing number of us are saying: "The period of humanism is past! You cannot swim against the current! Those Messianic tidings, the charge of justice, were nothing but an expression of our weakness! So come, let us be strong!" Their only wish is to join the wolf pack. If we are not acceptable in the pack, it is enough to live on its fringes, in its neighborhood. And if we cannot be the head, it is also quite enough to be the tail. Of all the many kinds of assimilation in the course of our history, this nationalist assimilation is the most terrifying, the most dangerous.

If we consider all the reasons for anti-Semitism advanced by the Christian nations, we find that they are all superficial and transitory. But if we go deeper, we find that there is one deep and unconscious reason that is true for all periods of the Exile. It is that there has entered and become dispersed among them a people carrying a charge from heaven which is written in a book which became sacred for them too when they became Christians. It is unique in human history, strange and awesome, that heaven should make a specific demand (*Forderung*) in reference to human behavior, and that the demand should be recorded in a book, and that the book should be the heritage of a people that is dispersed among all the nations with this, its holy book, which is holy for all the nations as well. The demand hovers high over them as the comprehensive demand that their God makes of them.

And the nations refuse to submit to it. To be sure, they
wish to retain the God they have received, but at the same
time they would reject His demand. In so doing they rely
upon the teachings of Saul, a Jew from Tarsus, who asserted that it was impossible to fulfill the demand and
that it was necessary to cast off its yoke by submission to
another Jew, Jesus of Nazareth, who had died during Saul's
lifetime and was the Messiah, who had indeed fulfilled the
demand and abolished it at the same time, and who demanded nothing of his true believers save faith. Such was
the argument of the nations who went in the footsteps of
Saul, and a large part of their theology has been nothing
but a detailed interpretation of the utterance of Saul, the
apostle to the Gentiles.

Yet against all their opposition to the Torah stood that
unfortunate Jewish people, bearing the book which was
its own book and at the same time part of the holy book
of the nations. That is the real reason for their hatred.
Their theologians argue that God rejected this people,
who no longer have any heritage because that heritage has
now passed over to Christianity. But the Jewish people
continued to exist, book in hand; and even though they
were burned at the stake, the words of the book were still
on their lips. That is the perennial source of anti-Semitism. In this sense there is an essential truth in the verse of
the medieval Hebrew poet, "Hated we are, for Thee we
love, O Holy!" [3]

For that reason there was only one way to abolish the
hatred: realizing the truth. If we as a people had fulfilled
this requirement and had refuted the words of Saul of
Tarsus by our actions, and if we had actually shown the
nations by our actions the way to a better life upon the
earth, then we would have ceased to be contradictory and
terrifying to them, and we would have become what we
truly are—their older brother. The peoples accepted the

Gospel, but with it came the Torah of Israel, which comprehends three things: first, the history of creation, which develops into the history of Israel; second, the revelation of God, which was first of all His revelation to Israel; and third, the Messianic prophecy, whose center and focal point is the effort of the people of Israel for the redemption of humanity. And it is the books of the Gospel which relate the life of Jesus, the Jew in whom they see the redeemer himself as he lived among his people; and there he states expressly that he came only for the lost sheep of the house of Israel.[4] This was too heavy a burden for the nations to accept in full as their own faith. So they rose against it time and again. Saul of Tarsus, to be sure, maintained the unity of the Hebrew Scriptures and the Gospel. But a mere twenty years after his death a man was born who undertook to separate them.

That was Marcion the Gnostic,[5] who regarded himself as the disciple of Paul. At the time when the emperor Hadrian quenched the Bar-Kokhba revolt[6] in a sea of blood, transformed Jerusalem into a Roman colony, and set up a temple to Jupiter on the site of the Second Temple, Marcion came to Rome from Asia Minor, bringing with him his own Gospel as a kind of spiritual contribution to the destruction of Israel. In his Gospel he not only separated the Old from the New Testament and the history of Christianity from the history of Israel, but he also drew a line of demarcation between the Deities: on the one side the God of Israel, who is also the creator of this imperfect world and is himself imperfect, being only a just God, and not a good God; on the other side, the "alien," unknown God who has no concern with this world, yet takes pity on it and redeems it. The logical conclusion was the Gnostic transvaluation: There is no value to this material world, and no thought ought to be given to *its* correction.

Yet there is another conclusion which Marcion never

expressed and which quite possibly he did not even realize. If such is the case, then the world is in the hands of
the worldly powers. Jesus told his followers to render unto
Caesar the things that are Caesar's and to God the things
that are God's.[7] From the context we learn that he meant
them to pay to Caesar the tax Caesar required and not to
rebel against Caesar; but they were to give the whole reality of life to God. Marcion rendered this world unto Caesar and the other world unto God. In the teachings of Marcion the nations of the world are absolved of the demands
of heaven by an extreme dualism: the redeemed soul on
the one hand, and that of existing society on the other.
In the former there is not justice, but there is grace, while
in the latter there is not even true justice.

The Church did not follow Marcion; for it knew that
if its traditional link with the creation of the world and
the revelation were to be broken, the entire basis of its
influence upon the order of this world would be undermined. Protestantism, while approximating more closely
the doctrines of Marcion, did not accept them either. But
in the year 1920 the Protestant theologian Adolf von
Harnack[8]—who was not in the least an anti-Semite but a
representative of a broad liberalism and as such thought
that the greater part of Scripture, with the exception of the
Prophets and the Psalms, hindered the inner development
of Christianity—wrote in his book on Marcion[9]: "Any
retention of the Old Testament as a canonical document
in the Protestantism of the nineteenth century and later is
an outcome of religious and ecclesiastical paralysis."

Three years after the death of Harnack in 1930, his
idea, the idea of Marcion, was put into action; not, however, by spiritual means, but by means of violence and ter-
ror. The state of which Harnack was a citizen placed before the Church one of two alternatives: either to exclude
Judaism and the spirit of Israel entirely from its midst,

and thereby to renounce any influence over the affairs of this world, the affairs of the state and society; or else to be liquidated together with Judaism. The gift of Marcion had passed from Hadrian into other hands.

Meanwhile those hands have been severed. But we do not know into whose hands Marcion's gift will pass, we do not today know when the churches will again be faced with the alternative of renunciation, which is an inner death, and external overthrowal, which is actually the prospect of rebirth out of the darkness of the catacombs.

But this we do know: that the extrusion of the Jewish element from Christianity means an extrusion of the divine demand and concrete Messianism.

But what of us Jews?

We have no right to make use, as we have been accustomed to do, of the term "spirit of Israel" as a kind of epithet descriptive of the "prince" of our nation, one of the many warring "princes" on high, one of the conflicting national forces. We must not use this term as a kind of metaphorical mask for our own egotism. The true spirit of Israel is the divine demand implanted in our hearts. We should not take pride in ourselves because of it but should submit to it, for we have betrayed it. Our first step at the present time is to give a full account of our souls without concealing anything, without deceiving ourselves about anything; to make an inventory of the real, omitting fictitious values.

We are entitled to ask, as did the people in the desert, "whether we have the Lord in our midst or not" (Exodus 17:7), as long as we ask with the proper intention. In that case the meaning of the question becomes: Is there true devotion to God in our midst, or is there not? And true devotion to God in turn means: our will to realize His truth. That again means: to aid in accomplishing His purpose in creating man, in the establishment of a human people whose king He is. And how is it given us to fulfill this if not by building the social pattern of our own people in its land, from the pattern of family, neighborhood, and settlement to that of the whole community? For it is no real community if it is not composed of real families and real neighborhoods and real settlements.

By the same token, there is no real nation if it does not maintain its truthfulness in relations as well, the relationships of a fruitful and creative peace with its neighbors. For a true nation is a force of that great peace which radiates in all directions. We can resume the existence of the people that chose, at the beginning of its progress on earth, the Lord of the universe as its king only if, no matter how basically changed the conditions and ourselves, we are ready, both internally and externally, to live a life of truth.

If we seriously proceed to this realization within our own restricted circle, we shall also be entitled to set up the spirit of Israel against the overt and covert Marcionism of the nations; that is, to oppose to the dualism of the redeemed soul in a physical world abandoned to a state of unredemption, the life of responsible work in the service of unity.

II

Judaism and Civilization

To RECOGNIZE the nature of what we call a "great civilization," we must consider the great historical civilizations not at the time of their full development but at an early stage. We shall then see that each of them can be understood only as a life-system. In distinction to a thought-system, which illuminates and elucidates the spheres of being from a central idea, a life-system is the real unit in which again and again the spheres of existence of a historical group build up around a supreme principle. This principle achieves adequate consciousness and articulateness only in sublime moments of the spirit, but its effect pervades, in manifold ramifications and shapes, and, of course, also in varying degrees of intensity, the entire existence of the group. Its fundamental character is always a religious and normative one: a religious one, because it always implies an attachment of human life to the absolute, an attachment that, though susceptible of intellectual comprehension, is essentially concrete, means concrete things, and points to concrete things; and a normative one, because the principle, though always relating to transcendent Being controlling the universe, proclaims that Being as exemplary for man, as that which alone, if imitated by man in his life-attitude and social structure, brings order and meaning into earthly existence, and on whose realization on earth by man depends, in fact, the survival of man qua man.

Whether we take the Chinese principle of *tao,* the "way" in whose eternal rhythm all opposites contend with each other and are reconciled, or the Indo-Aryan *rita* (Indian form) or *urta* (Iranian form, usually transcribed *asha*), the primeval order of that which is right and just, or Israel's *zedek,* in which truth and justice combine, or the Greek *dike,* the inexorable course of world events, and the "measure" determined by it—everywhere transcendent Being has a side facing toward man which represents a shall-be; everywhere man, if he wants to exist as man, must strive after a suprahuman model; everywhere the outline of a true human society is traced in heaven. All spheres of existence are essentially determined by that principle, by the relationship to it; wisdom wants to explore its action, art to lend shape to it, and where one strives to set public life itself to rights, one looks up to the stars and beyond them.

Man as he is (who in all these doctrines appears more or less out of joint, having lost his original concord with transcendent Being) naturally resists the command which he, man, has either read from the universe or received directly from a power superior to him and to the universe. He wills and wills not to translate the heavenly truth into earthly reality. He rebels in practice against what he recognizes in theory, nay, what he sees and hears. But it is precisely in this mute struggle of man with the spirit that the rise of a great civilization originates. The spirit conquers and is conquered, it advances and is checked, it hits upon the human material and finds in it a barrier; and here, in the lulls of the fighting between heaven and earth, there emerge, again and again, the specific forms of a civilization which also determine all its wisdom and art.

Among the great civilizations of the ancient world
there was one in which the action of the religious and
normative principle upon all spheres of public life manifested itself with peculiar, unique pregnancy. All others
shared, though in varying degrees of development, the
basic doctrine of a heavenly-cosmic society to which the
earthly, human one corresponds or rather ought to correspond—to which it corresponded once, say in the Golden
Age, or will correspond some day, say after the complete
victory of light over darkness. In ancient Israel the place
of this doctrine was taken by that of the Lord of all being and all coming to be, who, just as He has set the sun
in the sky, has set the commandment of truth and justice
above the heads of the human race. True, in the other
civilizations as well, the normative principle was carried
and guaranteed by divine beings who ruled that upper society; but only Israel knew a God who had chosen a human people—just that people—to prepare the created
earth as a kingdom for Him by the realization of justice.
For Israel, the principle is the norm and the law; for Israel's God, it is the mobile foundation, symbolized by the
Ark with the Tablets, on which He wishes to place His
earthly throne. This is why the principle here binds the
deity and mankind together in the unparalleled concreteness of the Covenant. And this is also why here, and only
here, civilization is mysteriously both affirmed and ne-
gated: God wants man's entire civilization—but not as left
to itself but as hallowed to Him, God.

Now we generally observe that man's resistance to the
spiritual demand, a resistance which, as we said, manifests itself already in the genetic phase of a civilization,
increases decisively as the civilization approaches its
height. In proportion to the development of its specific
forms, every civilization strives increasingly to render itself independent of its principle. In the great Western civ-

ilizations, this manifests itself partly by their individual spheres isolating themselves and each of them establishing its own basis and order, and partly by the principle itself losing its absolute character and validity, so that the holy norm degenerates into a human convention, or by the attachment to the absolute being reduced, avowedly or unavowedly, to a mere symbolic-ritual requirement, which may be adequately satisfied in the cultic sphere. A civilization may now, in its isolated individual spheres, produce works more splendid than it has ever produced before; its spiritual unity is lost. Periclean Athens and the Italian High Renaissance may serve as examples.

The development of the Eastern civilizations was different. Here, the individual spheres never fully emancipated themselves from the unifying bond, but even here the principle became more and more an object of doctrine rather than of life-relationship, and its service, originally embracing real existence, both private and historical, became more and more a merely symbolic and formal one. And here as well, the civilization, by converting the principle by whose action it had first arisen from an active reality into a revered fiction, undermined its own foundations.

Everywhere there were men who recognized this movement toward the abyss for what it was and tried to halt it; but there was only one civilization in which an elemental protest, concentrating all the spiritual passion of the people, was raised against the invalidation of the principle. It was, naturally enough, that civilization in which, as in no other, the absolute had made a covenant with the entire domain of human existence and refused to abandon any part of that domain to relativity. At no other time or place has the spirit been served in the human world with such militancy, generation after generation, as it was by the prophets of Israel. Here, the men of spirit took it upon themselves to actualize that affirmation and negation of civilization in the reality of the historical hour. Their fight was directed against all those who evaded the great duty, the duty of realizing the divine truth in the fullness of everyday life, by side-stepping into the merely formal, the merely ritual, that is to say, the noncommittal— all those who taught and practiced such evasion and thereby degraded the divine name which they invoked to the status of a carefully guarded fiction. This fight was waged for the wholeness and unity of civilization, which can be whole and united only if it is hallowed to God. The men who demanded from those in power the abolition of social injustice for God's sake did not know the concept of civilization, but they staked their lives to save civilization. Thereby, the protest against the false emancipation of civilization was registered in such a way that it was bound to act, and did in fact act, as a reminder and warning upon the whole future of mankind and quite especially upon the problematics of the last following civilization, that of the Christian West.

To appreciate fully the significance of prophetic religion for mankind and its civilization, we must ask ourselves why it was precisely in Israel that the normative principle voiced its protest against any such development of civilization as tended to deprive it, the normative principle, of its absolute validity. In answer, we must point to that religious realism peculiar to Israel which has no room for a truth remaining abstract, hovering self-sufficiently above reality, but for which every truth is bound up with a demand which man, the people, Israel, are called upon to fulfill integrally on earth. Now integral fulfillment means two things: it must, in the first place, comprise the whole life, the whole civilization of a people, economy, society, and state; and secondly, it must incorporate the whole of the individual, his emotions and his will, his actions and abstentions, his life at home and in the market place, in the temple and in the popular assembly. That is to say, it means the wholeness and unity—not otherwise possible—of the civilization. Men, especially the possessors of power and property, naturally resist the demand for the integral fulfillment of divine truth and justice; they therefore try to limit the service of God to the sacral sphere, and in all other spheres recognize his authority merely by words and symbols. This is where the prophetic protest sets in.

A characteristic example may illustrate our point. In the ancient East, the king was generally regarded as a son of the supreme god; he was considered either as adopted or as actually procreated by the god. This conception, in the first-mentioned form, of course, was not strange to Israel, either: the Psalmist makes God say to the king at his anointment on the Holy Mount, "Thou art my son; this day have I begotten thee" (Psalm 2:7). His anointment in the name of God made the incumbent of the throne responsible to God, not only as a viceroy is responsible to his sovereign but as a son is responsible to his father. Other peoples of the ancient East also knew this relationship of the king to the god. In Babylonia it expressed itself merely by the fact that on the New Year holiday, as the day on which the world begins anew, the priest struck the king a symbolic blow on the cheek, which settled the matter for the rest of the year; in Egypt there were only intimate conversations between the king and his divine father without any visible result. Not so in Israel. Here, the prophet again and again appeared before the king and actually called him to account. This prophetic realism crystallized in the divine message transmitted to David by the prophet Nathan: God proposes to adopt David's son as His, God's, son, but if he sins, He will chastise him, as a father chastises his son, and He will do it by the hand

of man,[1] by the hand of the enemies of Israel, to whom
an Israel not upholding justice must succumb.

But the example of the attitude of the prophets to the
unfaithful kings is calculated still further to elucidate the
nature of the relationship between Judaism and civilization. The conflict appearing here is not to be understood
as one between civilization and religion: it proceeded
within a civilization (in the widest sense of the term),
namely between its guiding principle, whose action had
first produced it, and the spheres of life, which more and
more repudiated the sovereignty of that principle. Often
enough, therefore, the line of battle cut across religion itself, namely, when established religious authority, per-
sonified by the priesthood, sided with and sanctioned
power. In this case, religion, in order to maintain itself,
by virtue of its pact with power, in possession of the particular sphere which the latter had assigned to it, dissoci-
ated itself from the claim of the religious principle to be
the mover of the whole. That coalition of established
power and established authority was faced by the prophet
as the man who had neither power nor authority. It is
only in the early days of Israel, before the emergence of
the situation that called forth the protest, that we find personalities such as Moses and Samuel, endowed at once
with prophetic qualities and with history-making power
and authority. Later, the powerlessness of the prophet
was a typical feature of the age.

But the example chosen here can lead us yet deeper
into the nature of our subject. For the experience of the
divine demand remaining unfulfilled engendered the Messianic promise; and just as the experience centered around
the nonfulfilling king, the promise centers around the king
who will bring the fulfillment. He is called Messiah,
"the anointed," because he will at last carry out the mandate that the kings received upon their anointment. In

him, man will at last go to meet God. Around him, first
Israel and then the city of mankind will be built up as the
fulfilled kingdom of God. But the latter is not conceived
of as conquering and superseding a defective human civilization, but as hallowing, that is to say, purifying and
perfecting it. When the life of man, with all its various
spheres fully developed, becomes a united whole, hallowed to the divine, then, just as Abraham at the altar
once called out the name of God over Canaan,[2] the name
of God will be called out over the whole earth as the domain over which He assumed government.

According to the ancient Persian doctrine, a world-
smelting fire will transform the human substance; a new,
divine work will replace the dilapidated work of man.
Christianity, and also the apocalyptics of Hellenistic peripheral Judaism, developed this basic conception. Central
Judaism rejected it. It took with it into its long exile the
prophetic doctrine that, in answer to man's return to God,
the dislocated human substance will experience His redeeming force, which will perfect the creation of man with
man's cooperation. Civilization, despairing of itself, will
offer itself up to God and be saved by Him.

This realistic faith in the future of the divine image—
in whose loss Judaism has never believed—cannot be dismissed with the cheap slogan "civilization optimism." It
is the belief that just as every sinner can find forgiveness
by "turning" to God, so can a sinful civilization. Just as
man can hallow himself and gain admission to the holy
without curtailing his existence, without "primitivizing"
his way of life, thus human civilization, too, can without
curtailment hallow itself and gain admission.

Here as everywhere else, Israel's religious-normative
principle manifests itself as an essentially historical one.
Just as its revelation, in distinction to the revelations of
all other religions, presents itself as an incident of na-

tional history, so its highest goal, too, is historical in character. Here, the suprahistorical molds the historical but does not replace it.

With this historical faith—at once realistic and Messianic—inscribed both in its book and in its soul, the Jewish people went forth into its worldwide exile and thus, in its majority, into a civilization whose religious-normative principle was the Christian. This situation was decisively determined by the fact that Christianity had its origin in a deformative late phase of Jewish Messianism, in which it strove no longer to conquer history but to escape from it to purer spheres, while, on the other hand, the group of peoples among which Christianity established itself had just started out to conquer history. Into their existence with its contradiction, the Jewish people was inserted with its existence and the contradiction thereof, enjoined to dwell among them, history-less, with its unfulfilled historical faith—among them who controlled history and whose faith commanded them to overcome history. We know what developed from this basic situation in the course of time.

The principle of our faith, the truth and justice of God, which strives to fulfill itself in the domain of human life and human history and which paints the Messianic picture of fulfillment on the firmament of that domain, continued to radiate from our Book; and some protagonists of the Christian faith were hit by its rays, so that one or the other of them conceived the idea that his people, like Israel of old, was enjoined to become a holy people and to hallow its civilization in all its departments. We ourselves were denied actualization of our principle in the world. In the era of dispersion, great things have happened within the Jewish community, in relation to God and to the brethren; but the development of a national personality expressing the divine intent was now made impossible to us by the fact that we were no longer a free and independent community. The Messianic idea, cut off from its natural area of realization, lost itself in late-Gnostic speculation and collective ecstasy. And yet, in every hour of genuine self-rediscovery we knew: What matters is the test of history.

When at last we stepped out of the ghetto into the world, worse befell us from within than had ever befallen us from without: the foundation, the unique unity of people and religion, developed a deep rift, which has since become deeper and deeper. Even the event of our days, the re-entry of the Jews into the history of the nations by the rebuilding of a Jewish State, is most intimately affected and characterized by that rift. A home and the freedom to realize the principle of our being have been granted us anew, but Israel and the principle of its being have come apart. It is said that we are now assured of the renewal of a great Jewish civilization. But has a great civilization ever arisen otherwise than by the unfolding of such a basic principle? People try to conceal the rift by applying basic religious terms, such as God of Israel, and Messiah, to purely political processes; and the words, ready to hand, offer no resistance—but the reality which was once meant by them escapes any speech which does not mean just it, that is, the fulfillment of God's truth and justice on earth. True, it is a difficult, a tremendously difficult undertaking to drive the plowshare of the normative principle into the hard sod of political fact; but the right to lift a historical moment into the light of what is above history can be bought no cheaper.

So much for the new Jewish community. But how about the Diaspora—still vigorously alive despite the immense destruction and devastation? Nowhere in it, as far as one can see, is there a powerful striving to heal the rift and to hallow our communal life. And if in our own coun-

try the question of the existence of Judaism, that is, of the
survival of the principle of Jewish being, may still be
veiled by political controversy and danger, in the Diaspora
at this hour it confronts us in its nakedness. Are we still
truly Jews? Jews in our lives? Is Judaism still alive? And
in mankind, meanwhile, the great crisis of its civilizations
and its civilization, which is a crisis of man, has broken
out more and more manifestly. Every original tie seems to
be dissevering, every original substance disintegrating.
Man tastes nothingness and lets even it dissolve on his
tongue; or he fills the space of an existence emptied of its
meaning with the mass of his programs.

Where does the world stand? Is the ax laid to the
roots of the trees—as a Jew on the Jordan once said,[3]
rightly and yet wrongly, that it was in his day—today,
at another turn of the ages? And if it is, what is the condition of the roots themselves? Are they still healthy enough
to send fresh sap into the remaining stump and to produce
a fresh shoot from it? Can the roots be saved? How can
they be saved? Who can save them? In whose charge are
they?

Let us recognize ourselves: we are the keepers of the
roots.

How can we become what we are?

III

The Silent Question

FROM TIME TO TIME, I seem to hear a question echoing out of the depths of stillness. But he who asks it does not know that he is asking it and he to whom the question is addressed is not aware that he is being questioned. It is the question that the world of today, in utter unawareness, puts to religion. This is the question: "Are you, perhaps, the power that can help me? Can you teach me to believe? Not in phantasmagoria and mystagogy, not in ideologies or in party programs, nor in cleverly thought-out and skillfully presented sophisms that appear true only while they are successful or have prospects of success, but in the unconditional and irrefutable. Teach me to have faith in reality, in the verities of existence, so that life will afford some aim for me and existence will have some meaning. Who, indeed, can help me if you cannot?"

We can take it for granted that the world of today will vehemently deny wishing to ask or even being capable of asking such a question. This world will passionately maintain that religion is an illusion—perhaps not even a beautiful one—and will support this contention with a clear conscience, for such is the assuredness of its conviction. In the innermost recesses of the heart, however, there where despair abides, the same question surges timidly upward again and again, only to be immediately repressed. But it will grow in strength; it will become strong.

The question is addressed to religion generally, to religion as such. But where is religion to be found? The question cannot be addressed to the isolated religious individual, for how can he measure up to such a claim today? It is only to the historic religions—or to some of them—that such a question can literally be addressed. But it is neither in their dogma nor in their ritual that the answer may lie; not in the one because its purpose is to formulate beliefs that are beyond conceptual thinking into conceptual propositions, not in the other because its object is to express the relationship to the unlimited by means of steadfast and regular performance. Both have their specific spheres of influence, but neither is capable of helping the modern world to find faith. The only element in the historic religions that the world is justified in calling upon is that intrinsic reality of faith that is beyond all attempts at formulation and expression but exists in truth; it is *that* which constantly renews the fullness of its presence from the flow of personal life itself. This is the one thing that matters: the personal existence, which gives actuality to a religion and thus attests to its living force.

Whoever listens closely to the question of which I speak observes that it is also addressed to Judaism and, indeed, that Judaism is included in the foremost ranks of those religions to which the appeal is made. I have recently received communications from many parts of the world from which it can be sensed that clarification and leadership are expected of Judaism. It can be sensed, too, that many of these correspondents are speaking for the many more who remain silent. That the world expects something from Judaism is in itself a new phenomenon. For centuries the deeper spiritual content of Judaism was either unknown or given scant attention, for the reason perhaps that, during the period of the ghetto, the underlying reality of Jewish life was hardly glimpsed by the outside world, while, during the emancipation period, Jews only—not Judaism—appeared upon the open scene.

A change seems to be taking place. Why? Is it because of the massacre of millions of Jews? That does not explain it. Or is it because of the establishment of a Jewish State? That does not explain it either. And yet both of these events are basically part of the reason why the real content of Judaism is beginning to become more perceptible. These astounding phenomena of dying and living have at last brought before the world the fact of the existence of Jewry as a fact of particular significance, and from this point Judaism itself begins to be seen. Now the world has gradually begun to perceive that within Judaism there is something that has a special contribution to make, in a special way, to the spiritual needs of the present time. It is only possible to realize this if Judaism is regarded in its entirety (*Einheit*), in its whole way, from the Decalogue to Hasidism, in the course of which its peculiar tendencies have evolved in an increasingly comprehensive manner.

This "entireness," these fundamental tendencies and their evolution, are, for the most part, still unrecognized even by the Jews themselves, even by those who are earnestly seeking the pathway of truth. This becomes manifest when we consider those among our spiritually representative Jewish contemporaries whose religious needs have remained unsatisfied by Judaism. It is highly characteristic that, in the springtime of modern society, spiritually significant Jews turned to Christianity, not for the sake of Christian religion but for the sake of Christian culture, whereas today the sympathies worth noting that spiritual Jews feel for Christianity are rooted rather in a sense of religious lack and a feeling of religious desire.

Let us consider two examples which will make my meaning clear and which will plunge us deeper into our purpose of examining the religious significance of Judaism for the world of today. The one example is afforded by Bergson,[1] the thinker who, like Nietzsche, built up his philosophy on the affirmation of life but, in contrast to Nietzsche, regarded not power but participation in creation as the essence of life. Consequently, again in contrast to Nietzsche, he did not fight against religion but extolled it as the peak of human life. The other example is to be found in Simone Weil,[2] who died young, and the legacy of whose writings expresses a strong and theologically far-reaching negation of life, leading to the negation of the individual as well as of society as a whole. Both Bergson and Simone Weil were Jews. Both were convinced that in Christian mysticism they had found the religious truth they were seeking. Bergson still saw in the prophets of Israel the forerunners of Christianity, whereas Simone Weil simply cast aside both Israel and Judaism. Neither was converted to Christianity—Bergson probably because it went against the grain to leave the community of the oppressed and persecuted; Simone Weil for reasons arising from her concept of religion which, apparently, led her to believe that the Church was still far too Jewish.

Let us examine how Judaism appeared to each of these and how the Judaism they saw relates to the actuality of the Jewish faith, to that "entireness" which has developed in the course of time and of which, as I have already pointed out, most Jews today still remain ignorant.

The image of Judaism conceived by Bergson is the conventional Christian one, the origin of which lies in the endeavor to depict the new religion as a release from the yoke of the older one. This picture is of a God of justice who exercised justice essentially on His own people, Israel, being followed by a God of love, of love for humanity as a whole. For Bergson, therefore, Christianity represents a human conscience rather than a social conscience, a dynamic code as opposed to a static code, and the ethics of the open soul as opposed to the ethics of the closed soul.

Simone Weil takes the same line but goes much further. She reproaches Israel with idolatry, with the only idolatry she considers a real one, the service of the collectivity, which she, utilizing a simile of Plato, calls "the Great Beast." Gregariousness is the realm of Satan, for the collectivity arrogates to itself the right to dictate to the individual what is good and what is evil. It interposes itself between God and the soul; it even supplants God and sets itself up in God's place. In ancient Rome, Simone Weil sees the Great Beast as the atheistic materialist who worships only himself. Israel, however, is to her the Great Beast in religious disguise, and its God the God it deserved, a ponderous God, a God "of the flesh," a tribal God—ultimately, nothing but the deification of the nation. The Pharisees, whom Simone Weil obviously came to know only through the controversies of the New Testament, are defined by her as a group "who were virtuous only out of obedience to the Great Beast." Everything that was hateful to her in more recent history, such as capitalism and Marxism, the intolerance of the Church, and modern nationalism, was ascribed by her to the influence of what she called the "totalitarianism" of Israel.

Bergson accepted the principle of social life as a transitional stage; for Simone Weil, who, by the way, was for a while actively associated with the extreme Left, it was the great obstacle. For both, Israel was its embodiment, and both strove to surmount it through Christianity, in which Bergson found the purely human element, and Simone Weil, on the other hand, found the supranatural.

Seldom has it been so evident as in this instance how a
half-truth can be more misleading than a total error. (As
far as Simone Weil is concerned, it is, indeed, scarcely a
quarter-truth.)

The real definition of the social principle of the
religion of Israel is something considerably different from
Bergson's conception and something entirely different
from Simone Weil's.

It is true, the group that is welded together out of
families and tribes under the influence of a common belief in God and becomes a people is understood in Israel
as a religious category. But this is not the actual people,
not that which the prophet who harangues the people
sees assembled around him. The religious character of the
people consists emphatically in that something different
is intended for it from what it is now, that it is destined for
something different—that it should become a true people,
the "people of God." Precisely in the religion of Israel is
it impossible to make an idol of the people as a whole, for
the religious attitude to the community is inherently critical and postulative. Whoever ascribes to the nation or to
the community the attributes of the absolute and of self-
sufficiency betrays the religion of Israel.

What, however, does it mean to become a "people
of God"? A common belief in God and service to His
name do not constitute a people of God. Becoming a people of God means rather that the attributes of God revealed to it, justice and love, are to be made effective in
its own life, in the lives of its members with one another:
justice realized in the indirect mutual relationships of
these individuals; love in their direct mutual relationships
rooted in their personal existence. Of the two, however,
love is the higher, the transcending principle. This becomes unequivocally clear from the fact that man cannot
be just to God; he can, however, and should, love God.

And it is the love of God that transfers itself to man; "God
loves the stranger," we are told, "so thou too shalt love
him." [3] The man who loves God loves also him whom
God loves.

It is not true that the God of the Bible has, as Simone
Weil expresses it, "never until the Exile spoken to the soul
of man." He has always spoken to the soul of the individuals, even in the time of the Decalogue; to whom other, if
not to the soul of the individual, can the injunction be
given not to covet, that is to say, not to be envious of
what is another's? But God speaks to individuals according to their real existence, and this means, in the pre-
exilic period, as members of the people into which they
are incorporated and from which they are undetachable.
The Ten Commandments are not addressed to the collective "You," but all of them to a single "Thou"; this
"Thou" means every individual, and as every individual
is yet thoroughly embedded in the nation, he is thus addressed as a part of it. It is only in the degree to which the
individual, in the course of historic reality, discovers
himself and becomes aware of himself that God speaks
to him as such. But even in the most highly individualized
times, that "Thou" still concerns every single individual
so long as he does not intentionally shut himself away
from it.

Bergson's conventional differentiation between Jewish particularism and Christian universalism is equally
unfounded. According to Amos, the earliest of the "literary" prophets, who significantly takes as his example
the archenemies of Israel, the wanderings of all peoples
are directed by God Himself.[4] The prophet states this not
as something new but as something generally known. This
is, indeed, a universalism not of the individuals but of the
nations, through which it reaches out to the individuals.
Within this universalism, however, there is a particulariza-

tion of vocation: Israel shall begin the work of the realization of God's justice and love on earth; Israel shall be "the first fruits of His harvest." [5]

It is not true that Israel has not accorded spiritual inwardness its rightful place; rather, it has not contented itself with it. Its teachings contest the self-sufficiency of the soul: inward truth must become real life, otherwise it does not remain truth. A drop of Messianic consummation must be mingled with every hour; otherwise the hour is godless, despite all piety and devoutness.

Accordingly, what may be called the social principle of Israel's religion is fundamentally dissimilar from any "Great Beast." It is concerned with social humanity, for human society is here legitimate only if built upon real relationships between its members; and humanity is taken in its religious meaning, because real relationship to God cannot be achieved on earth if real relationships to the world and to mankind are lacking. Both love of the Creator and love of that which He has created are finally one and the same.

In order to achieve this unity, man must indeed accept creation from God's hands, not in order to possess it but lovingly to take part in the still uncompleted work of creation. Creation is incomplete because discord still reigns within it, and peace can emerge only from the created. That is why, in Jewish tradition, he who brings about peace is called the companion of God in the work of creation. This concept of man's vocation as a co-worker with God is emphasized by Bergson as the goal of that mysticism which he glorifies and which he does not find in Judaism; it is, however, a fundamentally Jewish concept.

Both Bergson and Simone Weil turned away from a Judaism they did not know; in actual fact, they turned aside from a conventional conception of Judaism created by Christianity. But while Bergson was close to true Juda-

ism, which he did not know, Simone Weil was remote from
it, too. When she referred to the God of Israel as a "natural" God and to that of Christianity as a "supranatural"
God, she failed entirely to understand the character of the
former, inasmuch as He is not "natural" but is the God of
nature as well as the God of spirit—and is superior to both
nature and spirit alike. But even if Simone Weil had known
the true God of Israel, she would not have been satisfied,
for He turns toward nature, which He dominates, whereas
Simone Weil sought flight from nature as well as from
society: reality had become intolerable to her and, for her,
God was the power that led her away from it. But that is
definitely not the way of the God of Israel; such a way
would be the very opposite of His relations toward His
creation and His creatures. He has placed man in the
center of reality in order that he face up to it. Simone Weil's idea was to serve mankind and so she again
and again took to heavy manual labor on the land, but her
soul was always put to flight by reality. And she began with
her own reality: she contested the "I"; it was one's duty,
she thought, to slay the "I" in oneself. "We possess nothing in this world," she wrote, "other than the power to
say I. This is what we should yield up to God, and that is
what we should destroy." Such a basic orientation is, indeed, diametrically opposed to Judaism; for the real relationship taught by Judaism is a bridge that spans across two
firm pillars, man's "I" and the "I" of his eternal partner.
It is thus the relation between man and God, thus also the
relation between man and man. Judaism rejects the "I"
that connotes selfishness and pride, but it welcomes and
affirms the "I" of the real relationship, the "I" of the partnership between I and Thou, the "I" of love. For love does
not invalidate the "I"; on the contrary, it binds the "I"
more closely to the "Thou." It does not say: "Thou art
loved" but "I love Thee." The same applies to the "We,"

about which Simone Weil said, "One should not be I and even less should one be We." Judaism rejects the "We" of group egotism, of national conceit and party exclusiveness, but it postulates that "We" which arises from the real relationships of its components and which maintains genuine relations with other groups, the "We" that may say in truth: "*Our* Father."

Simone Weil knew neither the old religion of Israel nor its later way, in which the changed conditions of history brought about a new display of its basic elements. Bergson knew the prophets of Israel, yet without realizing how in their messages the principle of justice he found in them was complemented by the principle of love; but he knew not the road taken by the Jewish religion, and consequently he did not consider the prophets in connection with the whole of Jewish religious history. The prophets protested against the religious failure of Israel, against the fact that God's demand to create a place on earth for His justice and His love has not been sufficiently complied with—neither by the people nor by the individuals within it—at least not in the measure compatible with the strength available and under the prevailing conditions. And the seed of the prophets is springing up; though late, it is sprouting into stronger and stronger growth. In the Diaspora, it is true, a comprehensive realization of the principle of justice could not be aspired to, since that would have required an autonomous national entity, autonomous national institutions, which could only be hoped for with the return to the Holy Land; but the higher, the decisive principle, which alone can knit together the relationship to God and the relationship to man—the principle of love—requires neither organizations nor institutions but can be given effect at any time, at any place. The will to realization was not, however, confined to the individual. Within the communal form of life adopted in place of a

state—that is, the local communities—active love, in the
guise of mutual help, recurs as a basic social element. This
structure found its perfection about two centuries ago in
Hasidism, which was built on little communities bound
together by brotherly love. An inner religious development of the highest significance corresponds to that tendency, the striving to bridge the gulf between love of God
and love of man. Again the hasidic movement succeeded
in giving full effect to this striving. It teaches that the true
meaning of love of one's neighbor is not that it is a command from God which we are to fulfill, but that through it
and in it we meet God. This is shown by the interpretation
of this command. It is not just written, "Love thy neighbor as thyself," as though the sentence ended there, but
it goes on: "Love thy neighbor as thyself, I am the Lord"
(Leviticus 19:18). The grammatical construction of the
original text shows quite clearly that the meaning is: You
shall deal lovingly with your "neighbor," that is, with everyone you meet along life's road, and you shall deal with
him as with one equal to yourself. The second part, however, adds, "I am the Lord"—and here the hasidic interpretation comes in: "You think I am far away from you, but
in your love for your neighbor you will find Me; not in his
love for you but in yours for him." He who loves brings
God and the world together.

The hasidic teaching is the consummation of Judaism.
And this is its message to all: You yourself must begin.
Existence will remain meaningless for you if you yourself
do not penetrate into it with active love and if you do not
in this way discover its meaning for yourself. Everything
is waiting to be hallowed by you; it is waiting to be disclosed in its meaning and to be realized in it by you. For
the sake of this your beginning, God created the world.
He has drawn it out of Himself so that you may bring it
closer to Him. Meet the world with the fullness of your

being and you shall meet Him. That He Himself accepts
from your hands what you have to give to the world is His
mercy. If you wish to learn to believe, love!

Bergson speaks of an "active mysticism." Where is
this to be found, if not here? Nowhere else is man's essential doing so closely bound up with the mystery of being.
And for this very reason the answer to the silent question
asked by the modern world is found herein. Will the world
perceive it? But will Jewry itself perceive that its very
existence depends upon the revival of its religious existence? The Jewish State may assure the future of a nation
of Jews, even one with a culture of its own; Judaism
will live only if it brings to life again the primal Jewish
relationship to God, the world, and mankind.

IV

The Dialogue between
Heaven and Earth

I.

THE MOST IMPORTANT of all that the biblical view of
existence has opened up for all times is clearly recognized
by a comparison of Israel's Holy Writ with those holy
books of the nations that originated independently of it.
None of those books is, like it, full of a dialogue between
heaven and earth. It tells us how again and again God addresses man and is addressed by him. God announces to
man what plan He has for the world; as the earliest of the
"literary" prophets puts it (Amos 4:13), God lets him
know "his soliloquy." He discloses to him His will and calls
upon him to take part in its realization. But man is no blind
tool; he was created as a free being—free also vis-à-vis
God, free to surrender to Him or to refuse himself to Him.
To God's sovereign address, man gives his autonomous answer; if he remains silent, his silence, too, is an answer.
Very often we hear God's voice alone, as in much of the
books of the prophets, where only in isolated cases—in
certain accounts of visions, or in the diary-like records of
Jeremiah—does the prophet's reply become articulate, and
sometimes these records actually assume a dialogic form.
But even in all those passages where God alone speaks, we
are made to feel that the person addressed by Him answers
with his wordless soul, that is to say, that he stands in the

dialogic situation. And again, very often we hear the voice of man alone, as generally in the Psalms, where only in isolated cases the worshipper indicates the divine reply; but here, too, the dialogic situation is apparent: it is apparent to us that man, lamenting, suppliant, thanks-giving, praise-singing man, experiences himself as heard and understood, accepted and confirmed, by Him to whom he addresses himself. The basic teaching that fills the Hebrew Bible is that our life is a dialogue between the above and the below.

But does this still apply to our present-day life? Believers and unbelievers deny it. A view common among believers is that though everything contained in Scripture is literally true, though God did certainly speak to the men chosen by Him, yet, since then, the holy spirit has been taken from us; heaven is silent to us, and only through the books of the written and oral tradition is God's will made known to us as to what we shall do or not do. Certainly, even today, the worshipper stands immediately before his Creator, but how could he dare, like the Psalmist, to report to the world words of personal reply, of personal granting, as spoken immediately to him? And as for the unbelievers, it goes without saying that the atheists need not be mentioned at all, but only the adherents of a more or less philosophic God-concept, with which they cannot reconcile the idea of God's addressing and being addressed by man; to them, the entire dialogies of Scripture is nothing but a mythical figment, instructive from the point of view of the history of the human mind, but inapplicable to our life.

As against either opinion, a faithful and unbiased reader of Scripture must endorse the view he has learned from it: what happened once happens now and always, and the fact of its happening to us is a guarantee of its having happened. The Bible has, in the form of a glorified remembrance, given vivid, decisive expression to an ever recurrent happening. In the infinite language of events and situations, eternally changing, but plain to the truly attentive, transcendence speaks to our hearts at the essential moments of personal life. And there is a language in which we can answer it; it is the language of our actions and attitudes, our reactions and our abstentions. The totality of these responses is what we may call our responsibility in the proper sense of the word. This fundamental interpretation of our existence we owe to the Hebrew Bible; and whenever we truly read it, our self-understanding is renewed and deepened.

II.

But in Scripture, not only the individual but the community too is addressed from above, in such a manner as is found in no other of the holy books of mankind.

Here the people, as a people, confronts God and receives, as a people, His never ceasing instruction. It, too, like the individual, is called upon to participate in the realization of the divine will on earth. Just as the individual is to hallow himself in his personal life, the people is to hallow itself in its communal life; it is to become a "holy people." Like the individual, it is free in its answer to the divine call, free to say yes or no to God by its doing and its not doing. The people is not a sum of individuals addressed by God; it is something existing beyond that, something essential and irreplaceable, meant by God as such, claimed by Him as such, and answerable to Him as such. God leads it and requires it to follow His sole leadership. He has created not only man as an individual, men as individuals, but also the human peoples; and He uses them, like the former, for His purpose, for the completion of His world-creation. He takes care of them in their history; not only Israel but all peoples are, as the prophet proclaims, led by Him to freedom when enslaved by other peoples,[1] and in freedom they shall serve Him, as peoples, each in its own way and according to its own character.[2] Though He reprimands Israel with especial severity because, contrary to its mandate, it has not fulfilled divine justice in the life of the community, yet He reprimands the other peoples as well, because they, who are also His children, do not act toward each other as brothers should. Some day, however, so the prophecy runs, the representatives of all of them will crowd around Mount Moriah and there, as Israel once did, alone, at Mount Sinai, receive that divine instruction on the great peace between the peoples (Isaiah 2). "The noble ones of the peoples are gathered together," so the Psalmist says, "as the people of the God of Abraham" (Psalm 47:10) —of Abraham, who is called "the father of a multitude of nations" (Genesis 17:5), a description meaning more than genealogy. Since world history is the advance of the peoples toward this goal, it is, essentially, sacred history.

This is also why in Scripture the divine voice addresses man not as an isolated individual but always as an individual member of the people. Even before there is a people of Israel, its father-to-be, Abraham, is addressed as such: he is to become "a blessing" in his seed. And in the legislation, both in the Decalogue and in the injunctions supplementing it, God again and again addresses Himself to a "thou" that is certainly the "thou" of each individual in each generation of the people, but as he is conceived in his connection with the people, at whose communal life that legislation is aimed, so that everyone, when a commandment conveys to him the will of God with regard to his own life, conceives himself as the individual condensation of the people. This basic view unfolds itself up to the highest level of human existence: "Thou art My servant, the Israel in whom I will be glorified," says God (Isaiah 49:3) to His elect; the man who fulfills the mandate given to the people embodies the truth of the people's existence.

From this vantage point, modern life, both of peoples and of persons, is judged and sentence passed. This life is split in two: what is thought reprehensible in the relations between persons is thought commendable in the relations between peoples. This is contrary to the prophetic demand: the prophet accuses a people of sinning against another people because it "remembered not the brotherly convenant" (Amos 1:9). But that split naturally continues into the life of modern man as an individual: his existence is divided into a private and a public one, which are governed by very different laws. What he disapproves, in his fellow man and in himself, in the former sphere, he approves, in his fellow man and in himself, in the latter: lying degrades the private person, but it well befits the political partisan, provided that it is practiced skillfully and successfully. This duality of moral values is intolerable from the point of view of biblical faith: here, deceit is under all circumstances regarded as disgraceful (also, e.g., in the case of the patriarchs, as we see from the prophetical criticism of Jacob and from some other indications), even if it is prompted by a desire to promote the cause of justice; in fact, in the latter case, it is the more pernicious, since it poisons and disintegrates the good that it is supposed to serve.

If the first biblical axiom is: "Man is addressed by God in his life," the second is: "The life of man is meant by God as a unit."

III.

As we have seen, in the biblical conception of existence God addresses the human person and the human people with a view to what shall be, what shall be realized through this person, through this people. This means that man is placed in freedom and that every hour in which he, in his current situation, feels himself to be addressed is an hour of genuine decision. In the first instance, of course, he decides only upon his own behavior, but by doing so he participates, in a measure that he is neither able nor authorized to determine, in the decision upon what the next hour will be like, and through this upon what the future generally will be like.

It is from here that the great biblical phenomenon of prophecy must be understood. The essential task of the prophets of Israel was not to foretell an already determined future, but to confront man and people in Israel, at each given moment, with the alternative that corresponded to the situation. It was announced not what would happen under any circumstances, but what would happen if the hearers of the message realized God's will, and what would happen if they refused themselves to its realization. The divine voice chose the prophet, as it were, for its "mouth," in order to bring home to man again and again, in the most immediate fashion, his freedom and its consequences. Even when the prophet did not speak in alternative form, but announced unconditionally that after such and such a time the catastrophe would happen, this announcement—as we learn from the paradigmatic Book of Jonah—nevertheless contained a hidden alternative: the people is driven into despair, but in precisely this state kindles the spark of "turning": the people turns to God—

and is saved. By an extreme threat to existence, man is
stirred to the depths of his soul and brought to a radical
decision for God, but his decision is at the same time a
fateful decision in the strictest sense.

Post-biblical thinkers have pondered how the freedom of the human will and the resultant indetermi-
nation of the future can be reconciled with divine foresight
and predetermination. Outstanding among all that has
been said in the effort to overcome this contradiction is
the well-known saying of Akiba's, "All is foreseen, yet the
power is given," [3] whose meaning is that to God, who sees
them together, the times do not appear in succession but
in progressless eternity, while in the progression of times
in which man lives freedom reigns, at any given time, in
the concrete moment of decision; beyond that, human
wisdom has not attained. In the Bible itself there is no pon-
dering; it does not deal with the essence of God but with
His manifestation to mankind. The reality of which it
treats is that of the human world, and in it the immutable
truth of decision applies.

For guilty man this means the decision to turn from
his wrong way to the way of God. We see most clearly
what this means in the biblical view that our responsibility
is essentially our answering to a divine address. The two
great examples are Cain and David. Both have murdered
(for so the Bible understands also David's deed, since
it has God's messenger say to him that he "slew Uriah the
Hittite with the sword") and both are called to account by God. Cain attempts evasion: "Am I my brother's
keeper?" He is the man who shuns the dialogue with God.
Not so David. He answers: "I have sinned against the
Lord." [4] This is the true answer: whomever one becomes
guilty against, in truth one becomes guilty against God.
David is the man who acknowledges the relations between

God and himself, from which his responsibility arises, and realizes that he has betrayed it.

The Hebrew Bible is concerned with the terrible and at the same time merciful fact of the *immediacy* between God and ourselves. Even in the dark hour after he has become guilty against his brother, man is not abandoned to the forces of chaos. God Himself seeks him out, and even when He comes to call him to account, His coming is salvation.

IV.

But there is, in the biblical view, a third, widest sphere of divine utterance. God speaks not only to the individual and to the community, within the limits and under the conditions of a particular biographical or historical situation. Everything, being and becoming, nature and history, is essentially a divine pronouncement (*Aussprache*), an infinite context of signs meant to be perceived and understood by perceiving and understanding creatures.

But here a fundamental difference exists between nature and human history. Nature, as a whole and in all its elements, enunciates something that may be regarded as a self-communication of God to all those ready to receive it. This is what the psalm means that has heaven and earth "declare," wordlessly, the glory of God.[5] Not so human history—not only because mankind, being placed in freedom, cooperates incessantly in shaping its course, but quite especially because, in nature, it is God the Creator who speaks, and His creative act is never interrupted; in history, on the other hand, it is the revealing God who speaks, and revelation is essentially not a continuous process, but breaks in again and again upon the course of events and irradiates it. Nature is full of God's utterance, if one but hears it, but what is said here is always that one, though all-inclusive, something, that which the psalm calls the glory of God; in history, however, times of great utterance, when the mark of divine direction is recognizable in the conjunction of events, alternate with, as it were, mute times, when everything that occurs in the human world and pretends to historical significance appears to us as empty of God, with nowhere a beckoning of His finger, nowhere a sign that He is present and acts upon this our historical hour. In such times it is difficult for the individual, and more so for the people, to understand oneself to be addressed by God; the experience of concrete responsibility recedes more and more, because, in the seemingly God-forsaken space of history, man unlearns taking the relationship between God and himself seriously in the dialogic sense.

In an hour when the exiles in Babylon perceived God's passage through world history, in the hour when Cyrus was about to release them and send them home, the anonymous Prophet of the Exile, who like none before him felt called upon to interpret the history of peoples, in one of his pamphlets made God say to Israel: "From the beginning I have not spoken in secret" (Isaiah 48:16). God's utterance in history is unconcealed, for it is intended to be heard by the peoples. But Isaiah, to whose book the pronouncements of the anonymous prophet have been attached, not only speaks of a time when God "hideth His face from the house of Jacob" (8:17), but he also knows (28:21) that there are times when we are unable to recognize and acknowledge God's own deeds in history as His deeds, so uncanny and "barbarous" do they seem to us. And the same chapter of the Prophet of the Exile, in which God says, "Ask Me of the things to come" (45:11), states that in the hour of the liberation of peoples the masses

whom Egypt put to forced labor and Ethiopia sold as slaves
will immediately, with the chains of serfdom still on their
bodies, as it were, turn to God, throw themselves down,
and pray: "Verily Thou art a God that hideth Himself, O
God of Israel, Savior!" (45:15). During the long periods
of enslavement it seemed to them as though there were
nothing divine any more and the world were irretrievably
abandoned to the forces of tyranny; only now do they
recognize that there is a Savior, and that He is one—
the Lord of History. And now they know and profess:
He is a God that hides himself, or more exactly, the God
that hides Himself and reveals Himself.

The Bible knows of God's hiding His face, of times
when the contact between heaven and earth seems to be
interrupted. God seems to withdraw Himself utterly from
the earth and no longer to participate in its existence.
The space of history is then full of noise, but empty of the
divine breath. For one who believes in the living God, who
knows about Him, and is fated to spend his life in a time
of His hiddenness, it is very difficult to live.

There is a psalm, the 82nd, in which life in a time of
God's hiddenness is described in a picture of startling
cruelty. It is assumed that God has entrusted the government of mankind to a host of angels and commanded
them to realize justice on earth and to protect the weak, the
poor, and the helpless from the encroachments of the
wrongdoers. But they "judge unjustly" and "respect the
persons of the wicked." Now the Psalmist envisions how
God draws the unfaithful angels before His seat, judges
them, and passes sentence upon them: they are to become
mortal. But the Psalmist awakes from his vision and looks
about him: iniquity still reigns on earth with unlimited
power. And he cries to God: "Arise, O God, judge the
earth!"

This cry is to be understood as a late, but even more

powerful, echo of that bold speech of the patriarch arguing with God: "The judge of all the earth, will He not do
justice?!" [6] It reinforces and augments that speech; its
implication is: Will He allow injustice to reign further?
And so the cry transmitted to us by Scripture becomes our
own cry, which bursts from our hearts and rises to our
lips in a time of God's hiddenness. For this is what the
biblical word does to us: it confronts us with the human
address as one that in spite of everything is heard and in
spite of everything may expect an answer.

In this our own time, one asks again and again: how
is a Jewish life still possible after Auschwitz? I would like
to frame this question more correctly: how is a life with
God still possible in a time in which there is an Auschwitz?
The estrangement has become too cruel, the hiddenness
too deep. One can still "believe" in the God who allowed
those things to happen, but can one still speak to Him? Can
one still hear His word? Can one still, as an individual
and as a people, enter at all into a dialogic relationship
with Him? Can one still call to Him? Dare we recom-
mend to the survivors of Auschwitz, the Job of the gas
chambers: "Give thanks unto the Lord, for He is good;
for His mercy endureth forever"? [7]

But how about Job himself? He not only laments, but
he charges that the "cruel" God (30:21) has "removed
his right" from him (27:2) and thus that the judge of all
the earth acts against justice. And he receives an answer
from God. But what God says to him does not answer
the charge; it does not even touch upon it. The true answer that Job receives is God's appearance only, only
this that distance turns into nearness, that "his eye sees
Him" (42:5), that he knows Him again. Nothing is explained, nothing adjusted; wrong has not become right, nor
cruelty kindness. Nothing has happened but that man
again hears God's address.

The mystery has remained unsolved, but it has become his, it has become man's.

And we?

We—by that is meant all those who have not got over what happened and will not get over it. How is it with us? Do we stand overcome before the hidden face of God like the tragic hero of the Greeks before faceless fate? No, rather even now we contend, we too, with God, even with Him, the Lord of Being, whom we once, we here, chose for our Lord. We do not put up with earthly being; we struggle for its redemption, and struggling we appeal to the help of our Lord, who is again and still a hiding one. In such a state we await His voice, whether it comes out of the storm or out of a stillness that follows it. Though His coming appearance resemble no earlier one, we shall recognize again our cruel and merciful Lord.

Notes

PREFACE TO THE 1923 EDITION

1. The mystics taught that, in the primeval creation which preceded the creation of our world, the divine light-substance burst and the "sparks" fell into the lower depths, filling the "shells" of the objects and creatures of our world.
2. Exodus 19:16 ff.
3. *Shekhinah* ("indwelling"): divine element indwelling in the world and sharing the exile of Israel; divine Presence among men.

JUDAISM AND THE JEWS

1. Genesis 32:23–33.
2. Moritz Heimann (1868–1925), German-Jewish writer; author of *Das Weib des Akiba*, 1922.
3. This refers to the social and economic conditions of East European Jews at the time of writing.

JUDAISM AND MANKIND

1. Jakob Wassermann (1873–1934), German-Jewish novelist; he expressed his views on Judaism in *Mein Weg als*

Deutscher und Jude, 1921 (*My Life as German and Jew,* 1933).

2. Genesis 3.

3. E.g., Genesis Rabba XCVII, 2.

4. Luke 10:42.

5. Enoch 93:17.

RENEWAL OF JUDAISM

1. Moritz Lazarus (1824–1903), philosopher and psychologist; a leader in German-Jewish liberalism. Author of *Die Ethik des Judentums,* 1898.

2. Ahad Ha'am (Asher Ginzberg, 1856–1927), Jewish thinker, advocate of spiritual Zionism. His collected essays appeared as *Al Parashat Derakhim* (*At the Crossroads*), 1895–1913. See *Nationalism and the Jewish Ethic: Basic Writings of Ahad Ha'am,* 1962.

3. *Die Erneuerung des Judentums* appeared posthumously, in 1909.

4. Philo of Alexandria (*ca.* 30 B.C.E.–40 C.E.) harmonized Hebraic tradition and Greek critical philosophy, revelation, and reason.

5. *Sephirot:* the mystical and organically related hierarchy of the ten creative powers emanating from God, constituting, according to the kabbalistic system, the foundation of the existence of the world.

6. "God or Nature": a principal concept in Spinoza's philosophy.

7. Sayings of the Fathers II, 17.

8. Yohanan ben Zakkai: leading teacher of Jewry after the destruction of the Second Temple in 70 C.E.; founder of the Academy in Jabneh.

9. Pesikta de Rav Kahana 40a–b.

10. Rehabites: a religious community in the period of the First Temple; it led a nomadic life and prohibited the drinking of wine. Jeremiah 35.

11. *See* Preface, note 1.

12. *See* Preface, note 3.

13. Ezekiel 1:3; 3:14.

14. John 4:22.

THE SPIRIT OF THE ORIENT AND JUDAISM

1. Novalis (1772–1801), religious poet in the era of early German romanticism.

2. Joseph von Goerres (1776–1848), German writer; interpreter of myth, national poetry, and medieval culture.

3. Luke 10:42.

4. Amos 9:9–11.

5. Romans 7:15.

6. Deuteronomy 6:5.

7. Genesis 1:2.

8. Cf. Pesahim 54a.

9. Meister Eckhart (*ca.* 1260–*ca.* 1320), German Dominican mystic and theologian; his pantheistic thought was influenced by neo-Platonism and by Moslem and Jewish tenets.

10. Seder Eliyahu Rabba IX.

11. Simeon Bar-Kokhba led the unsuccessful Jewish rebellion against Rome, 132–135.

12. Genesis 27:27 f.; 37:7.

13. Ben Sira 7:15.

14. Nebuchadnezzar II (died 562 B.C.E.), king of Babylon, conquered Palestine in 586. Cyrus (died 529 B.C.E.), founder of the Persian Empire, conquered Babylon in 540–539 and allowed the Jews to return to Palestine.

15. Rome conquered Judea in 70 C.E.

JEWISH RELIGIOSITY

1. The Baal Shem (Israel ben Eliezer, the Baal Shem Tov, abbreviated the Baal Shem), 1700–1760, founder of Hasidism.

2. *See* Martin Buber, *Tales of the Hasidim: The Early Masters,* 1947, p. 48.

3. Berakhot IX, 5.

4. Tanhuma on Genesis 3:22.

5. Sifre on Deuteronomy 33:5.

6. Berakhot 34b.

7. Sayings of the Fathers IV, 22.

8. Zaddik ("the righteous one"): title of leaders of the hasidic communities; in the course of Hasidism's history, the Zaddik was considered by his followers to be the intermediary between God and man.

9. Talmud, Abodah Zarah 20b.

10. Sifra on Leviticus 20:26.

11. Abba Shaul: a second-century talmudic master.

12. Mekhilta on Exodus 15:2. The scriptural *anvehu* ("I praise Him") is here interpreted as *ani vehu* ("I and He").

13. Simeon bar Yohai, a second-century talmudic master.

14. Sifre on Deuteronomy 33:5.

15. Zohar II, 32b.

16. Sanhedrin IV, 5.

17. Exodus 32:26 ff.

18. I Kings 18:21.

19. Aggadah: the non-legal (ethical, religious, historical, biographical, folkloric) portions of the Talmud, as distinct from Halakhah, the legal portions. Aggadic material is collected also in the Midrash literature.

20. Therapeutae: members of a Jewish religious sect in Egypt, first century C.E. Their teachings and customs are described by Philo in his treatise *De vita contemplativa* ("On the Contemplative Life").

21. Lurianic Kabbalah: the school of Jewish mysticism that followed the teachings of Isaac Luria of Safed (sixteenth century). *See* G. G. Scholem, *Major Trends of Jewish Mysticism,* revised edition, 1961, Seventh Lecture.

MYTH IN JUDAISM

1. Benvenuto Cellini (1500–1571), Italian goldsmith and sculptor.

2. David Neumark (1866–1924), author of *History of Jewish Philosophy* (in Hebrew) and numerous essays.

3. Joseph Karo (1488–1575), author of *Shulchan Arukh*, authoritative code of Jewish law.

4. Elijah, the Gaon of Vilna (1720–1797), famous talmudist; opponent of Hasidism (founded by the Baal Shem).

5. Isaiah 27:1; Psalm 74:14; Job 38:7 f.

6. Genesis 3:8, 32:25; Exodus 3:2.

7. A concept of "Merkabah mysticism"; *see* Scholem, *op. cit.*, pp. 67 ff.

THE HOLY WAY

1. Gustav Landauer (1870–1919), German socialist thinker; victim of assassination by antirevolutionary troups. Buber published his letters, *Gustav Landauer, ein Lebensgang in Briefen*, 1929.

2. Talmud, Shabbat 119b.

3. Genesis 2:7.

4. Genesis 12–22.

5. Exodus 19:5 ff.

6. Shabbat 88a.

7. I Samuel 8:5.

8. Othniel: Judges 3:9; Ehud: *ibid.*, 3:15; Deborah: *ibid.*, 4:4; Gideon: *ibid.*, 6:11; Samson: *ibid.*, 13:3 ff.; Samuel: I Samuel 3.

9. Nathan: II Samuel 12:1–15; Ahijah: I Kings 11:29–39; Elijah: *ibid.*, 21:17–26; Amos: Amos 7:10 f.; Jeremiah: Jeremiah 22:10–30; 37:3–10; *et passim*.

10. Jeremiah 34:8–22.

11. Ezra "the Scribe" reorganized the Jewish community

in Palestine about the mid-fifth century B.C.E. and established the Torah as the official law.

12. Alcimus. I Maccabees 7–9.

13. In *Quod omnis probus liber sit* ("Every Good Man is Free"), which includes a description of the Essenes' way of life.

14. John 18:36.

15. Mark 12:17.

16. *See* "Renewal of Judaism," note 8.

17. *See* "The Spirit of the Orient and Judaism," note 11.

18. Matthew 6:24.

19. Matthew 5:39.

20. Romans 7:15.

21. II Corinthians 5:21.

22. Matthew 4:1–11.

23. *Tephillin* ("phylacteries"): leather cubicles containing scriptural texts inscribed on parchment and worn during weekday morning services.

24. A talmudic conception (Berakhot 6a).

25. II Samuel 7:23.

26. Exodus 12:38.

27. *See* Martin Buber, *Tales of the Hasidim: The Later Masters,* 1948, p. 232.

28. Cf. Ezekiel 20:32.

29. From the Morning Prayer.

30. The kabbalistic doctrine of *zimtzum* (contraction), according to which "the existence of the universe is made possible by a process of shrinkage in God" (Scholem).

31. *Urim* and *Tummim:* a part of the chief priest's equipment (Exodus 28:30) which served as a sacred oracle.

32. *See* note 6.

33. "Jüdische Renaissance (1900)," *Die jüdische Bewegung,* I (Berlin, 1920), p. 10.

HERUT: ON YOUTH AND RELIGION

1. Sayings of the Fathers IV, 3.

2. Exodus 32:3 f.

3. Saul Tchernichovsky's (1875–1943) poetry worships the might and beauty of cosmic nature and celebrates the gods of the ancient and classical worlds. Buber is referring to the poem "Before the Statue of Apollo."

4. E.g., Jacob Klatzkin (1882–1948), advocate of secular nationalism and "negation of *galut.*"

5. Hayyim Nahman Bialik (1873–1934), outstanding poet of the Hebrew renaissance.

6. E.g., Hermann Cohen (1842–1918), German philosopher; the most prominent representative of the neo-Kantian school.

7. Exodus 3:14, usually translated: "I am (that I am)."

8. Deuteronomy 6:4.

9. *See* "Renewal of Judaism," note 5.

10. I Samuel 15:9–23.

11. Sanhedrin 105a.

12. Mishnah Yoma VII, 9.

13. Sayings of the Fathers VI, 1.

14. A similar story is told about the Baal Shem's most noted disciple, the Great Maggid.

15. Traditional number of commandments (*mitzvot*) contained in Jewish law.

16. S. R. Hirsch (1808–1888), founder of Neo-Orthodoxy; author of *Horeb* (1837) and of biblical commentaries.

17. Moses Mendelssohn (1729–1786), philosopher, leader in German-Jewish enlightenment; author of *Jerusalem* (1783), a work on Judaism and religion.

18. Johann Kaspar Lavater (1741–1801), Swiss Protestant theologian; tried to persuade Mendelssohn to accept Christianity.

THE SPIRIT OF ISRAEL AND THE WORLD OF TODAY

1. Exodus Rabba XXI, 5.
2. Tanhuma (Yelamdenu), Noah 19.
3. Yannai. See *Almanach des Schocken Verlags,* 5699 (1938–39), p. 6.
4. Matthew 10:6.
5. On Marcion, cf. Martin Buber, *Two Types of Faith,* 1951, pp. 141, 167.
6. *See* "The Spirit of the Orient and Judaism," note 11.
7. Mark 12:17.
8. Adolf von Harnack (1851–1930), German Protestant theologian, author of *Geschichte der Mission und Ausbreitung des Christentums,* 1902, 1924 (*The Expansion of Christianity,* 2nd ed., 1908).
9. *Marcion: das Evangelium vom fremden Gott* ("The Gospel of the Alien God"), 1921.

JUDAISM AND CIVILIZATION

1. II Samuel 7:14.
2. Genesis 12:7 f.
3. John the Baptist: Matthew 3:10.

THE SILENT QUESTION

1. Henri Bergson (1859–1941), French philosopher, author of *L'Evolution créatrice,* 1906 (*Creative Evolution,* 1911).
2. Simone Weil (1909–1943), French social and religious thinker.
3. Deuteronomy 10:18 f.
4. Amos 9:7.
5. Jeremiah 2:3.

THE DIALOGUE BETWEEN HEAVEN AND EARTH

1. Amos 9:7.
2. Micah 4:5.
3. Sayings of the Fathers III, 19.
4. Cain: Genesis 4:9. David: II Samuel 12:9–13.
5. Psalm 19:2.
6. Genesis 18:25.
7. Psalm 106:1.

Editor's Postscript

BUBER's addresses on Judaism must be viewed against their historical background. They are not academic presentations but responses to actual situations.

The "Early Addresses" refer to the intellectual conditions prevalent among the young Jewish intelligentsia in the years preceding World War I and in the war years. They have been described by Hans Kohn in his Buber biography of 1930 and by Robert Weltsch in his introduction to Buber's collected Jewish essays (*Der Jude und sein Judentum* [Cologne: Joseph Melzer Verlag, 1963]). Both Kohn and Weltsch were members of the Bar-Kokhba Jewish student organization in Prague which had invited Buber to deliver the first addresses.

At the time, the Jewish student and young intellectual of Western Europe found himself in a world in which Judaism had all but lost meaning. Jewish tradition and Jewish communal institutions were devoid of appeal; the young Zionist movement held out a promise of a future solution for the Jewish problem (for whomever Judaism seemed to be a problem) but offered no "content" for the present, beyond an elementary Jewish affirmation. Many wished to ignore Judaism and hoped that the world of modern, progressive, cultured men would also be able to ignore it and accept Jews as individuals into the common-wealth of secularized, educated Europeans.

Some, however, sensed that there was more to Judaism than appeared on the surface. But what then was its true nature? Led by such men as Hugo Bergmann and Leo Herrmann (who personally had evolved a deeper insight into the issue), the Bar-Kokhba group approached Buber as the man who could perhaps point the way. The year was 1909.

Thirty-one at the time, Buber had behind him years of work in the Zionist movement which had ended in dis-appointment. After his withdrawal from the party he de-voted himself to the study of Hasidism; in 1906 he issued the first of his volumes on Hasidism, *Die Geschichten des Rabbi Nachman* (*The Tales of Rabbi Nachman* [of Bratz-lav]). At the same time he gave serious thought to prob-lems of society and the relations between man and man; from 1905 on he edited a series of monographs under the title *Die Gesellschaft* (*Society*). In the prologue to the first issue of the series (*Proletariat,* by Werner Sombart), he used the term "interhuman relationship" (*Das Zwisch-enmenschliche*), which remained a key concept in his social, ethical, and religious thought.

Responding to the call of the Bar-Kokhba group, Buber re-established contact with a live Jewish audience. The first three addresses (1909–11) relate the core of his message; the addresses were supplemented by informal meetings and discussions with Prague's Jewish students. Later (1912–14 and 1918–19) Buber continued and amplified his thinking in five new addresses.

He rejected both shallow Jewish assimilation and for-mal Jewish orthodoxy; the decadent and comfortable European materialism as well as self-sufficient nationalism; politicization of society as well as institutionalization of faith. He advocated a "renewal of Judaism," a term that

first appeared in one of his essays of 1900. Such renewal
seemed to him to be part of a process of similar renewal
among other ethnic groups. It was to be a renascence of
the total individual or ethnic personality, not a change of
one or another aspect of life. In the case of the Jew it
meant renewed awareness of the deepest layers of Jewish
thought, biblical and post-biblical; a new understanding
of the millennia of Jewish history, its triumph and its
tragedies; knowledge of the bond that unites Judaism with
the great spiritual movements of the East (the "Orient"
and "Asia" in Buber's text), and of what this East can
contribute to a regeneration of the declining West; realization that to be a Jew is to live a life of unconditional commitment, rejecting compromise—that what count are
constructive deeds, not abstract concepts or theories.
Nevertheless, the basis for renewal of Judaism must be the
rebuilding of a normal national life in Palestine.

Buber's ethical, personalist, religious nationalism finds
its parallel in Charles Péguy's "mystique" of French nationalism and in the humanist nationalism of Romain
Rolland and Rabindranath Tagore. As Hans Kohn has
shown, this pure form of ethical, natural, "interhuman"
affirmation of ethnic origin as the basis of renewal of one's
life as a whole was the very opposite of the militant, power-
hungry, oppressive nationalism that was in operation and
on the increase at the time. Buber valiantly fought for the
preservation and growth of the ideal form of the national
spirit. In this respect he attempted to do for the Western
European Jew what Ahad Ha'am had done for Eastern
European Jewry.

Buber speaks of "the blood" and "the fate," the memory of which activates the Jew to follow the summons to
true community. Today these terms sound woefully out of
place and are open to misunderstanding. But at the time
they were voiced they meant rootedness in one's origin,

heritage, and history, and awareness of one's destiny, i.e.,
of the destination one had decided to follow. The "community of blood" is my forefathers' community, the community into which I was born and in which I desire to
set my own life. It is not organization nor party member-
ship that is important but organic belonging and conscious
partnership. The Jewish intelligentsia had lost its roots
and felt the pain of being uprooted. Buber tried to help.

The center of the message, however, is religious. The
Jew's relationship to the absolute, the unconditioned, the
establishment of a living communion with it—it is this that
Buber called religiosity, as distinct from religion, which,
in his formulation, is but the sum total of laws and customs,
doctrines and set beliefs. Later, the abstract terms "the
absolute" and "the unconditioned" were translated into
the concrete "God," the "Thou," the "eternal Thou." To
Buber the priestly establishment, talmudic legislative tendency, and rabbinism of the Diaspora represented official
"religion," its rigidity, preservation of the old, and conformity. Against this he opposed the "underground" movements of biblical prophecy—the Essenes, the early Christian brotherhood, the talmudic Aggadah, medieval mysticism, and eighteenth-century Hasidism—as expressions
of Jewish religiosity, its vitality, call for decision, and realization of the Divine on earth.

Such a division between official and "underground"
Judaism is largely incorrect. Among the masters of the
law there were many saintly men, and Hasidism was no
safeguard against hypocrisy, evasiveness, and sheer inertia.
But, in his attempt to win the minds and hearts of his
audience, Buber could not permit himself a historian's de-
liberation; instead, he had to judge historical movements
polemically, in terms of black and white. Official Judaism
of the past was used by him as a foil for the institutional
Judaism of the present—rejected by the audience—and

the spiritualized tendencies of the past, which seemed to challenge the existing order and even to rebel against it, were presented as the true, daring testimony of the Jewish spirit. He expected the best of the younger generation to be ready to identify themselves with this authentic Judaism.

The appeal was effective. Audience and readers responded to the novel approach to Judaism. Buber's attitude was nonconformist, yet demanding; critical, yet constructive. Here was not "tradition" in the usual sense, but thinking that moved within the vast scope of Hebraic heritage; the accent was on "spirit," but the spirit was "realized" in deeds. Both individual and community, both Jew and the world, were involved in the intended effort. The special position of the people of Israel was affirmed, but only in the context of humanity at large. Despite the proud and consistent references to the Hebrew classics—the Bible, the Talmud, the Zohar, hasidic writings—there was nothing parochial in the outline of the "renewal of Judaism." To this must be added the brilliance and increasing acuity of Buber's style (which, naturally, loses something in translation) and the dramatic impact of the spoken word, which not infrequently penetrated the listener's innermost being.

At the time, men like Max Brod and Franz Kafka came under the influence of Buber. To the young Jewish generation of post-World War I, he was the unchallenged spokesman of Hebraic renascence and humanism. Christian thinkers were attracted to him long before the universal aspect of his thought was given pronounced emphasis.

When, in the early 1940's and in the early 1950's (this time in the United States), Buber again formulated his views on Judaism (the "Later Addresses" in this volume), he confronted his audience with the same major themes as those contained in the "Early Addresses," the same appeal to the total person, the same call to assess

things Jewish and human "from within," the same intensity
and pathos, the same serious recourse to Hebrew classics.
However, in the meantime, he had qualified his interpretation of early Christianity, his appreciation of Spinoza, and
his use of "Asia" as a spiritual entity. A more critical view
had replaced the former overly idealistic one. And his
language showed greater simplicity, greater directness.
And present throughout, overtly and between the lines, is
the keen, painful awareness that in the interval between
the addresses Jewry experienced its darkest period in history and that a new Jewry, in both America and Israel,
was only a hope.

In preparing the last authorized edition of the addresses
as they appeared in *Der Jude und sein Judentum,* Buber
simplified the phraseology of the early addresses and removed some superlatives. For example, "to redeem" became "to liberate"; "the Jew Yohanan" became "the
Baptist"; the combination "Jesus and the Baal Shem" was
eliminated; "creative" rebellions was replaced by "essential" rebellions, "irrational" by "suprarational." The English rendition required some additional changes in the direction indicated by Buber's own revision. Omissions are
indicated by [. . .]. The notes give the most basic (but
not all) references and incorporate a few of Buber's own
footnotes.

No one will claim that Buber's thought is universally
acceptable. His views, and some of his actions, evoked
criticism during his lifetime, and the critics included some
of his friends and followers. This process will no doubt
continue. But beyond agreement and opposition looms the
figure of a mighty man, deeply rooted in Hebraic sources
and partaking in the freedom of the modern era. As such
he addresses himself to us.

                                          N.N.G.

OTHER
SCHOCKEN BOOKS
OF RELATED INTEREST

DAYS OF AWE:
A Treasury of Jewish Wisdom
for Reflection, Repentance,
and Renewal on the High Holy Days
edited by S.Y. Agnon
Foreword by Arthur Green
0–8052–1048–2

THE MYSTIC QUEST:
An Introduction to Jewish Mysticism
by David Ariel
0–8052–1003–2

TALES OF THE HASIDIM
by Martin Buber
Foreword by Chaim Potok
0–8052–0995–6

EVERYMAN'S TALMUD
by Abraham Cohen
Foreword by Jacob Neusner
0–8052–1032–6

ENTERING JEWISH PRAYER:
A Guide to Personal Devotion and the Worship Service
by Reuven Hammer
0–8052–1022–9

ON BEING A JEWISH FEMINIST
edited by Susannah Heschel
0–8052–1036–9

JEWISH MEDITATION:
A Practical Guide
by Aryeh Kaplan
0–8052–1037–7

WHEN CHILDREN ASK ABOUT GOD:
A Guide for Parents
Who Don't Always Have All the Answers
by Harold Kushner
0–8052–1033–4